Fiji

a travel survival kit

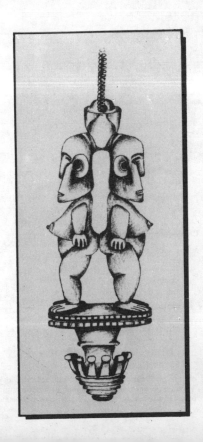

Fiji – a travel survival kit
First edition

Published by
Lonely Planet Publications
PO Box 88, South Yarra, Victoria 3141, Australia
Lonely Planet Publications
PO Box 2001A, Berkeley, California, USA 94702

Printed by
Colorcraft, Hong Kong

Photographs by
Rob Kay
Jim Parker
Fiji Visitors Bureau

First Published
March 1986

National Library of Australia Cataloguing in Publication Data

Kay, Rob, 1953-.
Fiji, a travel survival kit

First ed.
Includes index
ISBN 0 908086 87 3

1. Fiji – Description and travel – 1986 – Guide-books I. Title

919.6'1104

Rob Kay

Rob Kay is a 32-year-old Californian whose travel experiences are culled from having lived and worked in the destinations he writes about. He feels that only by rubbing shoulders with the local population can a travel writer even begin to transmit the true 'spirit of place'. Rob has worked as a freelance journalist in Tahiti and Fiji, a bartender and publicist in San Francisco, and a radio newsman in California's San Joaquin Valley. Rob contributes regularly to newspapers and magazines in San Francisco. He is fond of balmy climates, trout fishing and cold, dark beer.

This Edition

This book is dedicated to my adopted Fijian family – Waqa and Mere Nawaqatabu, and Iliese and Lele Duvuloco.

Special thanks to Dale Harvison, former *Fiji Sun*, chief sub-editor, for his editing, research and contributions to the Around the Island and History sections. My appreciation also goes to Fergus Clunie, Fiji Museum Director, for his sage advice; and to Elizabeth Kim, my editor.

I would also like to express my gratitude to Dick and Mimi Goodman of Oakland, California; Dick Lowe and Susana Tuivaga of the Fiji Visitors Bureau in Los Angeles; Malakai Gucake, manager of the FVB in Suva; Neil Jorgensen, former Peace Corps volunteer in Kadavu; Tevita Nawadra and Paul Geraghty of the Fiji Dictionary Project; Angeline Joyce of Rosie Tours; Lili Koroi, formerly of the Fiji Visitors Bureau; Professor Al Schutz of the University of Hawaii; Jeff Siegel of the University of the South Pacific; Dick Simmons of Network Travel Planners; William and Maria Tuivaga of New Zealand; Geoff Taylor of Savusavu; Len Usher, former mayor of Suva; Steve Yaqona, General Manager of Fiji Air; and Abe Yavala of the Fiji Visitors' Bureau.

And the Next

Travel guides are only kept up to date by travelling. If you find errors or omissions in this book we'd very much like to hear about them. As usual the best letters will be rewarded with a free copy of the next edition, or another Lonely Planet guide if you prefer.

Contents

A Warning on Pronunciation
There are some particular peculiarities in the pronunciation of words in Fijian. The letter *d*, for example, is pronounced *nd*. Similarly *b* is pronounced *mb*. Thus your aircraft lands at *Nadi* airport which is pronounced *Nandi*. And the island of *Lakeba* is pronounced *Lakemba*. This causes particular difficulties because some maps (including the ones in this book) spell things as they are spelt, others as they are pronounced. For more information see the Language section.

Introduction

On a recent press trip, several big-league travel writers with well over a million miles under their belts were informally polled as to their all-time favourite destinations. Without consulting one another, each of the journalists unhesitatingly answered 'Fiji.' The man who took the poll, himself a globe-trotting airline executive, was astounded. 'I've never been there. What makes it so great?' he asked. 'The people,' was the reply.

I happen to agree with the writers polled. Chances are a visitor would not find a more tolerant, hospitable and friendly people on the planet than in the Fiji Islands. It sounds like Office of Tourism hype but it's true. Fijians, who ironically were the fiercest cannibals in the South Pacific just over 100 years ago, are so gentle and kind that some visitors may even doubt the islanders' sincerity. The realisation of how ingenuous the Fijians are is more than enough to make you feel mean-spirited in comparison.

South Seas hands can talk about the aesthetic beauties of Bora Bora or the ethnological diversity of Papua New Guinea but the final measure of the 'spirit of place,' to quote Laurence Durrell, are the people who inhabit it. In this respect the Fijians are in a class of their own.

When you meet a Fijian an instant human dialogue is established. A Fijian will look straight into your eyes and an almost telepathic communication begins. From an early age Fijians are taught that family and friends are the most important things on earth. Children are instructed to pay attention to human beings and to understand their nature. It is not surprising that the islanders have amazing powers of observation and an intuitive sense when it comes to what people require and desire. Consistent with their comprehension of the human experience, Fijians will never forget a person they have met. Even the substance of a casual conversation will be vividly recalled over a long period of time.

In addition, the 300 islands that make

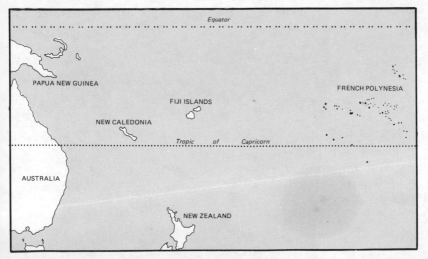

up the Fiji group offer clear blue water, fine beaches, world-class diving and snorkelling, excellent resorts, magnificent landscapes and seascapes, a varied cuisine, and cultures rich in tradition.

South Pacific islands have their own slow tempo and Fiji is no exception. Things don't move as quickly as in Sydney or San Francisco and you would be wrong to expect that they should. The sun is hot, the air is humid and no one – except a few misguided tourists – rushes around for any reason. If the bus is late (or doesn't show up at all), don't worry; there will be others. The Fiji Bitter you ordered may be slow in being served, but it will come and it will be cold. The hotel operator may not move like lightning to place your call, but he or she will place it eventually. In their own way and on their own time, people in Fiji do get things done.

When the airplane's rubber hits the runway at Nadi, slow yourself down and keep an open mind. If possible, soak up the sun and bask in the goodwill of these marvellous people. My hunch is that you may learn something from them and take it back with you.

Facts about the Country

HISTORY

The original homeland of the Pacific island peoples was South-East Asia. Early people, *homo erectus*, reached South-East Asia about two million years ago and modern man, *homo sapiens*, arrived approximately 60,000 years ago. Although evidence of human settlement in New Guinea dates back at least 25,000 years, the Austronesian migration from South-East Asia to New Guinea 6000 years ago marked a new stage in cultural evolution. Unlike their neolithic forbears, who were hunters and gatherers, the newcomers (who eventually were to populate Fiji) had adopted sail and outrigger canoes, methods of cultivating root crops, and pig farming.

According to archaeological evidence (mostly pottery) Fiji was settled in three different waves. The earliest wave dates from about 1600 BC and the migrants settled in within a few hundred years (which historically speaking is fairly quickly). This is evidenced by a number of bird extinctions and changes in distribution of birdlife, which indicates a massive environmental impact caused by a large, sophisticated population. These people, who came from the New Britain area (now part of Papua New Guinea) were most likely ancestors of present-day Polynesians. They practised agriculture, raised pigs and poultry, and fished.

Changes in pottery style indicate a probable second wave of migrants to the area between 400 and 100 BC. Scientists use the word 'probable' because they are not sure if the new pottery style was caused by an influx of new people into the area or if it simply was a local development. If the changes were caused by migrants, the newcomers probably mixed with the indigenous population and perhaps dominated them.

The final settlement of Fiji (1000 to 1800 AD) was a massive movement from Melanesia. This wave of people practised a sophisticated form of terraced agriculture which helped support a large population that may have grown to 200,000. People grew yams and taro, raised poultry, fished, and evolved a highly developed culture.

Pre-contact Society

As evidenced from their advanced form of agriculture, the pre-contact Fiji Islands were a highly evolved, stratified society, interlocked and interdependent through trade. Different clans were responsible for various crafts or activities such as pottery-making, mat-weaving, canoe-building and salt production. These items were traded throughout the Fiji group and even as far away as Tonga.

Women worked hard and aged early in life. In the division of labour, men did intermittent hard jobs such as breaking in land for crops. They also performed occasional social duties like warfare, housebuilding and ceremonial *lovo* cooking in large underground ovens. In other words, the more spectacular activities were usually in the man's domain, whereas the drudgery of weeding, washing and collecting firewood was (and still is) done by women.

Pre-contact Fijian society was dominated by a complicated class system. Chiefs often had tremendous personal power which was expressed in demands for tribute from conquered tribes and in many bloody human sacrifices. To outsiders, the chiefs seemed to have arbitrary and ruthless power based on 'club law.' Said one early observer: 'No eastern tyrants can rule with more absolute terror than the Chiefs do here; and few people are more thoroughly enslaved and trampled than are these islanders.'

Each 'tribe' was broken up into several

clans, each with its own function in society. There were chiefly clans, priestly clans, artisans, fishing clans and diplomatic clans whose purpose was to act as spokespeople for the chief.

Leadership in the tribal units was strictly hereditary and succession often a subject of debate. Rank was inherited through both parents, and in a polygamous society this could be very confusing. Thus a chief might have five different sons from five different wives, each with a different political status. To complicate matters even more, rank could be inherited from one's mother's brothers, and succession was usually through brothers before it passed on to sons. There might be a number of individuals qualified as chiefly candidates, but those who became chiefs had to stand out from the group.

Through intermarriage, incredibly complex relationships between tribes throughout Fiji were created. Tribal leaders looking to gain political power could thus draw support from different clans throughout the islands through their blood ties, and in the process just as easily make enemies. No one chief was dominant in Fiji. The political scene was in a constant flux of changing allegiances brought about by disputes over land, property or women, by quarrels, or by the rulers' petty jealousies.

Cannibalism

Cannibalism was an extremely important institution in pre-Christian Fiji, practised as early as several hundred years before the birth of Christ. According to Fergus Clunie, director of the Fiji Museum, it was a 'perfectly normal part of life.' The practise was a function of the religion – the great warrior-gods were cannibals and they required human sacrifice. Although some clans did not in fact eat human flesh for religious reasons (their totems were human), the practice of cannibalism was widespread throughout the Fiji group.

Victims were not just randomly selected but were almost always enemies taken during battles. Eating your enemy was the ultimate disgrace the victor could impose, and in the Fijian system of ancestor worship this became a lasting insult to the victims' families. This explains much of the sometimes extremely vicious infighting, internecine warfare and vengeance-seeking that went on in pre-Christian times. By all accounts, violence was a way of life and an accepted form of behaviour when directed towards one's foes. Chiefs generally always had some kind of grudge or power struggle against someone else and war could be an everyday occurrence. It was during these periods of warfare that cannibalism was practised.

Fijians were not without a gruesome

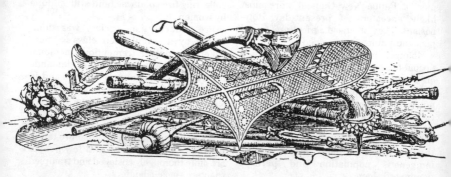

sense of humour. Cutting off some unfortunate soul's tongue or fingers, cooking them, commenting on how good they tasted and then offering the victim his own flesh to eat always got a chuckle. There are also horrifying accounts of missionaries who, in times of war, were given samples of cooked meat and were later told what they had eaten.

Eating human flesh was only one of many bloody practices in a society where extreme violence and extreme kindness existed side by side. Some examples of the darker aspects included hanging captured 'enemy' children by the feet or hands from the sail yards of war canoes; burying men alive at the post holes of new homes or temples being constructed; and strangling women at the graves of chiefs to accompany them into the next world.

European Exploration

Knowledge of Fiji and the other principal island groups of the south-west Pacific was a result of the search for the legendary 'South Land' *terra australis incognita*, which the geographers of the 16th and 17th centuries felt must exist to balance the land masses of the northern hemisphere. During the nearly one hundred years when voyages were made in search of this hypothetical continent, Spaniards from the coast of South America passed to the north of Fiji and established settlements in islands farther to the west, and Dutch sailors skirted the Tongan group, little more than three hundred km to the east.

The discovery of the Fiji archipelago was no organised affair, but was spread over a two-hundred-year period and included the talents of navigators such as Tasman, Cook, Bligh, Wilson and Bellingshausen.

Abel Tasman, skippering two vessels for the Dutch East India Company's service, sailed from Mauritius in September of 1642 seeking the hoped-for 'South Land.' He came instead upon Tasmania and later discovered New

Zealand, where he skirmished with the Maoris. Unwilling to risk further troubles, he headed north and came to Tonga where he was hospitably received. He set a course towards New Guinea and on 6 February 1643 sighted a low island now known to have been Nukubasaga, a sand cay upon a circular reef located west of Vanua Levu. Tasman luckily found a passage over the reef and later sighted points of land which were probably the peaks of Taveuni, lying to the north. Naming his discovery 'Prince William's Islands,' he turned north (probably in no mood to seek unknown continents in reef-infested waters), feeling his way among the reefs and islands until he passed Cikobia and so gained the open sea. He skirted the northern coasts of the Solomon Islands and New Guinea and brought his ships home to Batavia (now Jakarta, the capital of Indonesia) on 14 June 1643.

The next navigator known to have touched Fiji was Captain James Cook, who in the course of his second voyage in the Pacific sailed from Tonga and sighted a low, wooded island (Vatoa) in the southern Lau group, and a neighbouring reef on 2 June 1774. A few people were seen on the shore but they scurried inland at the boat's approach. Cook landed and left a few nails, some medals and a knife on some rocks. Having fixed the position, he named it Turtle Island.

Bligh's discoveries in Fiji came as a direct result of the famed mutiny on the *Bounty*. On 28 April 1789, when the *Bounty* was in Tongan waters, the crew mutinied, putting Bligh and 18 loyal officers and men in the ship's launch – an open vessel with very few provisions and no weapons. Bligh made for the smouldering volcanic island of Tofua, which was in sight, but the island had neither food nor water. Greeted only by a party of hostile Tongans and realizing he could not turn back to Tahiti, Bligh had no option but to sail for the Dutch colony on Timor. Though 6000 km away, it was the nearest European settlement he knew of.

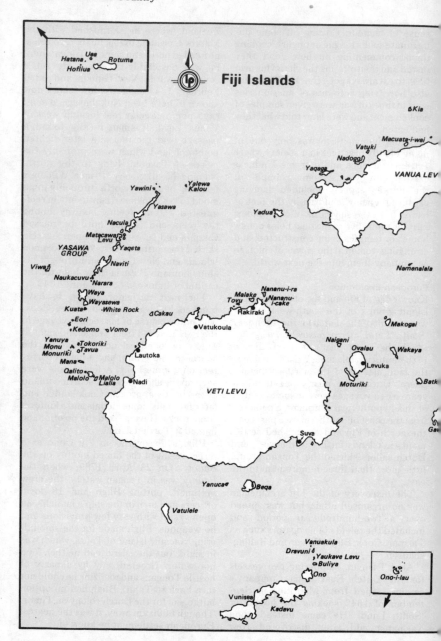

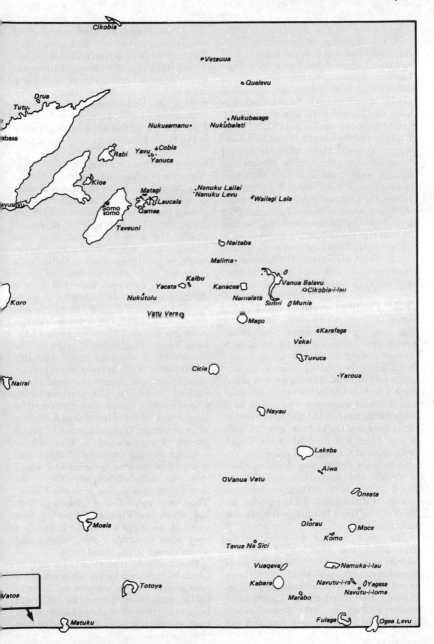

As master of the *Resolution* during Cook's third voyage in the Pacific, Bligh had seen Fijians and heard a great deal from the Tongans of their fierce reputation. However, there was no alternative but to sail through the uncharted Cannibal Islands, which is what Fiji was known as in those days. Late in the afternoon of the second day out from Tofua (4 May 1789), Bligh sighted the islands of southern Lau. During the next three days he passed through the very heart of the archipelago sighting numerous islands, including Nairai, Gau, Batiki, Koro, Wakaya and Ovalau. He eventually sailed between the two major islands, Vanua Levu and Viti Levu. Near the Yasawas on 7 May he met the first signs of unfriendly natives.

Bligh sighted two large canoes definitely in pursuit of his vessel. He fortunately made his way to a passage in a nearby reef but the wind dropped and the men took to the oars. Meanwhile, the canoes gained on them. The Fijian *drua* were speedy, seaworthy craft which clearly outclassed Bligh's skiff, but luckily for the Englishman a dark squall closed down on them, with thunder and lightning blotting out everything. When the weather cleared only one canoe was in sight. A fresh wind enabled Bligh's crew to barely hold their distance and at sunset the canoe returned to land while the launch headed into the darkness of the open sea. On 14 June, after 41 days at sea, Bligh was in sight of the Dutch settlement at Kupang on Timor.

Despite the distractions of foul weather, cannibals and uncharted reefs, Bligh found the time to record in great detail his numerous discoveries. To his credit, his chart of the 'Bligh Islands' is remarkably accurate.

The most notable advance in the exploration and charting of the Fiji Islands was made in 1840, in the brief period of three months, by a United States expedition led by Commandant Charles Wilkes. The headstrong American – whose actions in later years nearly precipitated a war between England and the USA – had an excellent staff of navigators, surveyors, geologists, zoologists, botanists, artists and philologists. The chart produced by the expedition was a remarkable achievement and long remained the standard chart of the archipelago. Unfortunately, the originals of the artists' highly detailed renditions of Fijian life during this era were lost in a fire in the United States.

Influence of the Europeans

When the first Europeans arrived, Fiji was divided into about seven different *vanua* or political confederations and the trend toward political centralisation was already under way. For a variety of reasons – chiefly the introduction of arms and Christianity – this political consolidation would be greatly speeded up through the influence of the white people.

The early explorers knew Fiji to be a dangerous place, an unknown area inhabited by unpredictable cannibals and strewn with dangerous reefs. In short, a place one avoided. However, people have been known to take great risks for the possibility of economic gain, and this accounted for Fiji's first sustained contact with Europeans during the sandalwood rush of 1804-1810. The precious wood, prized by the Chinese, was discovered by the survivor of the shipwrecked American schooner *Argo*, Oliver Slater, who found groves of sandalwood in Bua on the southern coast of Vanua Levu. Ships soon poured into the area, bringing a variety of men who included beachcombers – the first Europeans to live with the Fijians. They bartered nails and trinkets at first, but when the Fijians discovered how valuable the wood was to the Europeans they soon demanded axes, knives and whale's teeth in exchange for it.

Eventually the chiefs wanted more than goods to procure a cargo. They asked for men armed with muskets to aid them in battle, sometimes demanding this even before the crews were allowed ashore. The next several years saw the arrival of men who specialised in helping the Fijian chiefs in tribal warfare. Such were the exploits of Charlie Savage, a Swedish beachcomber/mercenary whose name became synonymous with modern warfare in Fiji and the rise of the Bauan empire.

Savage arrived in Fiji aboard the shipwrecked American brig *Eliza* in 1808, from which he managed to salvage Spanish silver dollars and muskets. The reputation of European arms grew in Fiji and Savage made his way to the tiny island of Bau, an up-and-coming political power. Savage managed to survive for five years on Bau, and acquired a number of wives for his help in subduing his host's enemies. The Swede was eventually ambushed in battle, his skull preserved as a kava bowl.

The second stage of European influence, which lasted from the 1820s to the 1850s, came about from the *beche de mer* (sea cucumber) trade. This era had greater impact on Fiji as it was more widespread and longer lasting than the sandalwood trade and involved far more Fijians as labourers. Beche de mer traders also introduced even larger quantities of guns which reinforced the Bauans' cause, already on the ascendant without the help of foreign arms.

The Rise of Bau

In the late 18th century there were seven main *vanua* or confederations: Rewa, Verata and Bau in south-eastern Viti Levu; Lakeba in the Lau group (an area often controlled by Tongans); and Cakaudrove, Macuata and Bua on Vanua Levu. Of these, Bau, a tiny island off the eastern coast of Viti Levu, was a recent vanua. Until the 1760s the island, which had been home to a few fishermen, traders and skilled canoe builders, was a vassal to nearby Verata. The original inhabitants were later driven out by the Verata confederation and Bau was occupied by the invaders.

Through a policy of intermarriage with leading families of Rewa and Cakaudrove and utilisation of the maritime skills of the exiled fishermen (some of whom were allowed to live on the island), the power of Bau grew. These factors, combined with the firepower of Charlie Savage, helped Bau defeat Verata in 1808. By 1829 Bau, which was allied closely with Rewa in the south-west, controlled northern and eastern Viti Levu and had crushed the supremacy of nearby Verata.

However, a factor that differentiated Bau from other vanua was the extent to which chiefly authority was personalised (as opposed to institutionalised). This was demonstrated by chief Tanoa, who refused to allow his warlords to capture European vessels, and especially by his son and successor Cakobau, who ruled with an iron-fisted power rarely seen.

Chief Cakobau's Reign

Cakobau, a brilliant and bloody Machiavellian strategist, was certainly the most influential chief in recorded Fijian history and a central figure for nearly half a century. It was during his reign that much of Fiji became politically consolidated and was eventually ceded to Great Britain. His rise to influence as chief of Bau must be understood within the context of the never-ending power struggle of Fijian chiefs and the emergence of European influence upon Fiji.

In 1849 Cakobau was described by Captain Erskine of *HMS Havannah*, who said: 'It was impossible not to admire the appearance of the chief: of large, almost gigantic, size, his limbs were beautifully formed and proportioned; his countenance with far less of the negro cast than among the lower orders, agreeable and intelligent; while his immense head of hair, covered and concealed with gauze, smoke-dried and slightly tinged with brown, gave him altogether the appearance of an eastern sultan. No garments confined his magnificent chest and neck, or concealed the natural colour of the skin, a clear but decided black; and in spite of his paucity of attire – the evident wealth which surrounded him showing that it was a

Cakabau

historical account of the Pacific wrote, 'Tales of his human sacrifices and punishments are legion ... at times Cakobau's anger was spontaneous, as when a chief was slow to pay tribute and was immediately clubbed to death.' On another occasion, Cakobau had the tongue of a Bauan rebel cut out which he 'devoured raw, talking and joking at the same time with the mutilated chief, who begged in vain for the boon of a speedy death.' Cakobau certainly had his moments but in general his behaviour was not out of character for any self-respecting chief of that day.

Cakobau's craving for power led Bau to a constant state of war throughout the 1840s and quarrels with his allies in Cakaudrove and Rewa. In 1844 a ferocious war broke out between Bau and Rewa which continued for another 12 years. At the height of his power, and having gone so far as to proclaim himself 'Tui Viti' (King of Fiji), Cakobau was increasingly resented by other Fijian tribes and the growing European settlement of Levuka on the nearby island of Ovalau.

Established in the 1830s by a handful of American and European beachcombers who took Fijian wives, Levuka became one of the most important ports of call in the South Pacific for whalers and trading vessels in the latter part of the 19th century. The men who lived there acted as pilots, interpreters and traders' agents. During the 1840s their once friendly relationship with Cakobau deteriorated and the town was razed by a fire in 1841 – under Cakobau's orders, it was believed, but there was no proof.

When Cakobau was not busy at war he monopolised the beche de mer trade, often committing himself to more of it than he could produce without resorting to arms. This was merely one of many obligations he had to assume as self-proclaimed 'King of Fiji.'

One incident in particular with an American trader in 1849 was to plague Cakobau for years. John Brown Williams

matter of choice and not necessity – he 'looked every inch a king'.'

According to historians, warfare and women were Cakobau's prime interests. His ambitions were no less than total supremacy over Fiji. Described by European observers as 'arrogant, cruel, cunning, devious, and bold,' he 'seemed to think of nothing else but war, and ... to desire nothing else but power.' As with all chiefs, who were considered semi-divine, the lives of underlings meant nothing to Cakobau. As K R Howe in his excellent came to Fiji in 1846 as the United States commercial agent. In 1849, a cannon set off during a 4th of July celebration exploded and set fire to Williams' home and store. In true island style the locals helped save as much merchandise as possible but naturally 'liberated' what they had saved, keeping it for themselves. Williams called this looting and held Cakobau responsible as king of Fiji. In 1851 an American man-of-war demanded Williams be compensated to the tune of $5000. Other incidents involving American property ran the figure up to $43,000 by 1855 and the king was summoned aboard a US warship and forced to sign a promissory note giving him two years to pay.

If the 1840s were the zenith of power for the great warlord, the 1850s were the beginning of his downfall. Fighting broke out with Verata and struggles were renewed against Rewa. The European settlers in Levuka became united against Cakobau when for the second time the town was burned to the ground. Although Cakobau was not at fault (at least this time), he was blamed and Europeans did all they could to direct shipping away from Bau and thus blockade the island.

It was clear Cakobau's authority was waning. He became ill, and as a final straw, his old allies at Kaba – an area from which he used to stage raids into Rewa – revolted. The force he sent in to quell them was thrashed and for the moment he seemed a defeated man.

The Christian Presence

The earliest Christian presence in Fiji was the LMS (London Missionary Society), which converted a chief from Oneata, near Lakeba, in 1830. The mission had a small following but failed to convert the powerful chief of Lakeba. In 1835 the Wesleyans, engaged in a running evangelistic war with the LMS, sent William Cross and David Cargill, along with an envoy of converted Tongans, to Lakeba. Several hundred of the local Tongans (who were under no obligation to the Fijians in matters of religion) took up Christianity. Once again the Fijian chief of Lakeba, undoubtedly fearing reprisals from Bau if he *lotued* (converted) refused to be swayed.

It was an uphill battle for Cargill and Cross, who realized the real power in Fiji lay in Bau and visited there in 1838. It was a period when Cakobau and his father Tanoa were seeking vengeance from their former enemies and not a serene time to visit. The mission was aghast at the savagery they witnessed and instead moved to Rewa where they were accepted by the Tui Dreketi, Cakobau's arch rival. Although the missionaries set up a base, they were by no means accepted by the populace.

American Captain Charles Wilkes explained the situation in this way: 'All the chiefs seem to look upon Christianity as a change in which they had much to lose and little to gain. The old chiefs, in particular, would often remark that they were too old to change their present for new gods, or to abandon what they considered their duty to their people; yet the chiefs generally desire the residence of missionaries among them. I was, therefore, anxious to know why they entertain such a wish, when they had no desire for their instruction. They acknowledged that it was to get presents, and because it would bring vessels to their place, which would give them opportunities of obtaining many desirable articles.'

Meanwhile the war between Bau and Rewa raged and missionary activity in the area ceased. Missionary progress in other areas looked dim except for the Tongans in Lau. It was clear the chiefs exerted a powerful influence in religious matters and unless they were converted, the rank-and-file would never *lotu.*

Ma'afu & Tongan Imperialism

Tongans had always traded with Fiji and had been present as residents in the Lau Islands of eastern Fiji for hundreds of years. Although they did mix with the local

Ma'afu

King of Tonga to convert and enjoy the support of Tonga or stand alone and face the dire consequences. He consulted with a missionary and his advisors and several days later converted.

Cakobau lost a great deal of influence, but soon re-established his power – at a price. Although he was still a force to reckon with in western Fiji, the Tongans clearly were the dominant influence in the east.

Despite the newfound legitimacy of Christianity, Howe explains that Fiji did 'not become a missionary kingdom in the manner of Tahiti, Hawaii and Tonga . . . . Christianity as an institution was not politically centralised because there was no political unification of the island group.' Despite the influence enjoyed by Ma'afu and Cakobau, they still did not have total control over their dominions, which were presided over by local chiefs. This was an extremely important aspect in the development of the country, especially regarding the preservation of culture and tradition. Among other things, it would mean less interference by outside forces – namely missionaries – in dictating what was good or bad for Fijians and may be a primary reason why modern Fiji still has so much of its culture intact. (See under 'Culture & Customs.')

The Baker Incident

One of the most celebrated incidents in the 'Christianisation of Fiji' was the murder of Reverend Baker, the only missionary ever to be killed by Fijians. In 1867 Baker, who had spent eight years in Fiji, set out to cross Viti Levu from the Rewa area via the upper reaches of the Sigatoka Valley, an isolated region where no missionary had ever ventured. The independent-minded residents of the area – the unruly *kai colo* (hill people) – wanted nothing to do with Cakobau, Christianity nor the coastal tribes who were likely to practise this strange religion. Baker's Fijian disciples who doubled as guides were well aware of this and imparted the

population, they were looked upon by Fijians as arrogant, conceited carpet-baggers. However, because of the Lau group's proximity to Tonga the Fijians were subject to the Tongan sphere of influence.

In 1847, Ma'afu, a cousin of the Tongan king and a Tongan in search of 'overseas adventure,' came to Fiji in the name of protecting Christian Tongan interests. In other words, he exploited, plundered, massacred and stole whatever he pleased in the name of Christianity. His 'good' works came to the attention of the King of Tonga and in 1853 he became governor of all Tongans in Lau – the *de facto* leader of of the Tongan-Wesleyan cause in Fiji.

Ma'afu's imperialistic ventures into Fiji worried Cakobau but pleased the Wesleyan missionaries, who saw the Tongan as one of their own. In 1853, under political pressure, Cakobau reluctantly allowed a missionary to live in Bau. A year later he was advised in no uncertain terms by the news to Baker. The expedition stopped at the recently converted village of Dawarau en route to Navosa, where the hill people lived. The missionary was well treated at the village but the chief refused to lead Baker personally to the Navosa area, saying it was too dangerous. Instead he sent two guides to accompany Baker. At the next village, Naqaqadelavatu, the evangelists were treated coldly. The following day the chief warned the expedition that someone was coming to kill them. Upon leaving the village the group was ambushed and Baker was murdered with a blow to the head from a steel axe. As was customary, the bodies of the slain men were cooked and since Baker was a person of rank, pieces of his body were distributed to villages throughout the district. Folklore has it that the kai colo attempted to eat the missionary's shoes.

But why was Baker killed at all?

The most credible answer is that the highlanders, who despised Cakobau, felt threatened by Christianity, which they considered 'Cakobau's religion,' and felt that the best way to rid themselves of the threat was to kill the man spreading it.

Cakobau was forced by the British consul to send warriors to avenge the killing, but his men were thrashed by the hill people. In 1903 the people from the area where Baker was killed took part in a special ceremony to atone for his killing. To this day, a sort of collective shame is still felt by the descendants of those who precipitated the crime.

European Settlement

European settlement in Fiji resulted in the almost immediate involvement of foreign powers. American, French and British war ships called regularly, often on behalf of aggrieved nationals. As the European population grew, settlers who lived under the protection and at the whim of local chiefs lobbied their respective governments in an effort to annex Fiji and establish a business-as-usual climate. Both the British and American consuls

living there were deeply immersed in Fijian affairs.

As self-proclaimed 'Tui Viti' (King of Fiji), Cakobau offered to cede Fiji to Britain in return for the payment of his long-overdue $45,000 debt to the United States. Four years later the offer was refused.

After the 1860s the European settlement evolved from a handful of scraggly beach-combers and vagabonds to a more orthodox settler society arriving mostly from Australia and New Zealand. Fiji became attractive because of the belief that the British were going to annex it, and economically as a cotton-growing centre for European markets which were deprived of this commodity during the American Civil War. By 1870 the European population numbered over two thousand.

Settlers purchased land, sometimes fraudulently, for firearms used in tribal conflicts. Claims and counter-claims often followed with no form of arbitration. There were also problems with labour. Men were needed to work the plantations, and the Fijians were reluctant to do so. Virtual slave labourers from the Solomons or New Hebrides were imported or 'black birded' to Fiji. With no set rules to govern these activities, anarchy sometimes reigned. The consensus among Fijians and Europeans was that a government was needed to sort things out.

Fiji's Foray into Government

The first attempt at a national government was a council of chiefs which met in 1865 but collapsed two years later because no one could agree on anything. This was followed by the creation of regional governments in Bau, naturally headed by Cakobau; in Lau, run by Ma'afu (with close links to Tonga); and in Bua. Although the latter two were moderately successful in establishing some kind of order, events were moving too rapidly for the chiefs' attempts at political reform, particularly with the influx of European settlers.

Levuka was attracting more and more

shipping, and the town's population, which had increased significantly by 1870, was in dire need of public amenities and law and order. *The Fiji Times* noted in 1870, 'It is not the natives that we want the government for, but ourselves.'

In the countryside the situation was also deteriorating. Disputes over land led to racial violence and as usual the tribes were at each others' throats. As if things weren't bad enough, the end of the Civil War in the United States created a depression in the cotton market and in late 1870 terrible hurricanes destroyed the crops. More than ever, a governmental solution had to be found.

In 1871 the Cakobau government was established at Levuka. Hopes were high on all sides that the effort would work. However, as Howe noted, 'the ministers could not satisfy the irreconcilable demands of merchants, planters and Fijians. The government became universally unpopular.' Again the situation deteriorated. Talk of race war was heard, and in order to prevent anarchy and bloodshed Cakobau was forced to cede Fiji to England. The English, realizing the responsibility they had towards the settlers and the Fijians, and not wishing the country to fall into another government's hands, accepted. On 10 October 1874 the deed of cession was signed in Nasova, near Levuka. Fiji had become a Crown Colony.

Arrival of the Indians

Fiji was now a colony, but a colony in need of economic growth. Large-scale plantations seemed the obvious answer but labour was scarce. Sir Arthur Gordon, the colony's first governor, and fortunately for Fiji a decent man, was dead set against using natives to work the fields. Not only did he take steps immediately to protect Fijians from being exploited as a labour force, he also made it illegal to sell native land. In addition, he set up a taxation system requiring Fijians to work their own land rather than that of a planter.

Thus Gordon set in motion laws that would forever benefit the Fijian people by making sure they would never be alienated from their land nor exploited as workers. Gordon, a true 19th-century romantic, took the role of protector seriously and developed an administration very paternalistic towards the Fijians.

However, the colony was still in a dilemma. The infant sugar industry did have potential but no one to work the fields. The planters were screaming for labour. Gordon had a plan. Having previously worked in Mauritius and Trinidad, he had seen indentured Indian labour. He convinced the planters to bring over Indians as the answer to their needs.

On 14 May 1879 the era of the Indian in Fiji began. On this day the *Leonidas* arrived from Calcutta with 463 immigrants aboard. Between May 1879 and November 1916, when the final labour transport ship arrived, 60,000 people had come to serve as 'coolies.' Of these, some 85% were Hindus, 14% Muslims, and the rest were mainly Christians and Sikhs. Most of the migrants were men 20 to 40 years of age from the poor, agricultural castes. Life in India was never easy, and economic conditions had pushed them to accept the inducement offered by the British Empire.

In theory, workers understood that the *girmit* or agreement was to work for five years with the option to return to India in another five years or to remain in Fiji. In reality many of the Indians recruited (usually from the poorest and uneducated castes) were often tricked by unsavoury characters or even unwillingly 'shanghaied' aboard the ships.

In Fiji life was usually abysmal for the workers. They were housed in 'coolie lines' – barracks of of 16 rooms in two rows of eight, each room measuring three metres by two metres (10 feet by seven feet) and housing three single men or a married couple with no more than two children. Residents of this type of accommodation called them *kasbighar* or brothels. According to Fiji-Indian scholar and leader Ahmed Ali, in these conditions 'privacy was non-existent, marriages fragile, morality a luxury, overtasking widespread, violence, including murder and suicide, not infrequent . . . .'

In *A History of Fiji* Kim Gravelle quotes an immigrant who described the conditions of servitude:

To a man with a wife and family, who had belonged to a middle or high caste in India, his new life was a miserable one, at best that of a well-treated animal – fed, looked after if sick, driven to work, and given a stable to live in . . . . Conditions in the factories and on the plantations in India were as bad, if not worse . . . but it was not without reason that the Indians called their life on the plantations in Fiji *narak*. Hell.

After girmit ended, workers became *khula* – free but not unfettered. There was still five years to wait before getting a ticket home, and signing on for another five-year agreement was not appealing. However, there was also the small matter of survival. For people willing to work, plenty of work was available.

Most importantly, traditional differences between Muslim and Hindu, upper and lower castes were forgotten. Because the caste system had broken down, those who would have been on the bottom rungs of society in India had opportunities in Fiji they never would have had in their own country.

Free Indian settlers applied their farming skills, and 30 years after the first indentures were completed, 6500 hectares were leased to former 'coolies.' Likewise, Indian cattlemen were raising 10,000 head of livestock and Indian entrepreneurs were opening shops around the country. Indian labour was particularly important in the sugar industry, which had become the lifeblood of the colony.

Still, as people brought over as beasts of burden to a strange land, the Indians were looked upon with disdain both by the Fijians and the Europeans. Fiji's Indians were not handed their human and civil rights on a silver platter; they had to fight hard for them.

The first political stirrings surfaced in 1910, when 200 Suva and Rewa Indians asked for representation in government. A year later, the British Indian Association was formed. Their first task was to ask none other than Mahatma Gandhi – who at this time was active in the struggle for Indian rights in South Africa – to send a lawyer to Fiji.

The man who responded was D M Manilal, a Gujarati lawyer from Mauritius who had built a reputation fighting against the indenture system in India. Manilal, or Manilal Doctor, as he was called, arrived in 1912 and immediately commanded a wide following. Four years later, when a pro-indenture Indian was named sole Indian representative to the Legislative Council, Manilal's supporters urged that their own man be considered for the job. The colonial government was not fond of the idea.

Manilal responded by railing bitterly against the government's indenture system. His publicity campaign along with anti-indenture activities in India whipped up support in that country and even persuaded the Viceroy of India to announce that the indenture system would cease 'as soon as possible.' However, this was not to be the case. The colonial government in India later announced that the indenture system would continue for another five years.

Fiji's planters were happy but Indians at home and in India were outraged. Protests were staged at the viceroy's office and Gandhi and his supporters worked vigorously against the indenture system. In the end, as Kim Gravelle described in *A History of Fiji*, 'The economy of a tiny few sugar producing islands wasn't worth the price of Britain's self respect in India. On 12 March 1917, all labour recruiting was stopped 'for the duration of the war (WW I) and two years after'. It would never restart. Indenture officially ended on 1 January 1920.

Although the anti-indenture forces had

won a victory, there was still the matter of civil rights for Indians in Fiji. Manilal and company presented the colonial government with a list of requests which included the repeal of various taxes and discriminatory laws, and establishment of a minimum wage. The appeal was ignored.

The potentially violent situation was aggravated by wartime inflation and a general dissatisfaction with the state of affairs. Strikes by Indians followed, and in a confrontation with police three Indians were hit by gunfire, resulting in one death. Manilal was deported and strike leaders were exiled to remote parts of the country. The strike did not appear to have accomplished much at the time, but in actuality it did effect some gains for the Indians, including repeal of certain taxes and the setting up of government advisors who were to work on improving the Indians' lot in life. In essence, this marked the beginning of the end of Indian serfdom and absolute colonial rule.

World War I
When WW I broke out 700 'Europeans' left for the trenches. The government had instructed the colonial office not to send native Fijians but somehow a handful made their way to the action. Among them was Ratu Sukuna, a young high chief who would later distinguish himself in government service. Sukuna, who was studying at Oxford, tried to enlist in the British Army but was refused. He responded by joining the French Foreign Legion and winning the Medaille Militaire, the highest honour awarded to a soldier. Wounded three times while assaulting enemy trenches under fire, Sukuna was one of 35 men to survive out of a force of 2500.

Back in the islands a German sea raider, Count Felix Von Luckner, was on the loose. The wily count's ship the *Seeadler* (Sea Eagle) was disguised as a Norwegian freighter, and preyed upon Allied ships by feigning friendliness until the last moment, when she unfurled the iron cross and displayed her cannon.

Stopping at remote Mopelia atoll near Tahiti for a respite, Von Luckner's vessel was severely damaged by a freak tidal wave and the sailors were marooned. Von Luckner salvaged the lifeboat – which was christened *Cecile* – loaded it with provisions and set sail with five of the healthiest crew members in search of a ship to steal. They sailed over a thousand km to the Cook Islands but failed to find a ship.

From there the crew of the *Cecile* made it to Katafaga in the northern Lau group. Here they found adequate food supplies in a home where the owner was absent, but still no ship. (A framed letter politely thanking the owner of the home now hangs for all to read at the Ovalau Club in Levuka.) The crew then sailed to Wakaya near Ovalau and finally found what they were looking for – a handsome three-masted schooner with all the qualifications to be the *Seeadler II*. The captain of the vessel even agreed to take them on.

Before Von Luckner got a chance to steal the ship, however, a Fiji government cattleboat called the *Amra* lowered a skiff that approached the sea raiders. Von Luckner recorded that the vessel contained 'an officer and four Indian soldiers who wore puttees and those funny little pants.' Only the officer was armed. According to Von Luckner, 'We could have easily shot them down, or thrown a hand grenade in their boat. Then we could have captured the ship and sailed away . . . . ' However, being out of uniform and a good German aristocrat who played the rules the old-fashioned way, he surrendered peaceably.

The prisoners were first taken to nearby Levuka and then to Suva, where Von Luckner described their arrival to be 'the event of the year. The only warlike happening that had come along to break the monotony of life on the dreary South Seas.' The Count was sent to New Zealand where he commandeered a boat, stole a New Zealand Army officer's uniform and was recaptured. In the midst of his plans for another escape, armistice was signed. Meanwhile, back on Mopelia, the rest of the *Seeadler* crew had lured a French vessel to the island, captured her and sailed safely to Chile.

Back in Fiji, anti-German hysteria was whipped up. Long-time residents of German origin were interned and sent to camps in Australia. A few months later, the war was over.

World War II

Unlike WW I, WW II saw Fijians recruited in earnest. In the early years, men were trained and fortifications were constructed (such as the well-preserved gun emplacements at Momi near Sigatoka). With the attack on Pearl Harbor, it seemed only a matter of time until the Japanese war machine would roll onto Fiji's shores.

By 1942 the Americans had established bases on Fiji and the Japanese no longer seemed a direct threat. Americans were actually being trained under Fiji commandos whom they regarded as experts in jungle warfare. In December 1942 Fijians had the opportunity to prove their worth in the Solomon Islands. Thirty commandos were sent to Guadalcanal and on to Tenaru where Americans were holding the beachhead. The Fijians, who were later referred to as 'death in velvet gloves' by an American journalist, had the unenviable responsibility of mopping up the dug-in Japanese who had survived the American shelling. This was the first of many actions which distinguished the Fijians as among the finest fighting men in the South Pacific.

With the Fiji Islanders' proven early successes the American command cabled for more soldiers, and in April 1943, 36 officers and 799 additional men joined the ranks of those already in the Solomons. The Fijians continued their trail of valour in Bougainville and through the end of the war. The cost in lives had been 57 dead. In later years, during the Communist insurgency in Malaya and as peacekeepers in Lebanon, the Fijians again proved their reputation as modern warriors.

Ratu Sukuna

In ancient times the exploits of certain chiefs became legend and were eventually woven into a kind of mythology. Years later, the individual was deified. Had Ratu Sir Lala Sukuna lived in ancient times he surely would be a god by now. Perhaps the greatest modern-day statesman Fiji has ever produced, Sukuna was born on Bau on 22 April 1888, of chiefly lineage from Bau and Lau. As a child he received the education due the son of a high chief as well as tutelage in English and Latin from the age of six. He later attended Wilkenson School in Auckland and graduated from Wanganui College. He returned to Fiji and worked briefly as a government clerk, after which he sailed to England to study law and political science at Oxford. In his second year of studies, during the beginning of WW I, Sukuna dropped his schooling and attempted to join the British army. He was refused. Undaunted, he crossed the channel, joined the French Foreign Legion, distinguished himself in the field of battle and was awarded the highest honour the French military could bestow.

After the war Sukuna returned to Oxford, received a bachelor of arts degree from Wadham College, and went on to qualify as a barrister. He went back to Fiji and started up the bureaucratic ladder, serving as District Commissioner, Commissioner for Native Reserves, Adviser on Native Affairs, Secretary for Fijian Affairs, and Chairman of the Native Land Trust Board – the position he distinguished himself most in.

Though Sukuna's day-to-day responsibility in this capacity was sorting out land disputes for the colonial administration, he was a man of vision who did much to lay the groundwork for the modern-day government of Fiji. As an editorial in *The Fiji Times* put it, he was 'the best of interpreters of his people to those in authority, and of the affairs of government and of the outside world to the Fijian villager.'

Sukuna was instrumental in sending Fijian soldiers overseas during WW II because he believed Fijians would never be taken seriously until they had spilled blood. It would not be an exaggeration to call him the father of modern-day Fiji. He died on 30 May 1958, 12 years before Fiji would attain independence from Great Britain.

Independence

Life had barely returned to normal in the years following WW II, when Fijian soldiers were called to arms again. The 'Emergency,' as it was called in Malaya, began in 1948. The British-Malayan negotiations for an independent Malaya were opposed by Chinese living in Malaya and by communist guerillas. Both groups began making raids to topple the new government. Britain then began assembling colonial forces to combat the guerillas and wanted troops experienced in jungle warfare. The Kings African Rifles, Rhodesian African Rifles, the Ghurkas of Nepal and soon the 1st Battalion, Fiji Infantry Regiment, were fighting in Malaya. The first detachment of Fiji soldiers arrived in January 1952 and saw action within 48 hours of taking up their positions. By 1954, the jungles around the Fijian camp at Batu Pahat were so safe that the first of 80 Fijian families moved in. The camp eventually included a school, and Fijian *mekes* (traditional dances) were performed for nearby villages. The Fijian battalion became one of the most decorated on and off the battlefield, collecting every sporting trophy it competed for.

Four years and four months after its first skirmish, the Fiji battalion was sent home with an enemy loss of 205 to its credit, and its own loss of 25 men. The modern Fijian reputation of ferocity in combat was still firmly intact.

On 30 May 1958, news of a tragedy reached Fiji. The chief who catapulted his people into the 20th century and sparked the vision of an independent nation had died at sea en route to England. The death of Ratu Sir Lala Sukuna stunned the colony. He had retired from public service only a month earlier and was sailing to England for a holiday that was not to be. Fiji mourned and thousands attended memorial services.

The Fiji that Ratu Sukuna left behind would travel the road to the independence he had dreamed of, but not without a few bumps along the way. The most serious were the labour unrest and riots in 1959-60.

Labour unions, flexing their new-found muscle for the first time, called a general strike in December 1959, which eventually led to rioting by Fijians and Indians against European property. The strike was short-lived but was followed by a huge sugar workers' strike the following year. A massive march on the capital by sugar workers was turned back at the Rewa bridge by Fiji military forces reinforced by the New Zealand Army.

The colonial government, realising that postponing independence any longer would be to no one's benefit, set the spring of 1963 for the first popular election of the Legislative Council. For the first time, common Fijians and Indians would vote, and women of all races would be enfranchised. The Legislative Council has existed in various forms since cession to Great Britain in 1874, but its members were chosen by different methods according to race. Thus the European members were selected by an election amongst European men, the Fijians were appointed by the Great Council of Chiefs, and Indian members were chosen by wealthy Indians.

The next moves toward independence occurred in 1964-65 when members of the National Federation Party and the newly formed Alliance Party met in London to draft a new constitution that would lead to self-government. But the parties clashed bitterly at every session and negotiations ended in a deadlock. The situation would remain that way for four years.

A ministerial system of government was introduced in 1967, with Ratu Mara appointed chief minister and members of the Executive Council in the Legislative Council becoming the Council of Ministers. Negotiations began again in 1969 between the Alliance Party led by Chief Minister Ratu Mara and the National Federation Party led by A D Patel, the party's founder. The main stumbling blocks were the issues of full self-government and communal roll elections. The Patel-led Indians wanted a republic with no ties to the British Commonwealth or Crown and a one-person-one-vote electoral system. The Alliance Fijians and other races, including a minority of anti-NFP Indians, insisted on maintaining close links to the Crown and rejected any idea of a republic. The Alliance Party was also insisting on a communal election system.

In October 1969, Patel died and was succeeded by Siddiq Koya, who had a good working relationship with Ratu Mara and was ready to compromise. In January 1970 a tentative date of 10 October 1970 was set for independence day. However, there was still no constitutional agreement. A solution would not be reached until 30 April – just five months before the planned date. Incredibly, the target date was met, and 96 years to the day after Fiji's sovereignty was handed to Britain, it became an independent state in the presence of His Royal Highness, Prince Charles, representing Queen Elizabeth.

In one of the first moves after independence, the government agreed to pay $10 million to the Colonial Sugar Refining Company for its holdings in the country's four sugar mills. This was the first step towards nationalising the sugar industry and forming the government-owned Fiji Sugar Corporation.

April 1972 saw Fiji's first post-independence election in which Ratu Mara's Alliance Party gained a 14-seat majority in the House of Representatives. The following January, the paramount chief of the Fijians, Ratu Sir George Cakobau, was sworn in as governor general, succeeding Sir Robert Foster, the last governor under colonial rule.

Fiji celebrated its 100th anniversary of the country's link with the British Crown and fourth independence anniversary in October 1974, and Prince Charles made his third visit to the country in four years. By the end of 1976 vast amounts of development work had been done and the ground was set for many other large projects such as the Monasavu hydro-electric scheme and the completion of the Nadi-Sigatoka highway. Electricity, roads and water systems were being taken to rural areas and remote islands; tuna fishing and pine-tree planting had been introduced, tourism was growing and the country was nearing self-sufficiency in poultry, pork and beef. In addition, several new export crops such as cocoa and ginger were being developed.

Thanks to a booming tourist industry and high sugar prices, Fiji's economy grew 5% per year from 1970 to 1980. But the economic turndown in the first half of the 1980s exposed Fiji's failure to diversify its economic base. Thus when sugar prices collapsed in 1980, Fiji was sent into a nose dive. Only the continued growth of tourism, falling petroleum prices and continued foreign aid have softened the blow.

Fiji's international stature, almost single-handedly shaped by Ratu Mara, has grown since independence. Perhaps the most visible manifestation of the nation overseas are the Royal Fiji Military Forces. In April 1978 Fiji offered to send a battalion to Lebanon as part of the United Nations Peacekeeping force for southern Lebanon. The first soldiers left two months later and at the close of 1985, 600 troops were still on duty in that war-torn country. At the time of writing nearly 20 Fiji soldiers have lost their lives in Lebanon.

Fiji sent a 24-man detachment to Zimbabwe in December 1979 as part of the Zimbabwe-Rhodesia cease-fire monitoring force, and in 1981 sent another 550 soldiers to the Middle East as part of the Camp David agreement between Egypt and Israel, which called for an international peacekeeping force to monitor the border between the two nations in the Sinai.

Fiji Today

Recently, Fiji has been wrestling with its economy, unemployment and a wide income disparity between Fijians and Indians which has contributed to tensions. A lack of jobs for school graduates has resulted in increasing crime in the urban areas. In the past the villages could easily absorb unemployed Fijians into the subsistence economy. This is impossible now because the numbers are too large and many of the Fijian youth are urban kids who are just as hard for the villagers to handle. One of the biggest challenges facing the Fiji government is to create jobs for the young population.

Like the rest of the developing world, Fiji is a nation with problems to overcome and to paint a picture of an idyllic 'South Seas paradise' would be false and unfair. Fiji has made tremendous strides in development since independence, especially in comparison to most of its South Pacific neighbours and the country is still a very stable place

From a visitor's point of view, the bright side of Fiji is easy to discern. Improved roads, air service and expanding tourist facilities are making this delightful country more and more accessible to the visitor. Tourism is now the number one earner of hard currency and will continue to play a very important role in the future. One can only hope that Fijians of all stripes choose to develop this industry in such a manner that preserves the natural beauty of the country and allows the great cultures within its borders to flourish.

Prime Minister Ratu Sir Kamisese Mara

Ratu Sir Kamisese Mara has been Fiji's only prime minister since independence in 1970,

making him one of the longest-serving democratically elected leaders in the world today.

Born 13 May 1920, Ratu Mara is a hereditary Fijian high chief, Tui (King) of the island of Nayau, and Paramount Chief of the Lau island group.

He received his primary education at Sacred Heart Convent in Levuka and Lau Provincial School before attending Queen Victoria School in Tailevu. From there he went to the Fiji School of Medicine to train as a medical officer. After two years at the school he returned to complete his secondary education at Marist Brothers High School in Suva and Sacred Heart College in Auckland, New Zealand, where he passed his university entrance exam. He then attended Otago Medical School, where he studied medicine for four years. Despite the medical education, Ratu Mara was not destined to become a doctor.

The forward-looking Ratu Sir Lala Sukuna, who was seeking intelligent Fijians as potential future leaders of an independent Fiji, tapped the young Lauan chief for a career in government administration. He was sent to Wadham College, Oxford, England, where he was the first Fijian to earn an MA degree.

In 1950 Ratu Mara joined the colonial service in London and returned to Fiji as an administrative officer. He quickly advanced through the ranks to commissioner eastern, a post that was responsible for the Lau group and the Lomaiviti and Kadavu areas. He later became a member of the Legislative and Executive Councils, forerunners of the Parliament and Cabinet.

When the ministerial system of government was established in 1967, he became chief minister and then prime minister three years later. He was knighted by the Queen in the New Year's Honours list of 1969 and sworn in as a member of the Privy Council in 1973.

The Prime Minister has built Fiji's reputation as one of the most stable developing countries in the world. He has made state visits throughout the world and was the first Pacific Island leader to hold state-to-state talks with a United States President.

Standing an impressive 1.93 metres (6 foot 4 inches), the prime minister was an athlete as a youth, active in cricket, rugby and track. Today he is an avid fisherman and golfer. Ratu Mara is married to Adi Lady Lala Mara, a hereditary high chief from Rewa. (Adi is the Fijian term for a woman chief.) The Maras have eight children.

ECONOMY

The economy of Fiji is primarily agrarian, with subsistence farming on a village level still an important way of life for much of the population. The largest earner of hard currency is tourism followed by sugar, the main export crop.

The canelands of Fiji lie along the seaboard from the south-west to the north-west coast of Viti Levu, the largest island; and in the northern portion of Vanua Levu, the second largest island. Cane is grown mainly on small holdings (averaging around 4.6 hectares) leased by Indian farmers from communally owned Fijian land. The cane is hand-harvested and sent by truck and small-gauge railway to regional mills. It is then crushed and partially refined by the government-owned Fiji Sugar Corporation.

The system of small-holder cane farming has played an important role in the economic and social stability of the country. When Indian migration ended in 1916 and indentured labourers no longer worked the land, a new system had to be found to harvest the crop. The best alternative, which is still used today, was to break up the large estates and lease out the smaller holdings.

Aside from sugar, other hard-currency earners are gold, copra, tuna, ginger, cocoa, light industrial products and coconut oil. Timber is gaining importance and it is hoped that by the end of the 1980s it will be an important export item. The government is also encouraging small-scale agricultural development, especially in traditional root crops such as taro, cassava and yams.

The aim of the government is to wean the country away from its dependence on sugar. The wisdom of this was evident during the hurricanes of 1985, which severely damaged the cane crop in Viti Levu and left farmers who literally had all their eggs in one basket with very little. Except for pine forest production, which will not be realised until later, no large-scale attempt at agricultural diversification

has begun. However, the country has achieved self-sufficiency in poultry, pork and beef production.

Of late, tourism has taken on the role of primary earner of foreign currency. Tourism first gained importance in the 1960s; currently the demand for hotel rooms has outstripped what is now available. From the direction the government is taking, it appears that hotels will continue to be built and tourism will be the leading industry in the country for years to come.

GOVERNMENT

Fiji became an independent nation on 10 October 1970, 96 years after cession to Great Britain. Its constitution provides for a bicameral parliament modelled on the Westminster plan with a House of Representatives elected by popular vote and a Senate with appointed members.

The House of Representatives, whose purpose is to enact legislation, consists of 52 members elected on a formula designed especially to accommodate Fiji's multi-racial society. Voters choose a representative of their own race and vote for a national ballot of candidates from any ethnic group. The 52 seats consist of 12 Indian representatives, 12 Fijian representatives and three general members (Europeans, Part-Europeans, Chinese, Polynesian, etc) elected from communal rolls; and 10 Indian, 10 Fijian and five general members from the national ballot. The parliament has a life of five years unless dissolved sooner by the House of Representatives.

The Senate has 22 members, eight of whom are appointed by the Great Council of Chiefs, seven by the prime minister, six by the Leader of the Opposition and one by the Council of Rotuma. The Senate's purpose is to review legislation from the House of Representatives, appoint select committees of inquiry and administer to questions of native land. The term of a Senate member is six years.

Fiji is currently ruled by the Alliance

Party, headed by Ratu Sir Kamisese Mara. Ratu Mara and his party, which consists mostly of Fijians, Europeans, Chinese and other islanders, have presided over Fiji since independence.

The opposition party, with a majority of Indian members, won briefly in 1977 but due to squabbling within the ranks, failed to form a government. The Governor General reappointed the Alliance Party as a minority government but it was dissolved at the first sitting. In a second election, the Alliance Party won again.

One of the major future problems the Fijian government and society in general will have to deal with is how political power can be passed along smoothly once the Alliance Party dominance is over. In other words, the political party dominated by the Fijians will lose one day and the Indian party will gain control. The government must insure that the transition is made properly and correctly – a feat more easily said than done.

Although Fijians number fewer than Indians, they wield disproportionately more power than Indians – a feature that seems to be built into the system. Naturally Indians resent this gap, but despite the numerical advantage they hold, they have been unable to elect a prime minister of their own. However, that day will inevitably come. Fijians dread this event but the political reality is that it could indeed happen. How the country deals with sharing political power will be the key to the future of this pluralistic society.

NATIONAL SYMBOLS

The Flag Fiji's flag flew for the first time on Independence Day, 10 October 1970. It includes the red, white and blue 'Union Jack' of Britain in the top left-hand corner and the shield from the Fiji Coat of Arms on a light blue background. The design of the national flag was selected through a competition won jointly by Mr R Wilcock and Mrs M Mackenzie, both of Suva.

Coat of Arms Fiji's coat of arms consists of the images of two Fijian warriors (one bearing a war club, the other a spear) on either side of a shield, a *takia* (Fijian canoe) at the top of the shield, and the motto *Rerevaka na Kalou ka Doka na Tui* (Fear God and Honor the Queen) below the shield. The shield itself bears the image of a heraldic lion holding a cocoa pod across the top. Sugar cane, a coconut palm, a bunch of bananas and the dove of peace occupy each of the four quadrants of the shield. The dove was the flag symbol of Cakobau's government, the administration of the self-proclaimed 'King of Fiji' that preceded the English colonial government in Fiji.

POPULATION & PEOPLE

Fiji is perhaps the most cosmopolitan of all South Pacific nations. Its population, just under 700,000, is an amalgam of East Indians (50%), Fijians (44.8%), 'part-Europeans' or half-castes (1.7%), Europeans (.6%), Rotumans (1.2%), Chinese (.7%), and other Pacific Islanders (1%). The late Fijian statesman Ratu Sukuna spoke of Fiji as a 'three-legged stool' requiring the support of Fijians, Indians, Europeans and other races to keep it erect. Fiji is a pluralistic, multi-racial society that prides itself on its tolerance and maintenance of a stable democracy.

Fijians

Fijians, the indigenous inhabitants of Fiji, are Melanesians who possess an admixture of Polynesian blood which is very strong in the eastern islands (such as the Lau group) but less apparent in the west and interiors of the main islands. Many of the present chiefly families trace their descent, through 11 or more generations, from strangers who sailed or drifted to these shores from distant islands, and who settled singly or in small groups among the Melanesian people already in occupation of the land. The strong Polynesian influence, both physical and cultural, is due primarily to visiting parties of Tongans, many of whom stayed in Fiji for years or settled permanently. Eastern Fiji is thus the frontier on which two streams of migration – of Melanesians from the west and of Polynesians from the east – met and mingled.

Melanesians are characteristically short and dark-skinned, with fuzzy hair. Polynesians are generally tall and well built, with fair skins and straight hair. The intermingling of these two races has produced in Fiji a variety of physical types, ranging from the people of southern Lau – fair-skinned and very tall, with aquiline features – to the *kai colo* or hill people who are dark-skinned, short and flat-nosed. Culturally the differences are not so obvious but social organisation does differ in detail between tribes from east and west.

Fijian customs reflect an utmost courtesy and dignity toward the visitor. There are ceremonies for every occasion, which may include the presentation of *tabua* (whale's teeth), food or other gifts, or more commonly the drinking of *yaqona* (kava), the national beverage.

Communal Life

Traditional Fijian society is based on communal principles derived from village life. People in villages share the obligations and rewards of community life and are still led by a hereditary chief. They work together in the preparation of feasts and in the making of gifts for presentation on various occasions; they fish together, later dividing the catch; and they all help in communal activities such as the building of homes and maintenance of pathways and the village green.

The great advantage of this system is an extended family unit that allows no one to go hungry, uncared for or unloved. Ideally it is an all-encompassing security net that works very effectively not only as a caretaking system but also by giving each person a sense of belonging and identity. On the negative side, the communal system can be restrictive for the individual, who has no choice but to toe the line. Ambition and any kind of entrepreneurial instinct are quickly stifled, sometimes by jealous relatives if someone actually gets too far ahead. Having to abide by the lowest common denominator means one can't really be too different or rebel too much.

Prior to independence there was a move on the part of the government to incrementally change or 'modernise' the village system by dispensing with some communal obligations. At times these changes, combined with a societal transformation in general, were not positive. The slackening of obligations combined with the outside influences of tourism and money coming in from new jobs sometimes meant more diversions and less chiefly authority. The results were higher consumption of alcohol, disrespect for traditional values and a general breakdown of the social fabric. Of late, elders have decided it best to go back to the more traditional way of doing things, and many villages have reinstated a return to the old ways that had been thrown out just a few years ago.

Although some individuals have broken away from the village to set up a business and/or separate identity in town, there are always the family obligations that cannot be ignored. The concept of communal property, in which anything that belongs to you can be claimed by friends or relatives, is still very strong. When someone says 'Kerekere... ' – which translates roughly as 'Please may I have... ' – it would be socially unacceptable to ignore such a request. Due to commitments to friends and relations Fijian businesses often go under.

One will never grow rich in the village, but there is stability, and the member will always be able to survive quite well. Land ownership and the security of village life have provided Fijians with a 'safety net,' but this has been a burden as well. In a sense, it has prevented Fijians (who own over 80% of the land) from competing with the Indians, who have never had the luxury of land ownership. The communal life has put Fijians at a disadvantage with people whose lot has always been to struggle and make the most of what little they have; Fijians have had to adjust to the transition from a communal, subsistence-farming society to a capitalist money economy much more than the Indians.

Indians

Although Fiji Indians come from a variety of subcultures and religious groups, they are seen as a people who share a common way of life, and for political and administrative purposes they have always been lumped together. Early migrants coming to Fiji were carriers of Indian culture only in a limited sense. Most were young, illiterate peasants whose connections with India ended the day their ship left port. Once in Fiji, social groups based on caste disappeared for the most part; and because of a shortage of women, migrants were compelled to marry across religious lines. In addition, communal kinship patterns found in the traditional Indian village gave way to more individualism due to the breakdown in social structure and heightened demands for personal survival.

Fiji's Indians can be divided into two broad cultural categories reinforced by physical differences. Those from the north of India – the 'Calcuttas' or 'Calcutta Wallahs' – came from Bengal, Bihar and Uttar Pradesh through the immigration point of Calcutta and spoke 'village'

Hindustani. The second group was the 'Madrassis,' who generally had darker skin and lacked the sharp features of those from the north. They were recruited from Madras, Malabar, North Arcot, Vizakapatnam and Tanjore in southern India and spoke Tamil, Telegu and Malayalam. From this amalgam of cultures 'Fiji Hindi' has become the lingua franca.

Fiji Indians are also distinguished by their institutions of family and marriage. Although individuals have more free will to choose their partners today than in times past, relatives continue to have influence in this realm. Arranged marriages are more common in rural areas and marriage occurs mainly within subcultural categories and religious groups. Strict marriage ties are especially observed by the more clannish Gujuratis and Punjabis (Sikhs).

Today the trend is towards nuclear-family households but in many areas, both urban and rural, the joint-family household persists. Financial and domestic arrangements may differ from home to home but families may consist of parents, grandparents and both married and unmarried siblings residing under the same roof. Sons are given a freer rein than daughters, who are traditionally kept under very strict supervision.

Thus, despite a diverse cultural background, Fiji Indians are generally united through the common experience of indenture, the use of Fiji Hindustani as the lingua franca, family organisation, cuisine and interests in sports and Indian movies.

The exceptions are the Gujaratis and the Punjabis, who arrived as free migrants from north-west India. They came as traders and merchants and today own most of the shops and businesses in Fiji's urban centres. Generally the Gujaratis and Punjabis have much stronger kinship ties and attachments to India.

Europeans

European settlement in Fiji dates from the beginning of the 19th century. None of the discoverers had any but chance contact with the locals; it was the 'beach-combers' – shipwrecked sailors and deserters – who first attempted to live with the natives. Despite intermittent trade, the first 50 years of the century ended with no more than 50 white residents in all of Fiji.

The demand for cotton in Europe caused by the Civil War in the United States and the belief that Fiji would be annexed by Great Britain brought entrepreneurs and planters, and by 1870 the white population grew to 2000. The primary European settlement was Levuka, the major port and centre of commerce.

Alternating periods of economic growth and decline kept the European population – which was generally involved in planting, commercial enterprises, or government service – fairly stable. It reached its peak in the 1960s at around 7000. After independence in 1970, many Europeans left seeking greener pastures in New Zealand, Australia or the United States. Today the European population numbers less than 4000.

Kai Loma

The part-Europeans, also known as *kai loma*, are a distinctive cultural group with one foot in the Fijian world and the other in the European. Many are descendants of Australians, Americans or Europeans who established themselves either in Levuka, on the isolated coconut plantations of Vanua Levu or on the outer islands of Fiji during the 19th century, and took Fijian wives. One of the most famous part-European families are the Whippys, direct descendents of David Whippy, an American seaman who came to Levuka in 1824 and became that town's leading citizen. By 1881 there were around 800 part-Europeans and they have increased steadily until today they number about 12,000.

The part-European's character can be a fascinating melange of the easygoing sensibilities of the Fijian and the business acumen of the whites – in effect, the best of both worlds. Part-Europeans generally speak fluent English and can at least understand Fijian, if not speak it fluently. Conversations may be carried on in both languages simultaneously, with jokes made in the tongue that best suits the story. Many still make a living in communities like Levuka or Savusavu in Vanua Levu, in the old-time professions of planter, ship builder or seaman. Kai loma proudly trace their cultural heritage on both sides and may even enjoy land rights to the family group to which the Fijian parent belonged.

Rotumans

The Rotumans are a distinct Polynesian ethnic group who come from the island of Rotuma (located 386 km north-west of Fiji). The Rotumans ceded their island to Fiji in 1881 and have been governed as part of Fiji since then. They enjoy full citizenship, and many have settled on Viti Levu in order to find greater opportunity. Some have intermarried with Fijians or Chinese. Although a separate racial and cultural group, Rotumans have always assimilated easily with others and see themselves as an intrinsic part of the Fijian nation. Today Rotumans number just under 9000, most of whom live outside of Rotuma.

Other Ethnic Groups

The Chinese, of whom there are about 5000, first came to Fiji in 1911. They have the reputation of being model citizens and generally make a living as merchants or restaurateurs. Many have intermarried with the local population.

The sum total of other ethnic groups of Pacific Islanders is about 7000. Tongans, who as traders and warriors have lived in Fiji for hundreds of years, are the largest part of this community. In the old days there was active commerce between Tonga and Fiji, and later in the history of this relationship the Fijians in the Lau Islands became vassals to the King of

Tonga. One particular reason Tongans and Samoans came to Fiji was to build *druas*, large double-hulled canoes, because of the lack of proper timber on their own islands.

The second most important member of this group numerically is the Banabans, who are Micronesians. Originally from miniscule Ocean Island, which lies just south of the equator near the 170th meridian of east longitude, the Banabans were employed by a British mining company to excavate the rich deposits of phosphate which covered their island home. When it became obvious the island was doomed to devastation by phosphate stripping, Rabi Island, located near Vanua Levu, was given to the Banabans as a new home in 1942 by the Great Council of Chiefs. However, before they could make any move towards occupying Rabi, Japanese troops landed on Ocean Island and the Banabans suffered greatly. At the war's end the survivors were gathered, some from Nauru, others from the Gilberts (now Kiribati) and the Carolines; and the process of settling Rabi began. There are about 2600 Banabans living on Rabi and throughout Fiji.

Other ethnic groups include Tuvaluans (formerly Ellice Islanders), Samoans and the descendants of Solomon Islanders. The Solomon Islanders were brought to Fiji during the 19th century by 'black-birders' (who might politely be called labour recruiters) as labourers to work the cotton and sugar plantations. Although these islanders have by now thoroughly mixed with Fijians, they still trace their ancestry back to the Solomons.

Modern Fijian Society

On the surface, Fijian life – especially in the traditional village setting – is a romance. People are almost always friendly and generous to a fault. The climate is pleasant, though humid by European standards. Food is plentiful, vicious tropical diseases like malaria are virtually non-existent, and culture is rich in ceremony and tradition. Society and environment seem to be in a kind of gentle harmony.

The visitor whose head is filled with images of the way the South Pacific should be, may feel Fiji is paradise. The verdant landscape is coloured by tropical flowers, the sound of guitars fills the air, and the gentle night breeze caresses the skin. Watching the muscular virility of even the average Fijian man and the graceful ambling stroll of women (who seem akin to fertility goddesses) adds to the ubiquitous sensuality.

However, pure sweetness and light exist nowhere except in people's minds. Even in paradise bills must be paid, people go to the hospital and other problems of day-to-day life must be faced.

Today's Fiji is a society of two main ethnic groups, the indigenous Fijians and the Indians, most of whom came to Fiji in the late 19th and early 20th centuries as indentured labourers. No two peoples could be more different. The Fijian is easygoing, open and communal in orientation towards family and society in general. Most importantly, the Fijian is tied to the land. On the other hand, the Indian is intense, harder to know, excitable, enterprising, hard-working and landless. Families are tightly knit because Indians had to break with the past to get to Fiji, but kinship groups are small. Like the overseas Chinese or the Jew, the Indian is a stranger in his or her own land and compensates for landless insecurity by working harder and valuing material gain.

The goals of the two races were different in earlier years when the Indian simply worked the estates and the Fijian lived undisturbed in the village. However, with the emerging industrial age and an economy based on money, the sets of goals have become the same. The Indian long ago ceased to be the simple farmer content to cut cane and tend goats. Indian children have become educated and

Top: Fijian Resort, Viti Levu (FVB)
Bottom: Snorkelling (FVB)

better off materially than the previous generation, and they continue to work hard in hope of an even brighter future. Likewise, the village life of the Fijian no longer interests many of the youth who have seen discos, fancy hotels and flashy clothing. Increasingly urban areas are becoming crowded with migrants who have drifted from the villages in search of employment or at least excitement.

With jobs and resources becoming ever more scarce, the peaceful coexistence the two races have always enjoyed may at times be strained. Still, they manage to preserve it despite the fact that both groups want the same limited number of jobs, as complete an education as possible for their children, and the material prizes the 20th century has to offer.

The government's task and indeed the key to Fiji's future will be to harmoniously accommodate the aspirations of both races.

CULTURE & CUSTOMS

The visitor to Fiji with even the vaguest sense of perception cannot help but notice the pride of the indigenous people which comes across in their carriage, their way of looking you squarely in the eye and their respect for tradition which manifests itself in hospitality towards the guest. While other South Pacific cultures are dying or long dead, Fiji's way of life remains strong and resilient in the face of outside influence.

What accounts for this?

The reasons can be traced to Fiji's recent history. Just prior to cession, during the early period of settlement, Fiji hovered on the brink of a race war. Settlers and natives fought over land, and the nation, which was primarily ruled by feudal chiefs, was near anarchy. The country was voluntarily handed over to the British by the chiefs under terms and conditions that would protect the Fijian people. A basically benign, paternalistic sort of colonialism was provided by rulers who wanted to prevent a race war (which was already occurring in New Zealand) and to make sure no other power would step in and take advantage of the situation.

Fortunately for Fiji, the first governor, Sir Arthur Gordon, was a 19th-century romantic who saw himself as a head Fijian chief. He was anxious to see that Fijians were not exploited and took the role of protector quite seriously. He realised that the best way to govern the country was to let the Fijians govern themselves in the manner they always had – with the chief as the authority. He also set into motion the protection of Fijian lands so that the Fijians would never be alienated from them, and laid down laws that prohibited Fijians from being used as labour for the white people's plantations.

Realising that somebody had to work the fields, Gordon set up the indentured labour system which opened the flood-gates to East Indian workers. After Gordon there were some governors who had planters' interests at heart and who perhaps would have liked to loosen the laws prohibiting the use of Fijian labour, but the scheme developed by Gordon held fast. Also, thanks to Gordon's foresight more than 80% of the land is still held communally by Fijians.

Thus in answer to the original question of what accounts for the strength of Fijian culture, the Fijians never really lost their land nor their leadership. The chiefs have always had political sway and were always recognised by the colonial government, which was in itself often loosely based on a traditional Fijian system. The colonial government merely put an end to political bickering and warfare. In this way, communities weren't disrupted by men being forced into labour. Fijians were left to live as they always had; there was no reason to change and they didn't.

Aside from Gordon's assistance, Fijians have always had a tremendous reverence for tradition and an innate conservatism. Today we see this reflected in the sanctity of the kava ceremony and other customs.

People still operate entirely on a traditional system or methodology when in the village. Despite modern education's trend towards individualism – the direct opposite of traditional society – Fijians generally remain deeply entrenched in and psychologically committed to the old ways: respect for chiefs and respect for the system.

Yaqona or Kava Drinking

We have slept through the night and day now dawns
The sun is high in the heavens
Go uproot the yaqona and bring it . . .
Prepare the root and proclaim it!
The acclamation rose skywards,
Reaching distant lands!

Perhaps nothing reflects the Fijians' reverence for tradition like *yaqona* or kava drinking. Visit any Fijian village or home, particularly on a weekend, and you will likely come upon the spectacle of a family sitting on the floor around a large wooden bowl filled with a dishwater-coloured liquid, drinking the contents from a half coconut shell. You will then be asked, *'E dua na bilo?'* (Try a cup?)

You definitely should try a cup, though don't expect ambrosia. The drink is prepared from the pulverized root of a plant related to the pepper family (*piper methysticum*), looks like muddy water and has a tingly numbing effect on the tongue. The taste, not unpleasant, takes some getting used to and from a visitor's point of view it is *de rigueur* to at least *tovolea mada* (try please).

The most important aspect of kava drinking is psychological. Sitting around a bowl in the village, exchanging *talanoa* (conversation) and listening to the guitars hammer away is a very pleasant experience. Most importantly, the act of sharing a bowl creates an invisible bond between the participants. The visitor feels a warmth and acceptance among complete strangers that is normally associated with

family or close friends. It is no accident that in Fiji many business deals or social contracts are consummated around a kava bowl.

Yaqona is a Fijian link to the past, a tradition so inextricably woven into the fabric of culture that life without it would be unimaginable. Fijians would scarcely be Fijians without their national beverage. It is consumed ritually when welcoming visitors, sending village members on journeys, christening boats, laying the foundations of homes, casting magical spells, making deals, settling arguments and, as is usually the case, chatting. It is also presented as a *sevusevu* (guest gift) to the host or as a token of respect to visitors of higher rank in official ceremonies.

Kava drinking was an ancient custom when the first Europeans arrived and their observations still accurately reflect its use today. Basil Thomson, 19th-century ethnologist, said, 'The chief's yaqona circle supplied the want of newspapers; the news and gossip of the day were related and discussed; the chief's advisors seized upon the convivial moment to make known their view; matters of policy were decided; the chief's will, gathered from a few careless words spoken while drinking, was carried by mouth throughout his dominions.'

Legend has it that yaqona was derived from the Fijian god, Degei (which translates as 'from heaven to the soil and through the earth'), who asked his three sons where they wanted to live and what they wanted to do with their lives. They replied with where they wanted to dwell and what they thought their tasks should be. Degei was pleased but told his sons that although they had power and strength, they lacked the wisdom to make decisions. He gave them two sacred crops, yaqona and *vuga* (a type of tree) from which to draw wisdom. The sons in turn gave them to the people and to this day, goes the legend, the crops grow where the Fijian descendants live.

A non-alcoholic beverage, yaqona has

varying effects on the individual, ranging from a fuzzy-headedness to mild euphoria. The drink always acts as a diuretic and has been used as such by pharmaceutical manufacturers.

Early explorers spoke in awe of yaqona's effects but no one knows for sure if these accounts were exaggerated or if the 'grog' was more potent in those days. One theory postulates that because the root was chewed (by young virgins) before mixing, the saliva somehow reacted with the active ingredients to intensify the effect. Another plausible theory is that additives – possibly hallucinogenics such as 'angels cap' and 'yaqoyaqona' (*piper puberulem*) – were added to the mix. C F Gordon-Cumming, a noted travel writer who visited in 1875, noted: 'Its action is peculiar, inasmuch as drunkenness from this cause does not affect the brain, but paralyses the muscles, so that a man lies helpless on the ground, perfectly aware of all that is going on. This is a condition not unknown to the British sailor in Fiji.'

Even though the chemical makeup of kava is known, organic chemists haven't figured out the specific active ingredient(s). A University of the South Pacific pharmacologist, Yadu Singh, has made an extensive study of the drug and believes the kick comes from recently discovered compounds known as *alpha pyrones*. Said Singh: 'Their nature is not like a stimulant such as cocaine but cannot be described as a depressant either. Yaqona has a calming effect somewhere in between.'

Although yaqona is used primarily as a social drink, native healers have cured ailments ranging from tooth decay and respiratory diseases to gonorrhea with it. Excessive yaqona drinking causes a host of disorders including loss of appetite, bloodshot eyes, lethargy, restlessness, stomach pains and scaling of the skin. The latter condition, known as *kanikani* by Fijians, is fairly common among heavy drinkers who may consume up to a gallon or more in the course of a day.

In villages the brew is generally consumed by men in a home or community *bure*, but occasionally women gather in the kitchen and drink among themselves. On other occasions an older woman may join the men and imbibe in an area that is usually all-male. A woman visitor will generally be offered a bowl with no compunction; however, unless she is someone of rank, a man will be given the first opportunity to drink. In the cities where yaqona drinking is not so compartmentalised by sex, men and women can freely take a bowl together.

While some missionaries discouraged kava, which they referred to as a 'filthy preparation,' some of the more enlightened students of culture saw its merits. Basil Thomson questioned the wisdom of the Wesleyan missionaries who denied Fijians their yaqona. He wrote, 'The path of virtue for the native has been made dull enough already by the prohibition of all his ancient heathen distractions .... ' Thomson felt that denied their grog the Fijians would inevitably be swayed by the Catholic missionaries, whose policy was to make the lives of the Fijians 'as joyous as they dare.'

Thomson also recognized yaqona as a cure for the 'great temptation' that afflicted his fellow Englishmen in lonely tropical climes – alcoholism. Yaqona, he claimed, when substituted for spirits, satisfied the craving for liquor without producing intoxication. 'In this respect,' he wrote, 'it is a pity that yaqona cannot be acclimatised in Europe.'

Today, although kava is central to the Fijian culture, it is controversial in terms of how healthy it is for economic growth. Whereas in the old days grog was strictly used for ceremonial purposes by chiefs or priests, today it is drunk copiously in villages, often to the detriment of gardening, fishing or other 'productive activities.' Because of the negative side effects of this drinking, which certainly do not promote hard work, some Fijian officials have asked if excessive grog drinking is good for the country.

The yaqona plant is cultivated like any other crop and is big business in Fiji. The plants thrive at altitudes between 150 and 300 metres and grow to a height of 3.5 metres at full maturity. Yaqona can be harvested after a year's growth but the longer it grows the more potent the brew. Potency also varies with geographic location, subspecies, and method of preparation. Generally the dried root is used in making grog, but on occasion the green root or stem is utilised. Retail market price is US$4 to 5 a pound and it can be purchased as a dried root or pre-ground. Both forms are suitable as gifts and should certainly be considered when visiting a village or a household.

No one knows the origins of the plant but botanists believe it may have come from Java via India; from Java it was transplanted throughout the South Pacific by means of various migrations of islanders. Whatever the origins, kava is or has been used in the majority of the central and eastern Polynesian societies as well as in areas of Melanesia and Micronesia. Its use is documented as far north as Hawaii, as far south as Tonga, as far west as New Britain and as far east as the Gambier group.

In Fiji yaqona was and is the social cement that bonds society. The importance of its use today can be illustrated by a recent incident at the University of the South Pacific campus in Suva.

During a weekend beer-drinking bout, the age-old rivalry between Tongans and Fijians surfaced and a Tongan and a Fijian got into a fist fight. The Fijian got the short end of it, and the next day the offending Tongan was severely thrashed by a group of Fijians. The other Tongans on campus took retribution and a vicious circle was set into motion. Soon no Tongans were safe on the school grounds and all had to be moved to another location.

One day the authorities got wind that both sides were going to meet en masse and police were summoned to prevent any bloodshed. However, instead of tribal warfare, the police found Tongans and Fijians sitting peacefully next to a kava bowl, where they played guitar and sang into the wee hours of the night.

Both cultures so respected the 'peace pipe' represented by yaqona that the score was settled over a bowl of grog and a public confession by the protagonists. The war was over.

Tabua

A *tabua* or whale's tooth (taken from Cacholot or sperm whales) is the highest token of respect one can receive in Fiji. While the use of yaqona is shared with other regions of the Pacific, tabua-giving is strictly a Fijian ritual. The tabua is presented to a distinguished guest – for example a high chief – or is given if a favour is requested. Tabua may be exchanged at betrothals, weddings, births, deaths or when a major contract or agreement is entered into. Likewise, tabua may also be used to exchange apologies after an argument. Like yaqona, the role of tabua has an intrinsic role in the social and economic fabric of Fijian life. The value of each tabua is judged by its thickness and length. Taking one out of the country as a souvenir is strictly forbidden.

The Meke

The *meke* is a communal dance/theatre combining singing, chanting and drumming. Traditionally it is performed in a village setting on special occasions – typically for visiting dignitaries. Today mekes are commonly presented at hotels for the benefit of tourists. However, the meke is much more than a colourful dance – it is a medium of transmission that allows important historical events, stories, legends and culture to be handed down from one generation to the next. Often the composer of a meke is unknown, but the dances are embellished and passed on by the *daunivucu* whose role it is to preserve the custom. Traditionally the daunivucu has links with the spirit world and when in communion with the spirit plane may go into a trance and begin to chant and sway. During this time the daunivucu's disciples will watch his motions, which may be added to a particular ceremony.

In the meke every motion and nuance has its significance. The positioning of the performers and even of members of the audience is extremely important. Villagers of high birth have special positions in the ceremony and to place them in a subordinate spot would be insulting and possibly misrepresentative of the community's history.

Firewalking

Fijian firewalking is an ancient ritual, which according to legend was given by a god only to the Sawau tribe of the island of Beqa off the coast of Viti Levu. The skill is still possessed by the Sawau tribespeople (who live in four villages on the southern side of Beqa), but in special cases members of other tribes adopted by the Sawau can also perform this mystifying ceremony. Nowadays firewalking is performed occasionally for Fijians but most often for the benefit of tourists at various resorts. The performances for the visitors are generally less steeped in custom than the one described below, but the demonstration of firewalking is just as genuine.

Traditionally, several male representatives are chosen from each village. All are immediate family of the *Bete*, traditional priest-*cum*-master of ceremonies. For two weeks before the event the participants must observe two strict rules: There must be no contact with women (an act of true sacrifice for most Fijian men) and eating coconuts is forbidden. Failure to observe these *tabus* may result in severe burns.

In preparation for the firewalking a circular pit a metre or more in depth and four to five metres wide is dug. It is lined with large, smooth stones, a third to half a metre in diameter and covered with large logs. Six to eight hours before the ceremony a huge bonfire is built. The burning logs are later removed by men with long green poles who chant '*O-vulovulo*' and clear the way for the participants. A long tree fern, said to contain the spirit of God, is laid across the pit in the direction of the Bete. Large vines are then dragged across the stones, levelling them for the actual firewalking.

When the stones are finally in position, the Bete jumps on them and takes a few trial steps to test their firmness. He then calls for bundles of green leaves and swamp grass, which are placed around the edge of the pit. Finally, the position of the tree fern is adjusted at the command of the Bete; the firewalkers will approach the pit from the direction in which it points. Meanwhile, the village men who have prepared the fire take their positions surrounding the pit, leaving a gap for the entry of the firewalkers.

The Bete surveys the scene and when satisfied, shouts '*Vuto-O*,' the signal for the firewalkers' approach. They appear from their place of concealment and walk briskly towards the pit. The tree fern is removed and the firewalkers walk single file across the red-hot stones around the circumference of the pit. The devotees jump out of the pit and the bundles of grass and leaves are spread out on the stones, which steam in the fiery heat. The performers re-enter the pit amid the clouds of steam and squat for a few minutes in their version of a Turkish bath. After this they walk off the stones unscathed by the ordeal. At this time, if the ceremony is held at a resort, the inevitable skeptic will cautiously approach the pit and place the palm of his hand over the stones. He or she will then walk away convinced it was no charade.

How do they do it?

No one has the definite answer but scientists point to the power of suggestion, especially when the religious element of the ceremony is considered as well as the fact that an insulating film of moisture on the skin may act as a protective layer.

Members of the British Medical Association came to these conclusions after witnessing a ceremony: First, the skin of the participants was neither thicker nor tougher than that of anyone else accustomed to walking barefoot all their lives. Second, there was no evidence of oil or any other substance applied to their feet, nor were the participants under the influence of opiates. Finally, the performers reacted normally to painful stimuli such as burning cigarettes or needles jabbed into their feet before and after the firewalking.

Those who claim the performers may be in a trance-like state are also incorrect. Get close enough to the firewalkers during a performance and you may hear them crack jokes. One reliable witness told me he saw a participant pull a cigarette from behind his ear, light it on a red-hot stone and have a leisurely smoke!

Even with its tourist trappings, the firewalking experience is definitely worth seeing. Schedules for the events are available at all of the hotels or in tourist publications like *Fiji Beach Press* or *Fiji Fantastic*.

EDUCATION

Fiji has a comparatively good system of education compared to most of its neighbouring countries and is a centre for learning in the South Pacific. Enrollment is nearly 100% for primary-school children and tuition for grades one through eight is free. Classes are taught in the pupil's mother tongue (the local Fijian dialect for the Fijians and Hindi or Urdu for the Indians) and in English for the first several years until students have grasped enough English to make it the medium of instruction. Thus nearly everyone – except some of the older generation – speaks English.

There are 660 primary schools, 140 secondary schools, 37 vocational schools, a theological college, and one university (University of the South Pacific) in the country. Vocational training includes courses in engineering, maritime studies, telecommunications, agriculture, carpentry, hotel and restaurant management and business. The University of the South Pacific, established in 1968, has an enrollment of about 2500 students from throughout the Pacific and is funded primarily by Fiji and grants from overseas. There is also a separate Fiji School of Medicine, associated with the university.

GEOGRAPHY

The Fiji Islands are situated in the southwest Pacific Ocean, where they occupy a central locale 2797 km north-east of Sydney, Australia and 1848 km north of Auckland, New Zealand. Fiji lies wholly in the southern tropics, that is, between the equator and the Tropic of Capricorn. The Fiji archipelago forms the eastern outpost of the chain of high volcanic islands of continental origin that extends eastward from Papua New Guinea through the Solomon Islands and Vanuatu. Fiji's closest neighbour to the east is Tonga and to the west Vanuatu (formerly New Hebrides). Longitudinally, Fiji is where the new day begins; on the 180th meridian the International Date Line makes a special eastward bend around the island group so that all of the country keeps the same time.

The territorial waters of Fiji are defined in the Deed of Cession as all that area 'lying between the parallels of latitude of 15 degrees south and 22 degrees south of the equator, and between the meridians of longitude of 177 degrees west and 175 degrees east of the meridian of Greenwich.' In 1965 the boundary was extended by one degree to take in Conway Reef, extending the limit to 174 degrees east. In latitude, the Fiji Islands correspond with Tahiti, Townsville in Australia, Zimbabwe, Rio de Janiero and northern Chile.

The area included within these limits is approximately 709,660 square km, about 97% of which is water. The remaining 3%, 18,376 square km, is land. The Fiji archipelago includes about 300 islands (depending on how many reefs and tiny islets you take into consideration), of which about 100 are inhabited. The largest island, Viti Levu, which has 70% of the population and an area of 10,388 square km, is the hub of the entire archipelago. Situated on it are Suva, the largest city, the chief port and the capital; Nadi, site of the international airport; and Lautoka, the second largest city and the second port of entry.

Vanua Levu, situated to the north-east of Viti Levu, is the second largest island, which with an area of 5538 square km is slightly over half the size of Viti Levu. Although more sparsely settled than Viti Levu, it is also a centre of population. Like Viti Levu, it produces sugar cane and also has large coconut plantations.

Taveuni lies to the east of Vanua Levu, being separated from it by the Somosomo Strait. With an area of 435 square km, it is verdant, mountainous and very rich agriculturally.

Tied with Taveuni as the third largest island in the archipelago (with an area of 409 square km) is Kadavu, which lies to the south of Viti Levu. It is a centre of traditional Fijian culture and not often seen by tourists.

All of the remaining islands of Fiji are small and are divided into two main groups, Lomaiviti and Lau.

Lomaiviti translates as 'middle' or central Fiji, which describes exactly where this island group is found on the map. It is composed of seven main islands, with smaller ones lying off the coasts. Their aggregate land area is 425 square km. Gau, Koro and Ovalau are large, each being about 100 square km or more in area. Ovalau derives its importance from the town of Levuka, which was the earliest European settlement in Fiji and the original capital. Gau is the largest, highest and southernmost of the group; Koro is a high, wedge-shaped island rising abruptly from deep water. Nairai and Batiki lie to the east of Ovalau; they are lower than their neighbours, and are surrounded by extensive reefs. Makogai, located north-east of Levuka, was once a leper colony serving the entire south-west Pacific. Wakaya, once a plantation, is now an exclusive real estate development. All of the islands can be seen from the old capital of Levuka on a clear day.

Lau, or eastern Fiji, the area most heavily influenced by the Tongan culture, includes numerous limestone islands and others of volcanic or composite structure, all set among widespread reefs. For administrative reasons all of Lau is one district, but it is geographically divided into four sub-groups: northern Lau, central Lau and southern Lau, which together form a chain of islands stretching 432 km in a north-south direction; and the Moala group, lying to the south of Lomaiviti.

Northern Lau includes the Exploring Islands (one large island and eight small ones, all enclosed within a barrier reef) and some 14 others, of which Naitauba, Kanacea, Mago and Cicia are the most important.

Central Lau includes five islands centering on Lakeba, which is the hereditary seat of the chiefs of Lau and the home of Prime Minister Ratu Sir Kamisese Mara.

Southern Lau is comprised of 16 islands as well as some clusters, most of them grouped within 100 km of Lakeba.

Beyond these, in the attenuated 'tail' of the archipelago, lie Vatoa and Ono, isolated from their nearest neighbours and from one another by wide stretches of open sea. The most outlying islands of southern Lau are actually closer to Tonga than they are to Fiji.

The Moala group is composed of three islands having an aggregate area of 119 square km and situated about halfway between Kadavu and southern Lau. Moala is the principal island; Totoya is the rim of an extinct volcano whose breached and flooded crater forms a beautiful landlocked lagoon; and Matuku is reckoned to be one of the garden spots of Fiji.

The Yasawa group, situated to the north-west of Viti Levu, the main island, includes six principal islands (four of them large) and many small ones, having a total area of 135 square km. These islands, which have been compared to a string of pearls, extend across the sea for 80 km in shallow water behind the Great Sea Reef. This area is the destination for two local cruise companies, Blue Lagoon and Islands in the Sun. It is a favourite of many tourists and lives up the white people's idea of what the South Seas 'should' look like.

Rotuma, a Polynesian outlier which lies 386 km north-north-east of the Fiji group, was ceded to Britain in 1881 as part of the Fiji Colony. Although politically part of Fiji, geographically and ethnologically it has nothing to do with the islands. Most Rotumans, who are Polynesians related to the Samoans, live on Viti Levu rather than their 'home' island. Rotuma's policy is to discourage tourism.

The islands most visitors find themselves familiar with are those of the Mamanuca Group, also an archetypally 'South Pacific' locale, situated just offshore from Nadi and Lautoka on Viti Levu. It is here that many of the popular resorts such as Beachcomber, Plantation Island, Castaway and Mana are located.

Some of the other smaller but well-known islands not mentioned in the above paragraphs are Beqa, home of the fire-walkers; Vatulele, famous for its sacred prawns; and Rabi, once inhabited by Fijians but now the adopted home of Banabans or Ocean Islanders (Micronesians) who moved there after WW II (see Facts About the Country – Other Ethnic Groups). Both Beqa and Vatulele are located off the southern coast of Viti Levu, while Rabi is off the coast of Taveuni.

Types of Islands

Sailors generally speak of 'high' and 'low' islands, but to be geologically correct there are three types of islands in the archipelago. The majority are high islands of volcanic origin and low islands which include coral and limestone varieties. The volcanic islands, of which Viti Levu could be seen as an example, have sharply defined, mountainous landscapes, ancient volcanoes, and rocky outcroppings and shorelines. Inland, the country is broken terrain with few stretches of flat land except in river valleys. In the windward areas where rains are frequent, the hills are covered with thick vegetation and are smothered almost incessantly with rain. Leeward, growth is sparse and hills are brown. A lively vestige of the active volcanic period are hot springs, which are always found at low elevations. The best-known in Fiji are the springs at Nakama, in the old coconut-plantation town of Savusavu on Vanua Levu.

Coral islands, although low and small, have their own peculiar Robinson Crusoesque charm. Generally located near the inner margin of a broad reef, they are usually only a few metres above sea level, flat as a table and have beautiful white sand beaches. Despite limited soil, they often support luxuriant vegetation including vines, grasses, broad-leaved trees and, of course, the coconut palm. A classic example is the resort of Beachcomber Island off Lautoka.

Limestone islands may also appear to be low and flat-topped but have steep, sharp sides suggesting that they are huge masses of rock upheaved from the sea, which is exactly what they are. They are often surrounded by a succession of precipitous cliffs, undercut by the surf. Because the limestone erodes easily, the rock may be pitted and bristling with sharp pinnacles or cut by ravines or narrow canyons. Inland, central depressions give the islands a basin-like appearance. The depression floors are commonly cut up into rolling hills, fertile and well wooded. A good example of a typical limestone island is Vanua Balavu in the Lau group.

Of the hundreds of islands in the Fiji group, only a few may be classed as true atolls. The typical atoll, of which so much has been written in the romantic literature of the South Seas, is basically long strips of broken coral and sand ranging from a few metres to half a km forming a circular or ring-like structure that surrounds a lagoon. Perhaps the best-known example of an atoll in Fiji is Wailagilala, located on the eastern side of the Nanuku Passage, the main shipping lane through the islands.

FORCES OF NATURE

Despite Fiji's volcanic history, strong earthquakes in the region are rare. Of much greater relevance are cyclones, which have struck Fiji over the last several years with greater frequency than they have within a century. Normally Fiji gets 10 to 15 cyclones per decade, with perhaps one of hurricane intensity. Since the beginning of 1985, Fiji has suffered 12 cyclones, of which half had devastating hurricane-force winds. The sudden increase in cyclone activity is inexplicable but scientists postulate it may be part of a meteorological cycle.

In early 1985 Fiji was hit with two hurricanes, Nigel and Eric, within 24 hours of each other. The result was 26 deaths and massive flooding that caused millions of dollars' damage to homes, crops and hotels, thus crippling the vital tourism sector for months. A few months later, not yet recovered from Nigel and Eric's wrath, Fiji miraculously escaped what would have been terrible destruction from Hurricane Hina. Hina had appeared to be headed directly for the country's most populated areas but suddenly veered into the ocean, away from the islands. The hurricane had gusts of up to 160 knots (about 300 kph), making it potentially more destructive than Tracy, the hurricane that flattened the city of Darwin in 1974.

The forces of nature in Fiji not only cause havoc to life and property but have caused problems within the tourism industry. Because the number of insurance claims have increased, insurance companies have upped the cost of premiums to resorts who in turn pass along the costs to the consumer.

FLORA & FAUNA

The indigenous flora and fauna of Fiji (and the south-west Pacific) are strongly Indo-Malayan in character. They entered the Pacific from the west, in the face of the prevailing winds and ocean currents, and as might be expected, their range and variety became progressively poorer with the increasing distance from the source. Thus, Fiji has less range and variety than

the Solomon Islands and Vanuatu, which are poorer than Papua New Guinea but richer in species than Tonga, Samoa and Tahiti. Even within the Fiji archipelago the same attenuation of species is evident, the flora and fauna of the eastern islands being much poorer than those of the large islands to the west.

When the Europeans first arrived in Fiji they found mangroves on the salt mud flats and estuaries; coconuts on the foreshores and coastal plains; rain forests, bamboos and ferns on the mountains and hills; and on the dry leeward sides of the islands reeds, grasses, casuarinas and pandanus. More than half of Fiji's total area is still covered with forest, principally tropical rainforest occupying the windward or wet slopes of the large islands. The forested area also includes large sections of intermediate forest and some 20,000 hectares of mangroves. Early in the 19th century, Europeans discovered sandalwood in the dry, natural environment along the west coast of Vanua Levu and within about a decade removed most of it. Later on, other indigenous woods ruch as dakua, yaka and vesi were discovered and are still exploited commercially.

Fijians had already utilised the coconut for food, drink and construction; large timber for canoe building; pandanus leaves for mats and baskets; bamboo and reeds for home building; hibiscus for twine; mangrove for firewood; kava or *piper methysticum* for the ceremonial drink known as yaqona; and mulberry bark for 'masi' or bark cloth.

Visitors flying over Fiji will note the many pine forests that cover the mountains. The 30,000 hectares of pine have been introduced and will some day make an important national resource.

One of the best places to see Fiji's flora as well as plants from throughout the South Pacific is Thurston Gardens (the museum grounds) in Suva.

Fiji's indigenous mammals are limited to six species of bat and the small grey

Polynesian rat. Four of the bats are fruit bats (otherwise known as flying foxes) and the two remaining varieties are insect-eating bats. Dogs and pigs were introduced at an early period by the Polynesian immigrants to Fiji. All other mammals now in the islands have been brought here during the last 200 years.

Cattle, horses and sheep were introduced to Fiji about the middle of the last century – cattle and horses by the missionaries, and sheep by the settlers. Goats were introduced by the missionaries in the early 1800s. In 1859 several cows and a bull were introduced to the island of Wakaya (near Levuka) for breeding purposes. The story goes that upon seeing the animals, the local people asked 'What are these?' and the reply was 'A bull and a cow.' According to folklore, the Fijian word for cattle, *bulumakau*, was coined from this reply. This would be a convincing story for lexicographers; however, according to historian R A Derrick the first two introductions of cattle to Fiji were one or two milking cows (no bull at all), and the word bulumakau was already in existence in pidgin talk throughout the Pacific. Similar stories exist for pig (*puaka* or *vuaka*) and dog (*koli*). Logically we might think the words have English derivations, koli from collie and puaka from porker. Derrick tells us that it is a pity the 'mere facts spoil a good story.' Both koli and puaka have Polynesian roots extending long before the Europeans arrived.

The mongoose, often seen darting across a road or lawn, was introduced from India during the 1880s as a means of controlling the snakes and rats which plundered the cane fields. Unfortunately mongooses also liked hens, native birds and the shellfish clinging to the mangroves. By 1890 they had become a pest and remain so today. They are restricted to the larger islands.

Birdlife in Fiji is varied and, for the ornithologically minded, quite interesting. There are over 100 species of birds, which include seven varieties of parrots, a honeyeater, a kingfisher, a fantail, owls, ducks, rails, cuckoos and large swamp fowl. The most numerous and well-known introductions to Fiji are the mynahs and bulbuls from India, which have chased many of the smaller native birds into the hills. For those interested in birdlife the best book on the subject (available only in Fiji) is *Birds of the Fiji Bush* by Fergus Clunie, director of the Fiji Museum.

Snakes are found on many of the islands, the most common being the harmless Pacific boa which may grow up to two metres in length and feeds on rats and ground-nesting birds. The one venomous land snake in Fiji, the bolo, is not aggressive and is rarely seen; there is no record of death from its bite. Sea-snakes, commonly seen along the coast, are highly venomous but normally very docile.

There are several varieties of lizard. The friendly gecko or house lizard, seven to 10 cm long, pays visits to hotel rooms but is a welcome guest because it preys on mosquitoes and flies. Several other varieties of lizards are often seen scurrying among the rocks and brush, as well as the rarely observed banded iguana that is up to a metre long. In recent years scientists have discovered an entirely new species of lizard in Fiji, the crested iguana, on a tiny island off the coast of Vanua Levu. The original home of the iguana is South and Central America and biologists speculate that the iguanas may have drifted from the Americas on large pieces of floating vegetation and ended up in Fiji. At any rate it was too far to swim. Both species of iguanas have been successfully hatched at Orchid Island, a tourist attraction near Suva that among other things has many different exhibits of local flora and fauna on display. This is the closest thing to a zoo in Fiji and the only place where the rare reptiles may be seen.

The giant toad was introduced from Hawaii in 1936 to help control slugs, beetles and millipedes, and has spread prolifically ever since. When the toad's natural food becomes scarce it turns cannibalistic and grows smaller, as most have in Fiji. The toads breed in still water; you can always see multitudes of black tadpoles in ditches and potholes. They come out en masse on lawns at night, or on the roads after a rain. One wit observed that the only predator the toad and the mongoose have in Fiji is the automobile.

The Fiji frogs occupy the extreme eastern outpost to which amphibian Pacific migration reached. Their appearance has been recorded on a number of islands, including Ovalau, Taveuni, Vanua Levu, Viti Levu and Beqa. These are frogs of damp, thick forests, whose eggs are attached to the surface of leaves and in which complete intra-oval metamorphosis takes place.

In the sea and on the reefs there are fish, turtles (some, unfortunately, killed for their shells), sharks, lobster, little crayfish, giant clams, beche-de-mer, trochus and the annelid seaworm called *balolo*. The balolo rises to the surface with uncanny punctuality twice a year, generally in the months of October and November. Fresh-water prawns in the streams and rivers of most of Fiji provide a source of food.

Last but not least, Fiji also has the mosquito, but thankfully not the malarial variety.

The Fijians have in some cases developed a friendly relationship with turtle, shark, eel and prawn, and claim to be able to call them up from the depths. In Koro turtles are called up for the benefit of tourists (with mixed results at best). Kadavu is also a spot where turtles will rise in response to a particular chant. The people of Korolevu, a village on the Sigatoka River, are said to be able to call up eels. In Vatulele, off the western coast of Vanua Levu and on Vanua Vatu in Lau, sacred red prawns can be summoned. In Lakeba, an island in the Lau group, individuals from certain clans can call sharks to the surface. (See section on Lakeba.)

RELIGION

Fiji is a meeting ground where some of the world's great religions – Christianity, Hinduism and Islam – are practised in tolerance of each other. Surveys indicate that almost all of Fiji's inhabitants belong to some type of organised religion. Church attendance is generally high and pastors and priests wield a great deal of power over their flock. Approximately 51% of the population are Christians, followed by 40% Hindus and 7.73% Muslims. Of the Christians the majority, Fijians, are Methodists, followed by Roman Catholics, Seventh Day Adventists, Assembly of God adherents, Anglicans, Presbyterians, Mormons and other Christian groups.

Ancient Fijian Religion

The old Fijian religion contained a myriad of gods and spirits. Along with the same gods worshipped in different parts of the country, each clan might have its own deities. The core of the system was ancestor worship in which people paid homage to their forebears, particularly the illustrious ones. Each clan had its own temples dedicated to one god or goddess – an ancestor with a specific role. Thus one ancestral spirit, perhaps descended from a great warrior, would be dedicated to warfare and cannibalism; others, perhaps descended from an agriculturalist, would be concerned with crop productivity; and others might be concerned with fishing or some other activity. Gods thus reflected the society they sprang from.

Deification of chiefs went on right into the last century. This was evidenced on the battlefield, when warriors were reluctant to kill chiefs because they were seen as demi-gods – people who stemmed from the gods and had the potential to become gods. When a chief fell in a battle, the ranks broke and the enemy was for all practical purposes vanquished. This aspect was not lost on unscrupulous chiefs who hired European mercenaries to shoot enemy chiefs on sight. Perhaps this explains why a small group of Europeans backed by a strong 'conventional' Fijian army could wreak havoc upon armies of thousands of Fijian warriors.

Christianity

Although the priesthood and many of the ruling elite were at first reluctant to accept Christianity, Fijians in general embraced the new religion once their leaders had done so. They saw that the Christian god was powerful; he could produce incredible things like guns, ships and other technology. He was certainly a god to be reckoned with, but by their thinking he was only one of many gods.

During the introduction of Christianity some Fijians were so impressed they built temples to the Christian god even before the missionaries attempted conversion. They saw little difference between the Christian god and their own deities except that the Christian god didn't like them to worship other gods.

Denominations In Fiji there is a church or denomination for just about everyone. Visitors are always welcome to a Fijian service, and participating in one – particularly in a village – is a wonderful Fijian experience.

Methodist
Suva: Centenary Church (10 am, 7 pm Fijian); Dudley Church (10 am Hindi, 5 pm English); Wesley Church (8 am, 9.30 am, 10.45 am, 7 pm English)
Sigatoka: Prem Methodist (10 am English); Olosara, tel 50 293 (7.30 pm at private home); Nasigatoka Village (10.30 am, 7.30 pm Fijian)
Korolevu: (10.30 am, 7.30 pm Fijian)
Nadi Airport: Bethany Church, Nakavu, tel 23 505 (10.30 am, 7.30 pm English)

Anglican
Suva: Cathedral, Macarthur St (7.30 am Eucharist, 10 am sung Eucharist, 5 pm Evensong); St Matthew's, Samabula, tel 25 316 (8.30 am every Sunday except third Sunday of month, 5 pm); St Luke's, Laucala Bay, (7.30 am Holy Communion, 7 pm Evensong)
Sigatoka: Church of the Good Shepherd (9 am Holy Communion)

Nadi Airport: St Christopher's Church off London Ave (10 am Holy Communion)

Roman Catholic
Suva: Sacred Heart Cathedral, Pratt St (7 am, 8.30 am, 10 am, 7 pm English; 5 pm Fijian)
Nadi: St Mary's Martintar, tel 31 625 (7.30 am, 9.30 am English; 5.30 pm Fijian)

Bethany Assembly of God Church
Suva: 391 Grantham Rd, Samabula (10.45 am, 6.30 pm)
Nadi: AOG Balevu Fijian Branch past Mocambo turnoff towards airport, tel 381 965 (11 am, 8 pm Fijian)

Evangelical Fellowship Church (Baptists)
Lautoka: 7 Wainunu St, tel 61 087 (10.30 am, 7.30 pm)

Nadi: Northern Press Laundry Rd, tel 72 427 (10.30 am, 7.30 pm)

Church of Jesus Christ of Latter Day Saints
Suva: 29 Des Voeux Rd (9 am to noon and 2 to 5 pm Fijian); 29 Helsen Street, Samabula (9.30 am to 12.30 pm English)
Nadi: Northern Press Rd, tel 312 455 at Suva Mission (9.30 to 12.30 pm)

Presbyterian
Suva: St Andrew's Church, corner of Gordon and Goodenough St, tel 22 204 (10 am)

Indian Religions
Basically the same religions (with the exception of Buddhism) exist in Fiji as in India, but several generations of separation from India have made the Fiji Indian a bit less orthodox in his or her practise. Less orthodox does not mean less religious; most Hindu homes have shrines where the family worships together. Although the caste system essentially ended for the Indians who arrived in Fiji, it still does carry weight with Hindus in the realm of religion. 'Pundits' or priests who officiate at weddings and the like must be of the Brahmin caste.

The Hindu Fiji Indians, who compose about 80% of the Indian population, celebrate Diwali, Holi and the birth of Lord Krishna. Diwali is the colourful 'Festival of Lights' which occurs in October or November and resembles Christmas in the west. Houses are decorated ornately to welcome Lakshmi, the goddess of wealth and prosperity. Traditionally it is a time when businesses end their fiscal year, paying up their accounts and opening new books.

Holi, held in February or March, is a spring festival. During this time *chautals* (holy songs) are sung and people amuse themselves by squirting coloured water at each other in the streets.

Sikhism, an offshoot of Hinduism, is an eclectic monotheistic religion. Sikhs have their own temples (Gurdwaras) where they carry out prayer meetings and read their holy book.

The Muslims, who make up about 15% of the Indian population, worship in numerous mosques throughout Fiji. The major holidays are the fasting period of Ramadan and the Prophet Mohammed's birthday.

Firewalking
Firewalking in Fiji is also practised by Indians at an annual purification ritual called Trenial. It is performed at the Mariamman Temple in Suva and other locations in July or August. Hindu firewalking differs from the Fijian custom (see under 'Culture & Customs') in that the Indians walk across a shallow trench of burning embers whereas the Fijians traipse across a large pit of hot stones. Trenial is accompanied by the placing of *theresual* (three-pronged forks, tridents) into cheeks, hands, ears, nose and tongue prior to walking over the red-hot coals.

During the 10-day period of preparation devotees must sleep on the hardwood floor of the temple where the firewalking will occur; eat two meals a day of bland food (not the usual spicy Indian fare which is associated with lust and bodily satisfaction); bathe in cold water twice a day; abstain from alcohol, tobacco and sex; wear a minimum amount of clothing; devote time to prayer, confession and holy scriptures; and refrain from ill-feelings amongst each other. If that isn't enough, the faithful must submit to the disciplinary whip of the priest. Whippings are held in the morning and evening, following prayer.

The idea of the self-denial is to make the devotees forget about their 'body consciousness.' According to one religious authority, Pujari Rattan Swami, 'All of us are conscious of our body . . . We are not prepared to leave our self body consciousness, therefore whipping and self-control methods make the devotees at least temporarily semi-conscious.'

The firewalkers go through a host of other activities, including soaking their clothing in turmeric water which acts as a germicide and insect repellent to keep the mosquitoes away from their more exposed and therefore more vulnerable bodies, and smearing themselves with ash from burnt cow dung to illustrate that if one conquers one's weaknesses, one will be become pure. In this same respect the devotees ritually crack open coconuts, meditating on the three layers (outside layer, fibrous layer and shell) which symbolize man's three weaknesses – ego, ignorance and attachment. (The last is hardest to crack literally and figuratively.)

On the day of the event, a ritual bath is taken in a nearby river followed by chants and drum beating. The participants are whipped into a trance-like state and may pierce their tongues, cheeks and skin on the forehead with sharp needles. They walk back to the temple chanting 'Govinda,' the name of God. Upon returning to the temple the chief priest works the firewalkers into another trance and leads them across the glowing embers, once more shouting 'Govinda.'

HOLIDAYS & FESTIVALS

Public holidays in Fiji include:

January – *New Year's Day*
March/April – *Good Friday*
March/April – *Easter* – Saturday, Sunday, Monday
April – *Auckland-Suva Yacht Race*
June – *Queen's Birthday*

July – *Bula Festival* – Nadi area
August – *Bank Holiday*
August September – *Hibiscus Festival* – Suva
September – *Sugar Festival* – Lautoka
October – *Fiji Day & Inner District Soccer Tournament*
October/November – *Diwali* – Indian Festival of Lights
November – *Prince Charles' Birthday*
November/December – *Prophet Muhammed's Birthday*
December – *Christmas*

LANGUAGE
FIJIAN

When the earliest inhabitants of Fiji arrived 3500 years ago, they brought with them the language of the homeland they had set sail from – an island in Vanuatu, or possibly the Solomons (but certainly not Africa!).

That language has changed and splintered over the years into a multitude of different 'communalects' now numbering over 300. This is because language divides naturally as people spread out, and there may have been some additional input from more recent immigrants from other islands lying to the west.

The Fijian communalects belong to the enormous Austronesian language family, which means they are related to thousands of other languages spanning the globe from Malagasy in the west to Rapanui (Easter Island) in the east, from Aotearoa (New Zealand) in the south to Hawaii and Taiwan in the north. The family includes such important national languages as Tagalog (Philippines) and Malay. After Fiji had been settled, the flow of population continued north and east. The languages of Polynesia (such as Maori, Tahitian, Tongan, Samoan and Hawaiian), the language of the tiny island of Rotuma to the north of Fiji, and of course their speakers, all originated from Fiji over 3000 years ago.

These relationships can be clearly seen in the following table of selected words.

	Indonesian, Malay	Nggela, Solomons	Standard Fijian	Rotuman	Tongan	Maori
ear	telinga	talinga	daliga	faliga	telinga	taringa
eye	mata	mata	mata	mafa	mata	mata
fish	ikan	iga	ika	i'a	ika	ika
two	dua	rua	rua	rua	ua	rua
six	enam	ono	ono	ono	ono	ono
liver	hati	ate	yate	afe	'ate	ate
skin	kulit	guli	kuli	'uli	kili	kiri

The early missionaries had a keen appreciation of the importance of using local language in their work, and by 1840 had already devised an excellent spelling system for Fijian as well as published a number of books in different communalects. When the need for a standard language became apparent, they selected the language of Bau, the tiny island off the south-east coast of Viti Levu which was, and in some ways still is, the seat of the major power in Fijian politics. Nowadays the spoken Fijian of the towns and the Fijian used in books and newspapers are both known as 'Bauan,' even though neither is quite the same as the language of the island of Bau.

While many of its Pacific relatives, such as Hawaiian and Maori, have been struggling for survival, Fijian has never been in serious danger of extinction, even though it was ignored for a long time in the schools. The vast majority of Fijians have always used it as their everyday language, and most Indians understand at least some. In rural communities like Levuka, Taveuni and Savusavu, the Indians all speak Fijian fluently. In general, however, English is the lingua franca in Fiji.

Since independence in 1970, Fijian has also been increasingly used on the radio, in books and newspapers, and in the schools. To ensure that future evolution of the language has a sound base, the government has set up a department to research and develop the Fijian language. The department's first major task is to compile a dictionary of Fijian for Fijians, with all definitions and other information in Fijian, which when completed will be the first of its kind in the Pacific.

The Fijian Alphabet

Fijian spelling will come as a surprise to visitors because it uses some familiar letters in an unfamiliar way. Upon arriving in Fiji, you will soon realize that 'Nadi' is pronounced 'Nandi' (rhyming with candy). As linguist Albert Schutz in his very fine primer *Say It In Fijian* explains, the reason for this alphabet system was 'due neither to any perversity on the part of the first linguists, nor to chance.' Instead, David Cargill, the missionary who devised the alphabet especially for Fijian students learning to read, found that they considered it simple and satisfying.

The result of Cargill's work is a spelling system that is economical and regular. This second quality is extremely significant to the learner of Fijian because it means there is a good chance the student will pronounce the words correctly when he or she reads them. Contrast this system with the English language, which is riddled with exceptions.

Pronunciation

Consonants Most of the consonants other than b, d, q, g and c hold no surprises, but there are some differences from the way the English counterparts are usually pronounced. Like the combination 'dr,' the letters b, d and q are pronounced with a nasal sound in front of them – ie 'ndr.' 'R' is rolled or trilled, as in Spanish. 'Y' has not nearly as much glide quality to it as does the English 'y,' as in 'yes.'

The consonant letters that seem unusual to English speakers are:

b – represents mb, as in member
d – represents nd, as in Monday
q – represents ng+g, as in finger
g – represents ng, as in singer
c – represents th, as in father

Vowels

a as in father
e as in day, without glide at end
i as in see, without glide at end
o as in go, without glide at end
u as in zoo, without glide at end

Useful Phrases

Ni bula or *Bula* (Ni mbula or Mbula)
This is probably the first Fijian phrase you will hear. *Bula* means literally 'health' and 'life.' *Ni bula* is a polite greeting but the less formal *bula* by itself is also commonly used.

Ni sa yadra (Ni sah yandra)
Good morning.

Ni sa moce (Ni sahm mothay)
This literally means 'sleep' but also means 'good-bye' or 'good night.'

Lako mai eke (Lahko my kay)
Come here.

Vinaka (Vinahka)
An indispensable word which means 'good' and 'thank you.' *Vinaka vaka levu*, also heard a great deal, means 'Thank you very much.'

O sa lako ki vei? (O sa lahko kee vay?)
Where are you going? Interestingly enough there are no literal equivalents for 'How are you?' Instead Fijians might ask a friend they see on the street this instead, which is as much a greeting as it is a question.

O ni lako mai vei? (O ni lahko my vay?)
Where do you come from?

Au lako mai Niu Siladi (Ow lahko my New Silandi)
I come from New Zealand.

A cava oqo? (Ah thava ongo?)
What's this?

E dua na . . . (Ay do-ah nah) . . .
(It's) a . . .

Useful Words

bad	*ca*	tha
beer	*bia*	bee-ah
big, many	*levu*	layvu
bird	*manumanu vuka*	mahnumahnu vukah
cassava, tapioca	*tavioka*	tav-i-oh-kah
child	*gone*	gonay
comb	*i-seru*	ee-seru
cup	*bilo*	bee-low
eat	*kana*	kahna
fish	*ika*	ee-kah
food	*kakana*	kakahna
handsome, beautiful	*totoka*	toe-toe-kah
happy, satisfied	*marau*	mah-rau
house	*vale*	va-lay
kava	*yaqona*	yang-go-nah
kava bowl	*tanoa*	tah-noah
man	*tagane*	tahng-ahnay

matches	*masese*	mah-say-say
money	*lavo*	lah-vo
pot	*kuro*	koo-row
sleeping house	*bure*	bur-ay
small	*lailai*	lie-lie
smart	*matai*	mah-tye
stone	*vatu*	vah-too
stupid or crazy	*lialia*	lee-ah lee-ah
taro	*dalo*	dahlo
tobacco	*tavako*	tah-vah-ko
today	*nikua*	nickuah
toilet	*vale lailai*	vah-lay-lie-lie
tomorrow	*ni mataka*	ni mahtahka
tree	*vu ni kau*	vu ni cow
village	*koro*	koro
whale's tooth	*tabua*	tam-boo-ah
woman	*yalewa*	yah-lay-wah
yesterday	*nanoa*	na-noa

Useful Concepts

cakacaka	thaka-thaka	work
moku siga	moku singah	killing time, fooling around
gade	gan day	wandering around
vaka malua	vaka-mahluah	go slowly, take your time
kana vaka levu	kahna vaka layvu	eat heartily
io	ee-oh	yes
sega	sayngah	no
tabu	tamboo	taboo, forbidden
isa, isa lei	ee-sah, ee-sah lay	exclamation of regret
madua	man-doo-ah	ashamed, shy
tovolea mada	toe-vo-lay-ah mahndah	go ahead and try
kerekere	kerri-kerri	a request

Those interested in further studies of Fijian will find Albert Schutz's *Say It In Fijian*, published by Pacific Publications, an excellent introduction to the language. The book is available in Fiji. Likewise, Schutz's *Spoken Fijian* is a good primer for more advanced studies. My experience in Fiji has been that even the most minimal attempt at learning a few words or phrases will be amply rewarded with kindness and a greater respect for the visitor.

FIJI HINDI

The language of the Fiji Indians is generally called Hindi or Hindustani, but it is quite different from the Hindi spoken in India. Fiji Indians call their language *Fiji Bat* (meaning 'Fiji talk') or simply Fiji Hindi. This lingua franca of Fiji Indians is a hybrid of many Indian languages, dialects and borrowed words from Fijian and English. As Jeff Siegel, author of *Say It In Fiji Hindi* aptly puts it, 'Fiji Hindi reflects the diverse origins of the Fiji Indians as well as their unique new culture which has developed in Fiji.' Linguists and scholars may argue about the legitimacy of this dialect, but there is no doubt that it is a living language with its own special grammar and vocabulary suited for Fiji.

The history of the language mirrors the history of the Indian experience in Fiji.

The Indians who settled here were a diverse group – Hindus, Sikhs, Muslims and Christians from numerous castes and subcastes. Some people came from the northern districts of India speaking Urdu or Hindustani and dialects such as Bhojpuri, Awadhi, Bagheli and Maithili. From the southern regions some spoke unrelated languages from the Dravidian family such as Tamil, Telugu and Malayalam.

However, passage on the vessels to Fiji and later plantation life necessitated living at close quarters. This quickly resulted in the breakdown of caste taboos regarding food and work. The coming together of all the different Indian cultures also demanded a common language so that everyone could communicate. Thus Fiji Hindi was conceived. Siegel theorises that Fiji Hindi possibly evolved out of a 'Bazaar Hindustani' that already existed in India with many words and features of the various Indian languages. English and Fijian influences were later incorporated.

The vast majority of Fiji Indians speak Fiji Hindi but some still speak a different language at home such as Gujurati, Tamil, Telugu or Punjabi. Some of these languages are taught in school, but mostly Indian Standard Hindi or Urdu are taught for use in connection with religion, literature or formal occasions. English is taught in all Fiji schools and is the lingua franca of the nation. The average Fiji Indian may thus speak Tamil at home, Fiji Hindi with the neighbours, the local Fijian dialect with the villagers, English at work and Standard Hindi at a religious gathering.

Hindi – Hindustani – Urdu

It's all very confusing. Hindustani is the language used in parliamentary debate yet Hindi is designated as the official language of Fiji Indians. The Fiji Broadcasting System uses Hindustani but newspapers are in Hindi. According to a government survey, nearly 90% of Fiji Indian households speak Hindustani but Hindus learn Hindi in school, while Muslims learn Urdu. How do we make sense out of this?

First of all, we must distinguish between spoken and written languages. Hindustani usually refers to the spoken language of north India. It evolved from the classical Indian language of Sanskrit (which is studied much like Latin in the west) but utilises a lot of borrowed Persian words. A formal style of Hindustani is used on the radio. Fiji Hindi is a colloquial form of Indian Hindustani.

Formal Hindi is a literary form of Hindustani utilising Devanagari script (the same writing as Sanskrit) but replaces the borrowed Persian words with Sanskrit. Urdu is also a written or literary form of Hindustani using Arabic script and Persian as well as Arabic words rather than Sanskrit ones. There are also important religious distinctions between Hindi and Urdu. Urdu, used exclusively by Muslims, developed from the Persian court language spoken by India's Moghul conquerors who were Muslims. Hindi, of course, is used by Hindus.

The bottom line is that Hindi and Urdu are very different in formal and written form but are almost the same spoken language.

Phrasebooks

Visitors interested in Fiji Hindi would be well advised to pick up a copy of *Say it in Fiji Hindi*, published by Pacific Publications and available in local bookstores.

Greetings

Only rarely will the visitor encounter a Fiji Indian who does not speak English. Just the same, Indians will appreciate the visitor who extends him or herself by learning a few commonly used expressions.

Many greetings are used but the most heard is 'Namaste,' meaning both hello and goodbye. Another common greeting, corresponding to the English 'How are you?' is 'Kaise?' The answers might be:

thik hai	teak high	I'm fine
rait	right	right, OK
accha	ach-cha	good

Useful Phrases

ap ke nam ka hai?	app kay nam key-yah high	what's your name? (formal)
tumar nam ka hai?	too-mar dam key-ya high	what's your name? (familiar)
hamar nam ... hai	hah mar nahm ... high	my name is ...
ham nhii samjha	hahm anh-hee sahm-jah	I didn't understand
fir se bolna	fear say boll nah	please say it again
pata nahi	patah na-hee	I don't know
ka hue?	key-yah who-way	what's happening?
ka bhay?	key-yah ba-hay	what happened?
ham thak gaya	hahm-tahk gah-hay	I'm tired
... accha lange	... ach-cha la-gay	I like ...

Eating Out

khana bahut accha hai	kana bahoot ach-cha high	the food is very good
thora thora	tora tora	just a little
bas!	bahs	enough!
khalas	kalas	finished
pet bhar gaya	pet bahar gah-yah	my stomach is full
nasa ho gaya	nah-dah ho gah-yah	I'm drunk

Shopping

kitna dam hai?	kit-nah dahm high	how much is it?
bahut mahaga	ba-hout mah-ha gah	very expensive
huwa sasta mili	who-wah sas-tah mill-li	I can get it cheaper there
dam thora kamti karo	dahm tora kam-ti car-ro	knock the price down
aur kamti	our kam-ti	lessen it more
khali dekhta	kali deck-tah	just looking

Facts for the Visitor

VISAS

Visitors who do not need visas can get permits on arrival to stay for one month; these may be extended up to six months. You must have a valid passport, an onwards or return air ticket and adequate funds for your stay.

Visas are not required for citizens of Commonwealth countries, nor for nationals of Austria, Belgium, Denmark, Finland, France, Greece, Iceland, Indonesia, Ireland, Israel, Italy, Japan, Liechtenstein, Luxembourg, Nauru, Netherlands, Norway, Philippines, South Korea, Spain, Sweden, Switzerland, Taiwan, Thailand, Turkey, Tunisia, United States, West Germany and Western Samoa.

Nationals or citizens of other countries require visas unless their stay in Fiji will not exceed three hours.

Passports and visas are not required by people who transit Fiji directly by the same ship or aircraft. (The term 'ship' does not include yacht.)

Conditions for a visitor's permit are (according to a government pamphlet) 'that while in Fiji he will not behave in a manner prejudicial to peace or good order, will not engage in any business, profession or employment whether for reward or not, except with the approval of the Permanent Secretary of Home Affairs, and will not engage in any religion, vocation, or research without the Permanent Secretary's approval. Permit may be subject to other conditions which the Permanent Secretary may impose.'

CUSTOMS

You may bring the following items into Fiji duty free: 200 cigarettes or 250 grams of tobacco or all three, but not exceeding 250 grams; one litre of liquor or two litres of wine or two litres of beer; and other durable goods not exceeding F$30 per passenger.

Meat, dairy products, plants, seeds and flowers are prohibited without necessary licences from the Ministry of Agriculture.

WORK PERMITS

Those wishing to reside and work in Fiji should be advised that work permits are nearly impossible to get. The only exceptions are visitors with skills the government thinks worth the permission to stay. The best procedure in this case is to apply to the Permanent Secretary for Home Affairs, Government Buildings, Suva, prior to entering the country.

MONEY

US$1	= F$1.10	F$1 = US$0.90	
A$1	= F$0.75	F$1 = A$1.33	
£1	= F$1.50	F$1 = £0.67	
C$1	= F$0.80	F$1 = C$1.25	
NZ$1	= F$0.65	F$1 = NZ$1.55	
DM1	= F$0.43	F$1 = DM2.30	

The currency used in Fiji is the Fiji dollar (F$). Notes come in denominations of $1, $2, $5, $10, and $20. Coins are in amounts of 1, 2, 5, 10, 20 and 50 cents.

There are five banking groups in Fiji, all of which have head offices in Suva and numerous branches around the country. They are: The Australian & New Zealand Banking Group (ANZ), five outlets; Bank of Baroda, 12 outlets; Westpac Bank, 17 outlets; National Bank of Fiji (NBF), nine outlets; and Bank of New Zealand (BNZ), 30 outlets. Banking hours are Monday through Thursday from 10 am to 3 pm, with a late closing of 4 pm on Friday. The Bank of New Zealand operates a 24-hour service at Nadi International Airport.

Major credit cards are accepted in Fiji at many shops, restaurants, rental-car agencies and most hotels. There are representatives in Fiji for three of the major credit cards: Diner's Club, Fiji

Insurance Building on Butt St (tel 313 099, 315 522 or after hours 25 547); VISA, Bank of New Zealand (tel 312 755); and American Express, Tapa Tours, 189 Victoria Parade (tel 315 344). MasterCard is also accepted, although seemingly less so than VISA and American Express.

I have found that VISA cardholders can quickly get cash advances from any of the 30 Bank of New Zealand branches around the country – a policy that comes in very handy for sometimes itinerant authors and other travellers in general. The American Express office will quickly replace traveller's cheques or lost cards, but the Fiji representative doesn't seem to offer any of the other much-vaunted cardholder services. You will find that travellers' cheques are readily cashed in any Fiji bank and in most hotels and duty-free shops. During non-banking hours the best rates for traveller's cheques are at Thomas Cook in Suva, at 21 Thomson St.

CLIMATE

Fiji has a tropical maritime climate, tempered by the ocean and trade winds. Fiji's weather is not, however, uniform throughout the islands. There is a range of climates, from the hot and dry to the warm and wet, providing conditions favourable for the growth of a variety of food and commercial crops. The leeward sides of the major islands (eg the Lautoka or Labasa areas) are dry, with clear skies, a limited temperature range and abundant sunshine. It is on the leeward or western side of Viti Levu that most of Fiji's resorts are located. Average annual rainfall here is 165 to 180 cm (65 to 70 inches). The windward sides of the islands are subject to cloudy skies and frequent rains with even temperatures and moderate sunshine. Suva is an example of a windward climactic area and averages 300 cm (120 inches) rainfall annually.

The cool, dry months – which are the best time to visit – are from May to October. The so-called 'winter' begins in July. During July and August the temperature may drop down to 18-20°C, and lower inland. Even during the winter months, however, these relatively low temperatures are by no means constant. Spells of cloudy, cool weather with occasional rains alternate with warm, sunny days, sometimes of high humidity. The hot, wet season may begin as early as November; but the conjunction of heat and humidity that most people from moderate climates find trying occurs during the first three months of the year. During this time the temperature ranges from 23°C to 31°C, and it may rain nearly every day.

HEALTH

Fiji is malaria-free and inoculations are not required except for those arriving from an area infected with smallpox, cholera or yellow fever, which exempts 99.9% of visitors. Water is safe and plentiful in most areas but for the skittish there is always bottled water, Coca Cola or Fiji Bitter beer. In some areas mosquitoes are pesky and numerous, so I suggest that you bring a good insect repellent.

Listed below are guidelines and suggestions gleaned from professional medical sources regarding several major concerns in the South Pacific. When in doubt, medical care is available and you should not hesitate to see a doctor but, unfortunately, medical care in this country does not come close to the standards in Europe, the USA, Australia and New Zealand. You should be aware of this, especially when dealing with local hospitals. That does not mean that there are not good local doctors available or that the hospitals are not safe to deal with for minor afflictions. Your best bet when ill is to get a recommendation from the management of a hotel, your embassy or consulate, or a friend.

Sunshine

No matter how hot it feels on a given day in the tropics, the sun is less filtered by the atmosphere than in other climes and is much more potent. Damage can be done to skin and eyes, so take heed. To avoid a horrendous sunburn, use sunscreen. Tanning can still occur with sunscreen, so don't be discouraged if you are not a bronzed god or goddess overnight. Remember that you will only peel that much sooner if you burn. A bad burn can ruin a vacation, and a severe burn will require medical attention. A minor burn can be treated with a cool shower or compresses, soothing cream or steroids. An aspirin two or three times a day will also ease the pain. Some folks are allergic to ultraviolet light, which will result in redness, itching and pin-sized blisters. For these unfortunates, clothing is the only answer. Fair-skinned people beware in the tropics!

Humidity

Humidity not only means discomfort but the possibility of rashes caused by yeasts and fungi which thrive in a warm, moist environment. The problem is compounded by tight-fitting clothing and moist, hot skin rubbing against the same. You don't have to be a doctor to deal with these difficulties. Keeping as cool and dry as possible is step number one. Loose-fitting clothing (cotton is best) is also a good idea,

as are open-toed sandals. To reduce chafing, talcum powder or corn starch can be applied to body creases (under arms, on necks, under breasts, etc). If all else fails, medications are available to combat fungal and yeast rashes.

Bacterial Infections

Aside from fungi and other microorganisms, the tropics are a prime breeding ground for staph bacteria. A common bacteria found on the skin, these little devils can multiply enormously under the right tropical conditions, especially if there is a cut, blister or insect bite on the skin releasing the fluids they thrive on. Infection can spread if you are not careful. To prevent this condition, wash the injury – no matter how insignificant – with soap, treat it with antibiotic ointment and cover with a clean dressing.

Gastrointestinal Problems

Perhaps the most common complaint of visitors anywhere is the 'traveller's trots,' which can stem from any number of causes. There are several things you can do to guard against this: 1) Make sure meals are cooked properly. Virtually all organisms that thrive at body temperature are killed in the cooking process. 2) Water in Fiji is nearly always potable (the only exception being the villages), but if you have the slightest fears, drink bottled water or soft drinks. 3) Peel or thoroughly wash any fruit or vegetables purchased in a market. Peeling fruit yourself is always a good idea. 4) Avoid swimming, walking barefoot or collecting seafood from beaches or lagoons directly in front of settlements. Raw sewage is often dumped or piped into the nearest convenient grounds – the beach that forms the villagers' front yard.

For those who have never been in the South Seas, the extreme changes in humidity, food and other conditions may tax the system. The best advice is to take it easy for the first few days until you are acclimatised. You would do well to be prepared and bring sunscreen, band-aids and any minor medications you require. If you forget anything, there are plenty of pharmacies (chemists) which stock all the medicines and accessories you will likely need.

INFORMATION

The main information office for the Fiji Visitors' Bureau (also known as the FVB) is in a quaint colonial-style building (formerly the customs house) in downtown Suva. There are two desks occupied by helpful Fijians with maps, brochures and plenty of patience. For visitors coming off the plane at Nadi, there is also an airport office manned by a congenial gentleman by the name of Abe Yavala. He is there at every incoming flight. Addresses of the Fiji Visitors' Bureau offices in Fiji are:

Thomson St
GPO Box 92, Suva
(tel 22 867)

PO Box 9217
Nadi Airport
(tel 72 433)

Overseas addresses of the offices are:

Australia
  38 Martin Place, Sydney, New South Wales 2000 (tel 231 4251)
Japan
  Embassy of Fiji, Noa Building, 10th Floor, 3-5, 2-chome, Azabudai, Minato-ku, Tokyo (tel 03 587 2038)
New Zealand
  Room 605, Tower Block, Canterbury Arcade, 47 High St, Auckland; postal address: PO Box 1179 (tel 732 133 or 732 134)

UK
  Marketing Services (T&T) Ltd, 52-54 High Holborn, London WC1V 6RL (tel 01 242 3131)
USA
  Fiji Visitors Bureau, 6151 West Century Blvd Suite 524, Los Angeles, California 90045 (tel 800 338 5686 inside California, 800 621 9604 nationwide USA, 800 647 7700 Canada)

BOOKS & BOOKSHOPS

There are quite a few bookshops in Fiji, but selection is generally poor. For avid readers staying any length of time, the best bet is to obtain a library membership at the Suva Public Library or to enquire about using the University of the South Pacific Library, which has an excellent Pacific collection (open 8 am to 4.30 pm). Better yet, bring your own books.

Desai Bookshops are the largest chain of bookstores in Fiji. They have six locations in Suva including: Vanua House, Corner Shop on MacArthur St, Machines Show Room, Dominion House on Thomson St, Fiji Institute of Technology Bookshop in the suburb of Samabula, the kiosk at the bus station, and the USP Bookshop. Other booksellers in Suva are the *Suva Book Shop* on Greig St, the *Arcade Book Centre* on Victoria Arcade, the *Sigatoka Book Depot* at 34 Ratu Mara Rd in Samabula, and *Kevat's Book Centre* at 97 Cumming St.

Desai shops around the country are in Nausori (King's Road), Lautoka (Naviti St) and Nadi (Queen's Road), as well as in Sigatoka, Labasa and Tavua. There is also a chain of booksellers on the western side known as the *Sigatoka Book Depot*, with shops in Nadi (Sahu Khan St), Lautoka and Sigatoka. Finally there is the *General Bookshop* in Nadi at 317 Main St in Nadi.

The Pacific Conference of Churches at 4 Thurston St in Suva (near the Fiji Broadcasting Commission) also has a library-*cum*-bookstore with a good selection of reference books about Fiji and the South Pacific.

Guidebooks

There are comparatively few books (guides or otherwise) written about Fiji, especially when you compare what is available on Hawaii or other South Pacific destinations. Here are some of the more popular books:

How to Get Lost & Found in Fiji by John McDermott (Waikiki Publishing, Honolulu, 1978). For years this was the only guide to Fiji available in North America. Of all of McDermott's 'Lost and Found Books,' it's the best, although now a bit dated. The book contains a lot of useful nuts-and-bolts-type information and good observations on the character of the people, but you have to wade through a lot of verbiage and chitchat.

Finding Fiji by David Stanley (Moon Publications, Chico, 1985). Stanley's was the first comprehensive guide to Fiji, solidly aimed towards the low-budget visitor. The guide offers detailed information and good maps.

Fiji Handbook & Travel Guide edited by John Carter (Pacific Publications, Sydney, 1980). The ultimate book of facts about Fiji – everything from banking to weather. Reads like an encyclopaedia rather than a guidebook; dull but full of useful data. Could do with an update.

Suva - A History & Guide by Albert Schutz (Pacific Publications, Sydney, 1978). A very fine booklet (52 pages long), painstakingly researched and well written. Schutz, who is a professor of Polynesian languages at the University of Hawaii, details virtually everything you ever wanted to know about Suva and its environs, including the people behind the street names and the history of every neighbourhood. Although more a historical work than a guidebook, it is a must for the serious Fijiphile.

The Fiji Explorer's Handbook by Kim Gravelle (Graphics (Pacific), Suva, 1985). Gravelle has put together a very fine road guide covering Viti Levu and Ovalau. This is the book to get for the serious driver – it has good maps.

Exploration & History

Where the Waves Fall by K R Howe (George Allen & Unwin, Sydney, 1984). This book is subtitled 'A New South Seas history from first settlement to colonial rule' and is thus not strictly a work about Fiji. Howe's perspective is 'new' in that he brings the islanders themselves into the centre of the picture and interprets how their lives were affected by the intrusion of the Europeans rather than how the islanders affected imperialistic concerns. It is a scholarly but very readable tome and one of the best books on the exploration and settlement of Fiji and its South Pacific neighbours available. Howe goes all the way back to the actual settlement of the Pacific by the Polynesians and Melanesians and utilises the latest historical and archaeological information. In areas where historians differ in opinion – for example the method by which early Polynesians discovered the islands – the author explores the varying theories so that all points of view are touched upon.

Fiji - A Short History by Deryk Scarr (George Allen & Unwin, Sydney, 1984). A very thorough work by a leading Fiji historian. Unfortunately, the writing style is heavy handed and almost unreadable.

Fiji Times - A History of Fiji by Kim Gravelle (The Fiji Times & Herald, Suva, 1979). The book is a collection of 50 stories originally published in a newspaper series by *The Fiji Times*, Fiji's oldest publication. It is probably the most entertaining of the historical accounts available, but its newspaper-like format spotlights only particular areas and thus is limited. Available only in Fiji.

A History of Fiji by R A Derrick (Government Press, Suva, 1946). The seminal work of Fiji history, written by a former director of the Fiji Museum and a man considered an all-time authority on the subject.

Matanitu by David Routledge (University of the South Pacific, Suva, 1985). According to the experts, this is one of the very best books on Fiji's history to date. It is an extremely comprehensive book, concentrating chiefly on the years up to cession. The title translates as 'Confederation of States,' a term that incorporates both the old and new systems of government. The book is very readable but available only in Fiji.

Modern Accounts
Tin Roofs & Palm Trees – A Report on the New South Seas by Robert Trumbull (University of Washington Press, Seattle, 1977). This is a serious socio-economic/ historical overview of the South Pacific nations with a particular emphasis on their emergence into the 20th century. Trumbull, a former New York Times correspondent, has distilled a great deal of useful background information into his Fiji chapter.

Fiji: Islands of the Dawn by Leonard Wibberly (Ives Washburn, New York, 1964). A wonderfully written account of one man's experiences in Fiji within a historical context. That is, the author alternates between chapters dealing with his own encounters and an entertaining history of Fiji. Wibberly, author of *The Mouse that Roared* and other books, has keen powers of observation and a wit to match. Unfortunately, he seems to be the only writer of stature in modern times to have drifted into Fiji and left us with something in print. The dearth of Fiji literature makes his book all the more important.

Under the Ivi Tree by Cyril S Belshaw (University of California Press, Berkeley & Los Angeles, 1964; in England published by Routledge & Kegan Paul, London). An exhaustive socio-economic study of the Fijian people drawn from the author's obviously considerable personal experience in the islands. Although put together in the late '50s and early '60s, this look at the interplay of individuals and the society that surrounds them is still right on target in discussing the limitations of economic growth faced in Fiji, particularly with regards to the indigenous population. Belshaw, a former colonial administrator and professor of anthropology at the University of British Columbia, demonstrates great sensitivity for the Fijian people and their culture. Though much of the book deals with economic models and village structure, there are many very practical gems of insight for the average reader if you are willing to wade through the verbiage. The book is highly recommended for the serious student of Fiji.

Art & Culture
Fijian Material Culture by Alan Richard Tippett (Bishop Museum Press, Honolulu, 1968).

Say It in Fijian by Albert Schutz (Pacific Publications, Sydney, 1979). A wonderful primer on Fijian by one of the world's foremost students of the language. It's 55 pages long and filled with historical information as well as basic grammar and pronunciation.

Spoken Fijian by Albert Schutz and Rusiate Komaitai (The University Press of Hawaii, Honolulu, 1979). A language study guide for the serious student of Fijian. Easy-to-follow lessons include exercises.

Flora & Fauna
Birds of the Fiji Bush by Fergus Clunie (Fiji Museum, Suva, 1984) describes basic birds of Fiji with illustrations by Pauline Morse. Best book available on the subject.

Fiji Literati
Alas, this is virtually a barren section. A number of great writers did drop in, namely Rupert Brooke, Jack London, Mark Twain, Rudyard Kipling and Somerset Maugham, but none of their visits resulted in exceptionally good literature. The great Fiji Novel, a la *The Marriage of Loti*, remains to be written. Kipling did write a short poem about the Old Capital of Levuka and Twain did comment on his short stay in Fiji in 'Following the

Equator' in 1897, but these are miniscule compared to the volumes of literature set in other parts of the Pacific. London wrote a short story called 'The Whale Tooth' which appeared in his *South Sea Tales* and was probably based on the Reverend Baker killing, but it is not one of his best. Perhaps the best book yet written about Fiji by a major author is Leonard Wibberly's contemporary account *Fiji: Islands of the Dawn* – out of print but worth looking for. If you are a Michener fan, he wrote an essay on Fijian-Indian relations called 'Fiji' which was at best a subjective if not vituperative blast at Indians. Likewise, his short story 'The Mynah Birds' portrayed Indians in an ugly and racist manner. Both pieces appeared in Michener's *Return to Paradise*.

ART & CULTURE

As throughout the world, Fijians have embraced western pop culture. Conspicuously displayed in duty-free shop windows are the latest in fashions, stereo systems, computers, photo equipment and all the other evidence of 'the good life.' However, despite the preponderance of material culture imported from the USA and Europe, Fijians and Indians are true to their own birthright.

While other countries such as Tahiti or Hawaii are experiencing a revival in traditional arts, Fiji has no such contemporary movement – the reason being, for the most part, that Fijians never lost their cultural heritage. Most of the folkloric crafts are practiced in the villages, and village life is still the foundation of Fijian society. Critics do point to the decreasing quality (primarily due to commercialisation of crafts due to the tourist trade) of woodcarving and pottery, but there are still people around who know what they are doing. Except for a few skills like traditional house-building, which will probably disappear within 15 years because village homes are not built with traditional materials anymore, the arts remain part of contemporary culture.

Mat-weaving is taught to nearly every village girl, and the making of *masi* or tapa cloth is widespread. Likewise, the *meke* or traditional dance continues to be handed down from generation to generation and is often performed.

The closest thing to a revival has been in the Dance Theatre of Fiji, a highly praised troupe that has travelled throughout the world. Produced by Manoa Rasigatale, young chief and former Fijian rock star, the theatre has revitalised Fiji dance by re-introducing old ceremonies, choreographing them and presenting them to modern audiences. Regular performances of the Dance Theatre can be seen at Pacific Harbour near Suva. Rasigatale is also currently involved in the construction of a *drua* or old-time double-hulled canoe he is building completely of wood, sennit and other traditional materials. Plans are to launch the vessel and sail it on the open sea in the manner of the much-heralded voyage of the *Hoku'lea* several years ago in Tahiti.

CRAFTS

Pottery A craft that dates from the original settlement of Fiji around 1290 BC, pottery-making is still practised in the lower Sigatoka Valley, the islands of Kadavu and Malolo, western Vanua Levu and the province of Ra. Each district bears its own distinct signature in its pottery style. Today the technique and division of labour differ little from pre-contact times. Sometimes the men dig the clay but it is almost always the women who are the potters. The clay is first kneaded and then sand is added to control shrinkage and to improve the texture. The mixture is left to dry for a short period before being worked into its final form.

The tools used by today's potters are also the same as in the past – a rounded stone, large pebble or a wooden paddle for beating; a piece of coconut husk for rubbing the clay; a shell or stick for ornamenting; and a cushion of leaves on which to place the work during the moulding process. Pottery wheels were unknown to ancient Fijians and still are not used. Instead, a saucer-like section is shaped for the bottom of the pot or bowl and the item is progressively built up with slabs, strips or coils. The sides are shaped by beating the clay with a paddle or pebble. Considering the implements used, the Fijians achieve remarkable symmetry.

After the object is shaped and finished with moistened fingers or a smooth stone, it is dried for several days and fired for an hour in a fire made from brush, reeds or coconut fronds. Fijian pottery is not glazed; instead, certain plants are rubbed on the finished objects as a kind of varnish to improve water-holding qualities.

Mat & Basket Weaving Whereas pottery is a skill shared by very few villages, basket and especially mat plaiting is a universally practised art – every village girl has learned how to weave a mat or *ibe* by the time she is 10 years old. Palm fronds or the long fibrous pandanus leaves are vital construction materials in Fijian culture. The traditional *bure* is constructed from plaited pandanus or palm fronds; pandanus mats are woven into floor coverings, bed rolls, fans and baskets. Almost every home in Fiji, whether in village or town, has at least several mats for use as rugs or for sleeping. They are considered an important element in the wealth of the Fijian family and are traditionally given at weddings, funerals or during the visits of high chiefs.

Masi *Masi* or *tapa* are names for bark cloth. This art form is practised in many regions of the South Pacific and in several areas of Fiji. Masi has many uses, including ceremonial dress, wall decorations and more recent innovations such as table mats and handbags. It also makes a fine souvenir for visitors.

Masi is produced from the inner bark of the paper mulberry tree (*broussoneua papyrifera*), which is cultivated by Fijians expressly for this purpose. The process of making the bark cloth is arduous, time consuming and is typically a job given to women. The bark is stripped from the tree, soaked, scraped clean and pounded with a rolling-pin-like beater on a wooden anvil.

Masi can be purchased in many shops. The most inexpensive place to buy it is from villagers who make it themselves. The thicker the masi the better the quality.

Woodcarving This is a declining art in Fiji, no doubt another victim of the modern era. The woodcarver's role was a highly specialised one, important because of the cultural value of the items he produced. The war club, for example, was a vital part of Fijian culture. Not only was it the primary weapon in a warrior's arsenal, it was a symbol of authority used in ceremony and dance. Likewise, the *tanoa* or kava bowl also played (and still plays) an important part in Fijian society. Artist clans were so specialised that carvers in the old days only produced one particular artefact – say clubs or kava bowls – and that was it.

THE MEDIA & ENTERTAINMENT
The government-owned Fiji Broadcasting Commission (FBC) operates two national networks of AM transmitters: Radio Fiji 1 (which broadcasts in English and Fijian) and Radio Fiji 2 (which broadcasts in Hindustani and English). In addition, Radio Fiji 3 (FM) in Suva carries English programmes. Programming includes American, Fijian and Indian pop music, sports, locally produced news, international news from the Australian Broadcasting Commission, Voice of America and BBC as well as locally produced educational and quiz shows. In 1985 a privately owned radio station, FM 96, went into business, opening up the airwaves for the first time to a non-governmental enterprise. FM 96, which broadcasts only in the Suva area, is modelled after an American or Australian

pop music station. It provides entertaining listening, playing a variety of rock, R&B and occasional Fijian or Indian tunes. It also broadcasts sports, news and occasional interviews. When in Suva, tune in. In several years it is expected that the government will broadcast television. The TV venture, a controversial issue, will be produced in cooperation with an Australian network.

Currently the nation is being swept by a video craze. On practically every corner there is a video tape rental shop and nowadays it is a common sight to see Fijians of all ages huddled before a colour television, watching a grade C Hollywood movie or a pirated television show from the USA or Australia. In general, Fijians seem to be winding up with the poorest, most socially unredeeming programming that Hollywood has to offer. Hopefully the government's new TV project will bring quality television to the people of Fiji, who seem to be well on the way to becoming televisior junkies.

Newspapers & Magazines

Fiji is served by two daily English-language newspapers – *The Fiji Times*, founded in 1869; and *The Fiji Sun*, established in 1974. In years past *The Fiji Times* was the premier paper both in circulation and quality, but recently the *Sun* has not only picked up circulation, it appears to have equalled the *Times* qualitatively. Both publish Sunday editions. The Fiji Times group also publishes a weekly Fijian paper, *Nai Lalakai*; and *Shanti Dut*, a weekly Hindustani publication. The Fiji Sun group publishes *Siga Rama*, a bi-weekly Fijian newspaper; and *Sunsport*, a sports edition.

Available for visitors are the monthly 'throwaway' publications *Fiji Fantastic* and *Fiji Beach Press*, which are free of charge in many hotels, shops and travel agencies. They are commercial in nature but include quite a bit of valuable information for the traveller – including events, tours, accommodation, restaurants, cruises, shopping guides and miscellaneous information. *Fiji Fantastic* is published by the Fiji Sun Group and *Fiji Beach Press* by News (South Pacific) Ltd.

The finest publication to come out of Fiji is *Islands Business News*, a monthly South Pacific-oriented news and business journal. This slick, professionally edited magazine would be of interest to business-people as well as visitors who wish to understand what's going in this region.

Other magazines such as *Pacific Islands Monthly (PIM)* and *Pacific* are also available. *PIM*, published in Sydney, is an excellent regional publication and a venerable institution in the Pacific, oriented mostly toward the old Anglo colonies. *Pacific*, (formerly *New Pacific*), published in Honolulu, is a younger upstart that also covers the Pacific basin but has better reportage of former US Trust Territories and current dependencies than its rival. The old standby, the Pacific edition of *Time*, is sold here, as is a recently introduced hybrid which combines *Newsweek* and Australia's *Bulletin*.

Cinemas

There are movie houses in every major town in Fiji and 10 in Suva alone. The theatres are divided into two categories: the standard houses showing American and other English-language films, and the 'Indian' theatres featuring Indian-made movies exclusively. Many of the American movies are trashy, grade B, 'shoot 'em up' or 'karate 'em up' clones, but those with more discriminating tastes will find that some good flicks actually make it to Fiji. Admission price is F$1.50 and schedules are shown in the daily papers.

Sports & Games

Like most South Pacific Islanders, Fijians are sports fanatics. Soccer and rugby contests between major clubs and overseas tournaments are listened to religiously. Fiji has facilities for golf, tennis, basketball, volleyball, track and field, swimming,

ST: Cloudy, some light rain. Details, Page 26.

The Fiji Times

THE FIRST NEWSPAPER PUBLISHED IN THE WORLD TODAY.

Suva is just west of the International Date Line where the new day begins

soccer, cricket, boxing, lawn bowling and of course rugby, which is the closest thing to a national sport. Over the years Fijians, who have the build and stamina ideally suited for rugby, have excelled at the game, often winning in international competition.

Golf Courses

Golf has been popular in Fiji for years with the Anglo sector of society – many of the courses were actually laid out to meet the recreational needs of the old Colonial Sugar Refining Company. The finest course in the country is the facility at Pacific Harbour resort, which was designed by Robert Trent Jones. The only other 18-hole course in Fiji is the Fiji Golf Club in Suva. There are also nine-hole courses at Nadi, Lautoka, The Fijian Resort Hotel, Naviti Beach Resort, Reef Hotel and Taveuni Estates on the island of Taveuni.

POST

The Fiji postal system is generally efficient. Because of numerous international flights to and from Australia and North America, delivery time to destinations outside the country is usually no longer than a week. Like many smaller nations, Fiji earns a substantial amount of income from its stamps. Collectors can purchase special sets at the philatelic office in the Ganilau Building, across the street from the main post office in Suva.

Those wishing to receive mail at the post office may do so at the general delivery window. American Express clients can receive their mail at the American Express representative located at Tapa Tours Ltd, 189 Victoria Parade in Suva.

Telegrams and phone calls can also be made from any post office.

TELEPHONE

Phone service in Fiji gets a passing grade, but with some qualifications. Service can sometimes be frustratingly slow (especially switchboard operators in hotels), but that's the South Pacific. For the visitor on the street, the main problem seems to be lack of functioning public phones. In an emergency a shopkeeper or neighbour will always oblige. Cost for a local call is about F$0.20.

Long-distance service is quite adequate; Fiji is linked with every country in the world via satellite. Calls or telegrams can be placed at post offices, where there are also public phones for local calls. To make a long-distance call or send a telegram in Suva, the best idea is to visit the modern Fiji International Telecommunications (FINTEL) office on Victoria Parade, just down the street from the public library. Long-distance and local calls can also be made from any hotel.

TIME

Fiji skirts the International Dateline (180th meridian), so arrivals from the west coast of the United States will find

upon landing that they have lost a day. Thus, Sunday becomes Monday, Tuesday becomes Wednesday – you get the idea. When you go the opposite direction a day is gained back again.

Fiji is two hours ahead of Australian Eastern Standard Time, 12 hours ahead of GMT, 20 hours ahead of US Pacific Standard Time. Thus when it is noon Monday in Fiji it is 10 am Monday in Sydney, midnight from Sunday to Monday in London and 4 pm Sunday in Los Angeles. Once in Fiji you realize it doesn't matter what the clock hands or digital readout say. Fijians are a time standard to themselves, regulated by 'Fiji time' – usually two hours behind what you had planned.

Business Hours

Government and business offices are open five days a week. The usual hours are 8 am to 4.30 pm (4 pm on Fridays), with at least an hour for lunch between 1 and 2 pm. Most shops and commercial outlets (including the public markets) are open five days a week and Saturday mornings. Most locals do their Sunday shopping on Saturday, because very few shops are open on Sundays (and holidays). Banking hours are 10 am to 3 pm Monday through Thursday and until 4 pm on Friday. The Bank of New Zealand maintains a 24-hour service at Nadi International Airport.

'Fiji time' does not necessarily coincide with the split-second punctuality you may be used to back home. Social and even business appointments tend to be later than scheduled, so if someone is late in appearing, don't fret. Late arrivals and even no-shows are endemic to this part of the world. This can be very frustrating to the uninitiated but there is nothing that can be done except to adopt the same behaviour.

GENERAL INFORMATION
Electricity

Throughout Fiji the current is 240 volts, 50 cycles AC. Most hotels have 110-volt converters for razors. Outlets are in the Australian/New Zealand mode – a three-pronged configuration. Adaptors are available in the numerous duty-free shops and in electrical supply stores around the country.

Security

In recent years locals have shaken their heads sadly when speaking about the rise in crime and lack of respect among the youth. This may be true by Fijian standards but compared to the rest of the world, crime in Fiji is still minimal. Occasionally a visitor may be subject to a petty theft, but reports of this are very rare. Despite the fact that many people live in poverty, Suva is extremely safe by American big-city standards. In my experience, Fijian respect for the visitor means that the traveller has little to worry about even in the lowest-class dives. This does not preclude taking common-sense precautions when storing valuables or camping in remote areas, but in general, serious crime – especially a crime against a visitor – is almost unheard of.

ACCOMMODATION

Accommodation in Fiji is divided into four basic categories:

Inexpensive guest houses or hotels catering to local traffic or the 'backpacker' crowd may range from quiet, spartan but clean hotels and rooming houses to raucous, shabby dives frequented by locals seeking a hideaway for liaisons. Prices range from US$5-15 for a single. Some of the better examples of this category are the Old Capital Inn (Levuka) or the Seashell Cove Resort (Nadi).

Government guest houses are a very specialised accommodation, generally for use by government workers in the field. They are located either on the outer islands or in remote areas of Viti Levu or Vanua Levu. Although mostly utilised by the civil service, visitors can also use them providing that a government official is not already occupying them. Always check first with the local district office to see if there is a vacancy. Cost is usually F$4 to 5 per night.

The moderately priced hotels and resorts are mostly for tourists but are sometimes occupied by locals. These may represent the best bargains for visitors who want a modicum of luxury but do not feel they need the most expensive hotel to enjoy their vacation. Amenities may include air-conditioning, pool, restaurant, bar, beach frontage and gift shop. Prices range from US$20-45 for a single. Fine examples in this category are the Crow's Nest (Sigatoka) and the Dominion International Hotel (Nadi).

The top end or upscale resorts are generally located on the Coral Coast or Nadi/Lautoka area on Viti Levu but are sometimes on very remote islands. They are luxurious and aimed exclusively at the high-rolling visitor. These facilities usually include beach frontage, air conditioning, pool, bar, restaurant, gift shop, free use of snorkelling gear, bicycles, transportation to and from airport, and sometimes tennis courts and golf. Prices for this type of accommodation start at US$50-60 for a single and go up to US$100 or more. Typical hotels in this league are The Regent (Nadi) or The Fijian (Coral Coast).

Accommodation marked with asterisks in this book indicate my choices as best in their class.

Camping in Fiji without permission is prohibited on native land, but there are two licenced campsites on private property in Ovalau (Rukuruku), and Seashell Cove Resort (Nadi). Camping in some recreational areas such as Nadarivatu in Viti Levu is legal but you must have permission from the Lands & Survey Section of the Ministry of Lands.

FOOD

There are four types of cuisine in Fiji: 'local' or Fijian, European, Chinese and Indian. Fijian fare is more or less the same as fare in the rest of the South Pacific –

fish, shellfish, breadfruit, taro (*dalo*), cassava (*tavioka*), pork, beef, chicken, yams, rice, coconut milk (*lolo*), tropical fruits such as bananas, and various greens such as taro leaves or ferns. A typical Fijian meal at any given time might consist of beef or fried fish, boiled taro leaves (*roro*) topped with coconut cream, and starchy boiled cassava or taro on the side. Visitors may find this variety of cuisine heavy.

European cooking is that bland variety of food so many of us have grown up with and don't find particularly exciting in Fiji or anywhere else – overcooked steak, potatoes and vegetables. Excellent Chinese and Indian food are well represented in Fiji, though the Indian style may be a bit spicy by European standards.

Both modern supermarkets and local outdoor markets feature a variety of locally grown and imported high-quality fruit, vegetables, meat, poultry and every other conceivable household item. Those used to 'European' vegetables such as tomatoes, green onions, potatoes and the like need not fear they will be lost in a sea of exotic local food – there is always plenty of familiar fare to be had. Mutton, pork, chicken and beef are abundant as well. Imported, canned goods are available but tend to be expensive. There is also fine locally produced cheese, milk, eggs and other dairy products. Locally grown fruit you might enjoy include pineapples, guavas, mangos, oranges, limes, pawpaws, avocados and bananas.

If you purchase fresh fruit at the market, be sure to wash it thoroughly before eating. There are a plethora of nasty, tropical micro-organisms that may not agree with your system, so don't give them a chance to develop. Peeling the skins from vegetables and fruit is always a good idea.

The best good news for avid restaurant-goers is that of late the quantity and general quality of eateries has increased dramatically, especially in the Suva area. Newly opened, moderately priced Chinese, Indian, Indonesian and seafood restaurants have considerably brightened a previously bleak gastronomic landscape.

CONDUCT

To show up at a village uninvited and simply start wandering around is very rude – something akin to wandering around the suburbs of Los Angeles, entering strangers' backyards and perhaps peeping in their bedroom windows. It just isn't done.

Should you be fortunate enough to be invited into a village (a likely circumstance if you become friendly with the locals), there are certain rules of etiquette to be observed. Prior to the visit, if you have the opportunity, buy a pound or two of yaqona root (which can be purchased at any outdoor market or from local proprietors for F$4-5 per pound) as a *sevusevu* or traditional gift. This will surely start you off on the right foot and show your hosts you care about their tradition. Your host will gladly accept the gift and may perform a welcoming ritual that in effect says your visit is officially recognised by the village. In the course of the ceremony you will be offered a *bilo* (coconut shell) full of yaqona, which of course you should accept and drink (in one big gulp rather than sips).

After the initial ceremony you may be asked to sit with the gang around the *tanoa* (kava bowl) and *talanoa* (chat). This is the best way to get to know Fijians. Drinking 'grog' (kava) is a sacramental ritual with Fijians and cements friendships with strangers. After drinking awhile, perhaps your host will offer you something to eat or show you around the village. Children will inevitably be curious about your presence and will surround you as though you are the pied piper, asking innumerable questions. They will probably ask you to take their photo.

The visitor wishing to take photos of village life is free to do so, but is best accompanied by an adult or youngster from the community. Always ask per-

Top: Sugar cane country in west Viti Levu (FVB)
Bottom: Loading sugar cane near Nadi, Viti Levu (RK)

Top: Watermelons (FVB)
Left: Suva market, Viti Levu (RK)
Right: Wild pig hunter in Nausori Highlands, Viti Levu (RK)

mission when taking photos (which will almost always be granted), and as obvious as it sounds, never casually wander into someone's *bure* (house) and start shooting. During the yaqona ceremony do not stand upright and indiscriminately take snapshots without having asked permission beforehand. This is a solemn occasion, not a press photo opportunity.

Other points of etiquette to be observed are:

When entering a village, take off your hat.

When invited inside a *bure*, remove your shoes, place them outside the doorstep, and stoop slightly when entering. Avoid standing fully upright inside – it's bad manners.

Dress modestly when visiting a village. Men should not be bare-chested and women should wear slacks or a below-the-knee dress. Women should definitely not be in shorts or a bathing suit. Scanty clothing is disrespectful and might be construed as a moral reflection on the hosts. For women it would also send the wrong message to the village Lotharios.

As they told us in grade school, good manners will get you everywhere. Fijians are perhaps the politest and in many ways the most civilized people on the planet. They display good manners and should be treated reciprocally. They sense this respect and will go out of their way for a person they like.

Realize that the Fijians' culture dictates that they should always invite a stranger into their home whether they can afford to feed that stranger or not. I know personally of a family who couldn't send their child to school for a term because they spent her tuition taking care of an uninvited guest who stayed for a month.

If you are spending the night and are offered sleeping room in a *bure*, accept the accommodation rather than pitching a tent outside the home. Should you camp outside someone's home, the message advertised is that the host's house is an unpleasant place to sleep.

Try to avoid ostentatious displays of wealth. Remember that most villagers could never hope to own the kind of cameras, tape decks and other goods that we take for granted.

FILM & PHOTOGRAPHY

No self-respecting traveller or journalist comes to Fiji without a camera. Should you need them, film and photographic accessories are readily available in Suva's modern shops, which thanks to duty-free prices make photographic equipment and film probably the most inexpensive in the South Pacific.

There are several labs where same-day service is available for colour print developing – Caines Photofast Services, on the corner of Victoria Parade and Pratt St; Fiji Color Lab on 40 Cumming St; and Brijlal's Photo Service at Vanua House, Victoria Parade. Expect to pay just under F$10 for developing a roll of 04 shots. Film is about F$4 per roll of 36 (100 ASA).

Keep in mind that daylight is much more intense in the tropics, so if in doubt when shooting film, underexpose. That is, if you really want that photo, shoot according to what your normal meter reading dictates and then shoot one third to one full stop under. It's also a good idea to take photos at dawn or dusk for best light conditions – the mid-day sun is usually too harsh.

Always keep film dry and cool, and upon your return have your camera cleaned if exposed excessively to the elements – the humidity and salt air can ruin sensitive photo equipment in no time. If you plan to go through customs at airports frequently, it's advisable to buy a laminated lead pouch for film, available in any photo shop.

When taking photos of locals, smile and ask permission first. People will be happy to let you photograph them 99% of the time, but on other (rare) occasions some folks may not want to be part of your future slide show.

THINGS TO BRING

Dress in Fiji is almost always casual and, because of the warm climate, it is easy to subscribe to the adage 'travel light.' Unless you are planning to travel in the high mountains, you can be certain it will always be warm, even at night. Therefore, clothing should be light. Bathing suit and shorts (both for men and women) are practical and always fashionable around resorts but scanty clothing should never be worn outside these areas, especially in or near a Fijian village. Cotton shirts and dresses are also necessary, as are sandals, a windbreaker for the odd tropical downpour, a light sweater, a hat to shield you from the intense rays, sunscreen, sunglasses, insect repellent and perhaps small souvenirs or toys for Fijian children. Guitar strings and T-shirts make fine gifts for villagers.

THINGS TO BUY
Duty-Free Shopping

The most obvious thing about Fiji, even to the visitor who has just got off the plane, is the plethora of 'duty-free shops' in the country and the sometimes overly aggressive touts who work there. The most popular items are photographic equipment, tape recorders and VCRs, perfume, razors, telescopes, binoculars, sporting goods, radios, watches, liquor, tobacco and film. Duty-free shops can provide bargains for this merchandise, but buyer beware. 'Duty-free' is a misnomer for all the shops except the one in the departure lounge at Nadi Airport. All imported items sold in the so-called 'duty-free shops,' with the exception of photo equipment, carry at least a 10% duty.

If you're still interested, visit different shops, examine the merchandise and take a price survey. The best way to walk into a shop is to know exactly what you want and what its approximate retail market value is in your own country. Only then can you assess whether it is worthwhile to purchase the item. Some merchandise may in fact be more expensive in Fiji than where you come from.

In most stores the price is negotiated bazaar-style; the seller names a price and the buyer makes a counter-offer and so on until a bargain is struck. Don't be intimidated or afraid to drive a hard bargain. The seller will certainly not be afraid to relieve you of your money if he or she gets the chance. If you have local friends ask them to recommend a shop – or better yet, take a local along. There always seem to be local and tourist prices and you may benefit from this without excess haggling. Make sure that you get a docket and warranty to receive service when you return home. Also, try to watch the item you purchased being wrapped in front of you and insist that it be given a trial run. With electronic gadgets keep in mind the possible differences in electrical standards in your country and in Fiji. Be positive that the thing will work back in Peoria or Perth.

Although the airport shops are in fact 'duty free,' they must tack on some profit margin which may or may not make them cheaper than the stores in town. Again, the buyer should know his or her merchandise to really be sure. Prices at the airport shops are always fixed, so for those not interested in dealing with the bazaar method, they are the best places to buy.

For those who want to bargain but don't wish to deal with the hard sell, my experience is that the merchants outside of Nadi and Suva are certainly the nicest. Try your luck in the outlying communities of Lautoka and Sigatoka and you will readily note the difference.

Any complaints can be addressed to:
Suva Duty Free Merchants Association (tel 22249 or 22723)
Nadi Duty Free Dealers Association (tel 70088 or 70147)
Lautoka Duty Free Dealers Association (tel 60242 or 60536)
Sigatoka Duty Free Dealers Association (tel 50064 or 50534)

Arts & Handicrafts

Arts and crafts can be purchased from three different sources — private craftspeople, duty-free shops and the government crafts centre. The cheapest source is generally the individuals, but these people are hard to find. Sometimes villagers augment their income by selling mats, carvings, pottery or *masi* (tapa cloth) and you can always enquire. Duty-free shops are also a source of handicrafts, but quality varies. The official government crafts centre at Vanua House in Suva has some very fine items but they tend to be on the expensive side. The handicraft centre near the Suva Municipal Market has a wide variety of items, but you must check the stalls for goods and bargain. There is also a handicrafts shop at Pacific Harbour which is on the expensive side but has good merchandise. Outside of Suva, the craft centre at the Lautoka public market has some good bargains in varied items.

Keep in mind that you get what you pay for. Those interested in artefact-type replicas should first go to the Fiji Museum in Suva and carefully examine the relics therein. These are the models for the reproductions you are buying.

The travel experience is not complete without being approached by at least one 'sword seller.' These Fijian capitalists peddle souvenir 'swords' on the street with an individual's name carved on them. The swords are about as Fijian in origin as Snow White but might make the perfect tacky gift for that special relative you don't want to spend too much money on. Average price is about F$5. The sword sellers can be a nuisance but a simple '*Sega vinaka*' ('No thank you') will send them on their way.

Tailored Goods

Work done by tailors in Fiji can be quite good and very inexpensive. A Hawaiian-style shirt can be made for under US$10 for labour, and a fairly good array of fabric is available. Best bet is to bring to the tailor a shirt whose pattern you wish copied, along with material. Should you lose your suit on the airplane, South Seas Tailors (tel 22 725) at 155 Victoria Parade can replace it in 24 hours. For Hawaiian shirts I've had good luck and workmanship with Gangaram Tailors in Honson Arcade (across from Sunflower Airlines' office) in Suva. A locally made shirt (you supply the material) costs F$8.

CLOTHING

The national costume for men and women is the *sulu*, a rectangular piece of cloth about two yards (1.9 metres) long. It can be tied a number of ways, but is most popularly wrapped skirt-like around the waist and worn in combination with a T-shirt. For formal occasions men wear a kilt-like garment called a *sulu vakataga* and women wear a two-piece, ankle-length dress called a *sulu-i-va*. Like a sarong in Asia many men soon find that in Fiji's often humid clime it is a practical item of clothing to wear around the hotel. Get hooked and you will find yourself bringing a few sulus back home. They come in a variety of colours and patterns and in several grades of quality.

VILLAGE VISITS & TREKKING

Many travellers visit Fijian villages or Indian settlements, which certainly provide an insight into traditional life. While cultural exchange is the essence of travel, uninvited guests and trekkers who suddenly show up in a community can be extremely disruptive and, what's more, the government encourages the community to frown upon interlopers. Fijians, being the generous people that they are, will provide the visitor, even the uninvited freeloader, with their last spoonful of instant coffee or last tin of jam without uttering a peep. There is no question that when visitors are around, the normal routine of the village changes. Gardens do not get weeded, chores are put off and the attention goes to the entertainment of the guest. Visitors may not even realize the burden they can become.

Fijian culture dictates that the stranger be treated with the utmost hospitality and unfortunately some people take advantage of this. You should realize that although Fijians are rich in spirit, they are often very poor materially. You should always match your host's generosity by purchasing groceries and practical gifts if you plan to stay for a while.

Trans-island trekkers or visitors to outer islands where there are no visitor facilities should not camp on native land unless permission is given by the village. Nor should you assume that you can automatically stay in a village. Villagers are simply not equipped to handle guests nor to act as guides if someone wanders in looking for the right trail. Thus, even the best-intentioned visitors can become a nuisance. The government is reacting to this type of activity by considering ways of limiting backpackers to certain rural areas.

Aside from possible disruption of village life, hiking in the bush can be dangerous to the uninitiated and unprepared. Monsoon-like rains often wash out trails and it is easy to get lost in the rain forest. Backpackers have often been stranded, sometimes with injuries, in remote areas awaiting rescue from villagers or government officials – certainly not the way to spend a vacation. When in doubt about camping or hiking, always enquire at the local Lands & Survey Section of the Ministry of Lands (tel 241 250) or the Forestry Department.

DIVING & SNORKELLING

Most of Fiji's islands are bounded by reefs where tropical fish of every colour and description thrive. Those in the know say that three of Fiji's dive locales – Beqa Lagoon, Astrolabe Lagoon and Taveuni – are world class in calibre. What accounts for this? Just several hundred km from Fiji is the 'Tongan Trench' where upwelling waters rich in nutrients nourish Fiji's ocean life. This steady food supply provides for an abundance of sealife,

making it one of the best tuna grounds in the world. Locals say the sharks are not a problem for divers in the area, although for me sharks are always a concern.

Dive-shop owners in Fiji point out that because Fiji is a relatively remote destination, thousands of km of its reefs are as yet undived. Despite the remoteness of the destination, Fiji's reefs are more accessible for Australians than the Great Barrier Reef and cheaper for North Americans than Hawaii. However, you need not be a scuba diver to appreciate the fish – snorkelling is also excellent and easily learned. Nor should you feel that because you don't know how to dive this should prevent you from learning in Fiji. The warm waters of Fiji are more conducive to learning than the frigid waters of the United States west coast.

For a balanced diving itinerary, Lorraine Evans of Scuba Hire, a Suva-based dive shop, recommends two weeks in Fiji so that the experienced diver has time for:

An island resort – any of the Mamanuca Group, off Fiji's Western side.

Coral Coast – in conjunction with one of the larger hotels like the Hyatt or the Fijian.

Suva, Taveuni or Kadavu – to see deeper, more spectacular reefs. This may include time on a 'live-aboard charter' to allow a visit to a more remote reef. Charter should be pre-arranged.

The best time of the year to visit for diving purposes is the winter, April to November, when trade winds blow more favourably, the water is clearer and the fish are more active. Divers are advised to bring their own regulator, mask, snorkel and fins. Keep in mind that spearfishing in Fiji is not encouraged for conservation reasons.

Visitors can expect to pay F$260-420 for an eight day/seven night food-and-lodging package (depending on accommodation) with Scuba Hire. Lessons are F$230 for a course. According to Ms Evans a comparative course would cost US$350-600 in the USA.

Dive Specialists

Scuba Hire, PO Box 777, Suva (tel 361 241 or 361 458). Scuba instruction, photography, air-filling station, equipment sales, equipment repairs and diving excursions.

Dive Centre Fiji, PO Box 3066, Lami (tel 23 337 or 361 200). Scuba instruction, air-filling station, equipment sales, equipment repairs and diving excursions.

Diver Services of Fiji, PO Box 502, Lautoka (tel 60 496 or 63 034). Dive instruction, equipment hire, diving excursions.

In addition to the above dive specialists, the major resorts are affiliated with dive services and can arrange for dive excursions and equipment for their clients.

Dive Taveuni, CPO Matei, Taveuni (tel 406-M Taveuni), is a top-rated outfit with its own accommodation. They have equipment rentals and excursions to the famous Rainbow Reef.

Besides the dive shops you can check with the British Sub Aqua Club (BSAC). They organise dives for BSAC-licenced divers and will sometimes take snorkellers on their expeditions if there is room. Contact any of the dive shops for information.

Getting There

The vast majority of international flights land at Nadi (pronounced 'Nandi') International Airport. Although major airlines often market Fiji as a destination in its own right, it is in actuality an intermediate stop between major destinations in North America and Australia or New Zealand; most passengers on flights to Fiji are onward bound. Fiji is also linked to Hawaii, most of the major Pacific Islands and Japan, but not South America.

Carriers to Fiji include Continental, Air New Zealand, Qantas, Air Pacific, Japan Air Lines, Polynesian Airlines, CP Air and Air Nauru.

Upon leaving Fiji you must pay an airport departure tax of F\$5. The tax is payable in Fiji currency at the airline counter. This is usually a good time to get rid of your silver.

AIRPORT FACILITIES

Although a bit provincial by international standards, Nadi International Airport lacks nothing in the way of official services and amenities such as lockers, restaurant, snack bar, gift shops, post office, immigration service, health department, cargo and freight facilities, departure lounge, police station, customs department and quarantine department. There is also a full array of airline offices, tour companies, rental car agencies, and an office of the Visitors Bureau. Listed below are the facilities and their respective telephone numbers.

Airlines

Air Nauru	tel 72795
Air New Zealand	tel 72922
Air Pacific	tel 72499
Air Tungaru	tel 72499
CP Air	tel 72400
Continental Airlines	tel 72788
Japan Air Lines	tel 72199
Polynesian Airlines	tel 72499
Qantas	tel 72888

Agencies & Resorts

Burnmoore Travel	tel 72188
Atlantic & Pacific Fiji Tours	tel 72074
Yanuca Tours	tel 72809
Hunt's Travel	tel 72869
Rosie Tours	tel 72935
Tapa Tours (American Express)	tel 72100
United Touring	tel 72244
Japan Creative Tours (Jalpak)	tel 72640
Sun Tours	tel 72268
Tour Contractors Pacific	tel 72731
Turtle Island Lodge	tel 72780 or 72921
Musket Cove Resort (Dick's Place)	tel 72371, 72077 or 72488
Thomas Cook	tel 72377

Car Rental

Avis	tel 72233
Dominion Rentals	tel 72262
Hertz Rent-a-Car	tel 72771
Budget Rent-a-Car	tel 72735
Rosie's Rental Cars	tel 72935
The A-Team Rental Cars	tel 72052
Dollar Rental Cars	tel 73177

Fiji Visitors Bureau

The Nadi branch of the Fiji Visitors Bureau is manned by the very capable Abe Yavala, it is open in the daytime and during all aircraft arrivals.

Bank

The airport bank is a branch of BNZ, the Bank of New Zealand. It is the only 24-hour, seven-day-a-week bank in Fiji.

Post Office

Those looking for a post office in the terminal will be hard pressed to find one because it is located across the road, near the cargo building.

Duty-Free Shopping

There is plenty of duty-free shopping at the airport; however, it is only for 'last chance' outbound travellers who are either in transit or about to board their planes. Shoppers need not fear; there are plenty of shopping opportunities in and around Nadi, Lautoka, Sigatoka and Suva.

ROUND-THE-WORLD TICKETS

Round-the-World (RTW) fares are a comparatively recent innovation where two or more airlines link together to offer a round-the-world service using their combined routings. The RTW ticket they jointly market allows you to fly round the world with stop-overs at the various cities they serve. A number of these ticket possibilities can include Fiji.

There are often restrictions of some form on these tickets – apart from the limitation that they only apply to services of the two (sometimes three) airlines that get together to offer them. There may be limits to the number of stop-overs you are permitted, pre-booking requirements, penalties or additional charges if you change your routing, maximum/minimum period of validity and so on. The end result, however, should be a useful saving over other methods of getting to the places you want to go.

RTW tickets that can fly you through Fiji include the Qantas-TWA ticket which costs A$2699 and allows you to fly through Fiji between Australia or New Zealand and Honolulu on Qantas services. There are also Qantas-Air Canada and Qantas-British Airways combinations at the same cost.

Continental also fly through Fiji between the USA and Australia and offer a number of RTW combinations with other airlines. Continental-Air India or Continental-British Caledonian-Malaysian Airlines System is A$2300. Continental-Thai International-Scandinavian Airlines System is A$2460. Continental-KLM is A$2499. With Canadian Pacific Air you can fly via Fiji on their Vancouver-Australia services They have a variety of combinations with Alitalia, Cathay Pacific, Philippine Airlines and South African

Airways with costs from A$2399 to A$2950. You can also, at additional cost, add CP Air's South American services into these round-the-world routes.

Purchased in England RTW tickets through the South Pacific typically cost from around £1150. Possibilities include British Airways-Qantas £1328, British Caledonian-Continental-MAS £1150, TWA-Qantas £1250 or a whole host of combinations with Air New Zealand for £1265. London bucket shops will also put together their own RTW combinations at lower costs – see the From Europe section below.

CIRCLE PACIFIC TICKETS

Following the success of RTW fares a new variation, which can also include Fiji, is Circle Pacific Fares. Like RTW fares two airlines join to offer a round-the-Pacific route – which will usually mean travelling one way from Australia or New Zealand to the USA via the South Pacific and the other via Asia.

As with RTW fares there will usually be restrictions on booking, stop-overs and period of validity. Most Circle Pacific tickets give you either four or five stop-overs, additional stop-overs cost $25 to 50 each.

Examples of Circle Pacific fares going through Fiji include Continental-Thai International for US$1870 (A$2700). Continental-Japan Airlines offer combinations that go as far east as Honolulu for US$1820, to Los Angeles for US$1870 or all the way to New York for US$2267. Or try Continental-Philippine Airlines for US$1589 to Honolulu or US$1799 to Los Angeles.

Other Circle Pacific links include CP Air-Cathay Pacific for A$1817 or CP Air-Malaysian Airlines System for A$1628. Qantas-Northwest Orient get together for A$1932 to Honolulu, US$1982 to the US west coast.

OTHER PACIFIC AIRPASSES

Continental offer a variation on Circle

Pacific with UTA which allows you to take different South Pacific routes eastbound and westbound. You could, for example, fly via Fiji and Hawaii in one direction and return via Tahiti and New Caledonia in the other. Fares from Sydney range from A$1392 to 1938 depending on season, from Melbourne the range is A$1519 to 2065.

Another variation is offered by Continental-Qantas-Air New Zealand which allows you to do a circuit linking Australia-Fiji and New Zealand. The ticket is only valid for 60 days and costs A$684, NZ$970 or F$639, depending on where it is issued.

Or there's the Polynesian Airlines 'Polypass' which allows you to fly anywhere on the airline's route network for 30 days for US$799. Polynesian Airlines flies to Sydney in Australia, Auckland in New Zealand, Western Samoa, Tonga, Cook Islands, American Samoa, New Caledonia and Vanuatu. They also fly to Tahiti but that costs an extra US$100, which also extends the pass for another seven days. The airpass is not currently available in New Zealand or the French Pacific territories.

FROM AUSTRALIA

You can fly Australia-Fiji with Air Pacific, Qantas or Continental. Fares that might be of interest include regular one-way fares, excursion fares and group return fares. Excursion fares require a minimum stay of six days up to a maximum stay of 120 days. Group return fares are normally only available if you're going on an organised package tour but travel agents have been known to use their ingenuity with respect to these fares. The excursion fares and group return fares are seasonal– low season is most of the year, high season is basically most of December and January – the Australian school summer holiday period. Recently there have been special short term bargain fares on offer to Fiji from time to time.

One-way economy fares are A$450

from Sydney, A$548 from Melbourne. Round-trip excursion fares vary from A$531 to 675 from Sydney, A$648 to 823 from Melbourne. Group return fares are A$437 to 588 from Sydney, A$533 to 715 from Melbourne. Fares from Brisbane are the same as from Sydney.

An alternative to one-way or return fares from Australia are fares taking in Fiji as a stop-over between Australia and North America. CP Air, Continental and Qantas all fly this route and can include Fiji on their routings. Fares are the same to Vancouver, San Francisco or Los Angeles. The economy one-way fare is A$1795 from Sydney or Brisbane, A$1859 from Melbourne. Advance-purchase return fares from Sydney range from A$1392 to 1938 depending on season. From Melbourne the range is A$1519 to 2065. One way advance-purchase fares are not seasonal. From Sydney or Brisbane to the west coast is A$1000, from Melbourne it is A$1064.

Flight time from Sydney to Fiji is three hours 45 minutes, from Melbourne it's 4½ hours.

FROM NEW ZEALAND

Air New Zealand and Air Pacific fly Auckland-Nadi. The regular one-way fare is NZ$504. Advance purchase return fares vary with season from NZ$641 to 765. There is no minimum stay period and you can stay for up to 12 months. Fiji can also be a stop-over between New Zealand and the US west coast. The regular one-way economy fare is NZ$1629 or there is an advance-purchase one-way fare of NZ$1272. Advance-purchase return fares vary from NZ$1703 to 2434. Flight time from Auckland to Nadi is three hours 15 minutes.

FROM NORTH AMERICA

There are flights from the North American west coast and Hawaii to Fiji, most using Fiji as a stop-over en route to Australia or New Zealand. Airlines operating between North America and Fiji are Continental.

(out of Los Angeles and San Francisco), Qantas (ditto), Air New Zealand (out of Los Angeles) and CP Air (out of Vancouver). Flight time from the west coast to Fiji is about 11 hours. From Honolulu it's six hours.

Regular one-way economy fares from Honolulu to Sydney are US$720, to Melbourne US$770. From the west coast fares are US$800 to Sydney, US$850 to Melbourne. Excursion fares range from US$786 to 1086 from Honolulu to Sydney or Melbourne, depending on season. From the west coast fares are US$996 to 1296. Stop-overs are permitted on any of these fares. It is often possible to get slightly more attractive fares from agents, check the travel ads in papers like the *Los Angeles Times, New York Times* or *San Francisco Chronicle/Examiner*.

FROM EUROPE

Few people are going to go all the way around the world from Europe simply to go to Fiji but it can make an interesting stop-over en route to Australia or New Zealand. The various RTW fares covered above permit you to slot Fiji in or there are numerous special fares offered in London or other European cheap ticket centres.

In London you can check the travel ads in *The Times, Time Out* or give-aways like *Australasian Express* or try ticket specialists like Trailfinders or STA Travel. A typical ticket might take you to Australia via North America and Fiji and back through Asia for less than £850. One-way fares to Australia via Fiji are available for less than £500 if you shop around.

FROM ASIA

Apart from Japan Airlines there are no direct flights to Fiji from Asian nations, you have to connect via Australia. A rare exception is Air Nauru, the airline of the tiny but wealthy island of Nauru, who can connect you to Fiji via Nauru. Out of South-East Asia there are often interesting flight possibilities on offer via Australia or New Zealand and the South Pacific to the US west coast. This could be a good way to fly from, say, Singapore to the US via Fiji.

FROM OTHER PACIFIC ISLANDS

There are numerous connections between other Pacific islands and Fiji. Pacific airlines that fly into or out of Fiji include the Fijian airline Air Pacific, Polynesian Airlines, Air Nauru, Air Caledonie and Air Vanuatu.

FROM FIJI

Air Pacific, Fiji's national carrier, flies to the following South Pacific destinations:

flight	one-way fare
Nadi-Honiara	F$463
Nadi-Apia	F$216
Nadi-Vila	F$206
Nadi-Noumea	F$233
Suva-Tonga	F$159
Nadi-Auckland	F$357
Nadi-Melbourne	F$477

PACKAGE PLANS

Package plans may not appeal to the vagabond, but they are the way most visitors travel to the South Pacific. In Australia there are countless package tours available to Fiji resorts and any good travel agent can give you armfuls of colourful brochures. Costs depend upon the season, the resort and the length of time but typically an eight day stay on a share twin basis will cost A$200 to 400, plus air fares. The cheapest Viti Levu resorts are at the lower end of that bracket, the more expensive ones and the island resorts will be at the upper end. You can pay much more – eight days on Turtle Island will set you back over A$1250.

In other countries there may not be such a wide selection of Fiji packages but an agent should be able to answer questions such as: Does the hotel have a mountain or oceanside view? Will your accommodation be over the water, on the beach or in the garden? Is the hotel a super-deluxe one or more moderate? How far away is the beach? A specialist will be familiar with the tour packages available and should be able to answer these questions so that there are no unhappy surprises. A competent agent should also be able to prepare a tailor-made itinerary for the person who has special interests such as golf, diving, bird-watching, etc. Last but not least, a reputable agency can save you money.

ALTERNATIVE TRANSPORT

Unfortunately, the romantic days of catching a tramp steamer and working your way across the Pacific are gone forever. It is possible to book passage on a freighter by consulting an experienced agent or by contacting Freighter Travel Tips, a firm that has specialised in this type of travel for years. Local shipping agents can also refer you to the shipping lines that visit Fiji.

Once in Fiji, however, it is impossible to jump on a freighter to some other destination without having made previous arrangements. Freighter skippers simply do not want to deal with passengers, who will refer you to a shipping agent, who will probably just shrug his shoulders. Anything is possible, though, read the book *Slow Way Home* by Gavin Powell for a recent trans-Pacific ship trip.

It is possible to hitch rides on yachts either in Fiji or at ports in the US (west coast) or Australia. To find the boats headed in this direction, you must do some sleuthing at your favourite marinas and place notices on bulletin boards at yacht clubs and marine supply shops. The Lonely Planet newsletter once had some advice on hitching a yacht – from a yachtie – excerpts below:

Yachts are almost always crewed by couples or men only and are short of crew for the longer passages. No experience is necessary, just taking turns in keeping lookout for big ships

(call your skipper when in doubt). Yachts travel with the trade winds preferably and also in warm climates. This means they go west. Most land-travellers go via Boeing 747 and go east. Here might be a conflict.

How to find yachts: cruising yachts generally have the following characteristics (nice when you are looking around in Los Angeles): Foreign flags, wind-vane steering gear, generally sturdy appearance, laundry of the people who live on board hung out to dry.

Cost: Share food cost. This seems normal. I charged $50 a week for food and lodging and took care of all harbour dues, oil, propane, etc. Some people still think this is expensive. (Nobody realises that with depreciation, insurance, maintenance and operating expenses my boat ends up costing $50 a day).

The best way to approach a skipper is to state that you're not the seasick type (check this out) and have money to share food and money to travel home in case of emergency. Show your proof in travellers' cheques. Generally be helpful with work on board. With a bit of luck a good skipper will teach you the ropes as well as navigation. Go for a week's trial if the route and time permit.

Leave the boat at the appointed end of your joyride. The ship is also the skipper's home and, as you will experience, affords little privacy. Boating is the last freedom left but hassles with official permits, paperwork, visas, etc are getting worse, especially in the so-called 'free world.' Still it is beautiful to share the experience. And we do need more ladies out here (adventurous types naturally).

There have been various other letters in the Lonely Planet Newsletter about hitching yacht rides. The letters from yacht owners generally back up the statements above – that they're only too happy to take on crew. The letters from hitchers generally express amazement at how easy it was to pick a ride up – it's all a matter of luck.

Getting Around

The Fiji group is served by an extensive network of air routes, inter-island boats and an efficient bus system along its roads. Visitors will find that this infrastructure makes travelling within the larger islands and around the archipelago relatively easy. In addition, transportation is very reasonably priced, especially for Americans who have the benefit (at least for the time being) of a strong dollar. Despite the 'mañana' attitude that pervades Fiji, planes, ferries and buses generally run on time.

Many visitors to Fiji never leave the western side of the country, finding the hotels a self-contained vacation. They may venture only by local tourist bus or rental car to nearby attractions. However, those wishing to go to Suva or other parts of Viti Levu have the options of flying from Nadi or taking the 'scenic' route via rental car, local bus (which generally makes quite a few stops and takes four to five hours), or express, air-conditioned coach primarily for tourists (makes few stops and takes about three hours from Nadi to the capital). It is highly recommended that the first-time visitor travel overland (either Queens or Kings Road) rather than by air to get at least a cursory look at the Fijian countryside.

AIR
Although Fiji has its international airport at Nadi, the major hub for inter-island flights is Nausori Airport near Suva. There are some flights originating from Nadi to the outer islands (Vanua Levu, Taveuni, Kadavu and Malololailai) with Sunflower Airlines, but they are limited in comparison to the number of flights available from Nausori. The visitor wishing to fly to the majority of outer-island destinations must first fly to Suva (via Air Pacific or Sunflower Airlines) in order to feed into the Fiji Air (the major domestic carrier) route system. Sunflower also has several flights daily to Pacific Harbour, near Suva, but it is more convenient to fly Air Pacific from Nadi to Suva because Nausori Airport is closer to the capital than Pacific Harbour. The exception to the rule is during peak commute hours. Then, taking Sunflower to Pacific Harbour is faster and perhaps safer than fighting the traffic to Nausori.

Collectively, Fiji's domestic carriers provide service to every island where there is tourist accommodation. Naturally, many islands without visitor's facilities also have airstrips, but unless you are invited by local friends it is not advisable to simply drop in assuming there are some type of facilities. In one case – the prime minister's home island of Lakeba – it is not only ill advised to visit without permission, it is illegal.

Aside from regularly scheduled service, Fiji Air and Sunflower Airlines will charter planes for special groups or individuals. There is also a charter helicopter service, Pacific Crown Aviation (tel 361422), in Lami, near Suva.

In addition to local air service, two of Fiji's domestic carriers serve neighbouring South Pacific nations. Air Pacific (which is the main carrier shuttling passengers from Suva to Nadi) has flights on 737s to Apia, Western Samoa; Auckland, New Zealand; Brisbane, Melbourne and Sydney, Australia; Vila, Vanuatu; Honiara, Solomon Islands; and Tonga. Fiji Air also flies 'internationally' to Funafuti, the capital of Tuvalu.

Domestic Services
Air Pacific Though most of Air Pacific's services are international, the carrier averages about seven flights daily between Nadi and Suva for F$34. It also serves the sugar cane town of Labasa. Air Pacific's main ticket office is located in downtown

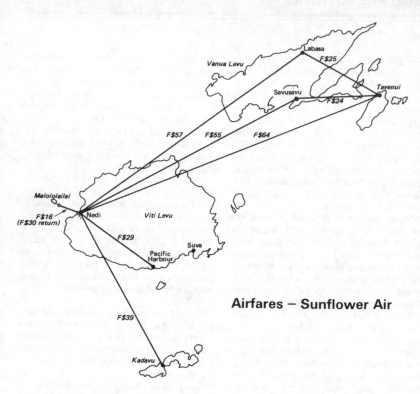

Airfares – Sunflower Air

Suva on Victoria Parade (across from the Westpac Bank and Queensland Arcade), at Nadi International Airport, and in every community served by the airline. Contact them at 313511 in Suva and 72499 in Nadi.

Sunflower Airlines Sunflower has a fleet of seven Britten Norman Islander twin-engined aircraft which use Nadi as a hub and operate every day. One of their biggest tourist destinations (four flights daily) is the island of Malololailai on which the resorts of Plantation Village and Musket Cove are located. Sunflower also flies to Pacific Harbour resort (three times daily) near Suva. From there the passenger must board a coach for the 45-minute free bus transport to Suva. Sunflower have offices at each of their destinations but the main contact is in Nadi, tel 73016 or 73477, telex FJ 5183.

Fiji Air Fiji Air, with a fleet of two 19-passenger Twin Otters and seven smaller aircraft, operates out of Suva and flies to 12 domestic and one international destination, covering more areas than any other local carrier. The airline features a special 'Discover Fiji' fare for visitors which allows you to fly anywhere on its route structure (with the exception of Rotuma and Funafuti) on an unlimited basis for 10 days. Their number is 313 666 in Suva and 72 521 in Nadi. Enquire also about standby fares, especially to Levuka.

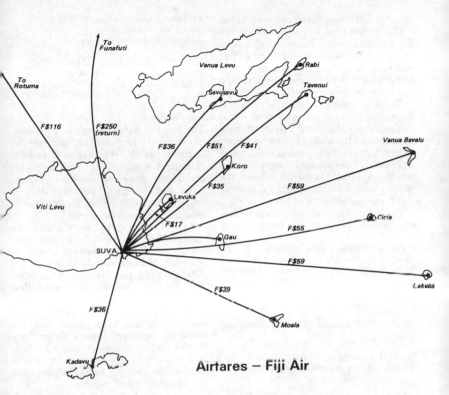

Airfares – Fiji Air

BY SEA

Although air transportation has become the preferred mode of long-haul travel, inter-island vessels remain a vital link for local travellers and cargo to the outer islands. In many instances, inter-island ferries, copra boats and small skiffs are the only way to reach isolated communities. For the visitor with time on his/her hands who doesn't mind roughing it, inter-island boats are a great way to travel and meet the locals. Voyages on these vessels may range from several hours to several weeks and are generally very inexpensive. Schedules are not posted; the best way to find out dates of departure is to call the various shipping companies listed below. Keep in mind that shipping companies

frequently give out inaccurate information regarding departure times and space availability. If you are determined to see the outer islands by boat, it is wise to check personally with the captain when the vessel is in port. He has the final say as to who goes. A pound of yaqona or a bottle of booze just may ensure your berth. This is almost mandatory for boats bound for Rotuma.

Copra Boats

Copra boats or inter-island steamers go to the outermost reaches of the archipelago. Quality of accommodation varies from vessel to vessel, as does space available – sometimes cabins can be had, sometimes only deck passage. Deck passage means just that – sleeping, eating and drinking on deck with the islanders who have chosen the economy route. Likewise, each ship has different eating arrangements. You may have the option (or the necessity) of bringing your own food along, or you might share regular meals with the crew.

There is something very basic about journeying on a copra boat; in a way, it is stepping into the past. You must have patience and the ability to weather minor inconveniences like choppy seas, sea-sickness, diesel fumes, engine noise, roaches and rain. On the other hand, the camaraderie, adventure, salt air, drifting and dreaming are hard to beat.

For information regarding schedules, call the following shipping firms:

D Chung Shipping Co (tel 315666)
Vessels: *Adi Lau, Malawai, Senikaloni*
Ports of call: Kadavu, Lau group, Lomaiviti group

Daisy Shipping Co (tel 44194)
Vessel: *Daisy*
Ports of call: Levuka, Koro, Makogai and Wakaya

Hasan Raza Shipping Co (tel 312339)
Vessels: *Akatere, Zepher II, Island Princess*
Port of call: Vanua Levu

Kaunitoni Shipping Co (tel 312668)
Vessel: *Kaunitoni*
Ports of call: One trip monthly to northern, southern and central Lau group

North West Shipping Lines & Agencies (tel 385388)
Vessel: *Princess Ashika*
Ports of call: Vanua Levu and Lomaiviti groups

Patterson Brothers Shipping Co (tel 315644 or 313088)
Vessels: *Ovalau II, Jubilee II, Deep Lagoon*
Ports of call: Nabouwalu, Savusavu, Labasa, Levuka (ferry boats and conventional vessels)

Tabusoro Co (tel 313939)
Vessel: *Adi Talei*
Ports of call: Lomaiviti group

Tui Levuka Shipping (tel 382174)
Vessel: *Tui Levuka*
Ports of call: Lomaiviti group

Wong's Shipping Co (tel 311888)
Vessels: *Adi Moapa, Belama, Evelyn, Tovata, Yatulau*
Ports of call: Lau and Lomaiviti groups

Ferry Service
The newest development in Fiji inter-island travel is ferry service. There are two of these vessels, the *Ovalau II* and the *Princess Ashika*, both of which mainly ply the waters between Viti Levu, Vanua Levu and Ovalau. They are modern, speedy and offer you the option of bringing your own car along.

Ferry service opens up a whole new vista of drive/sail travel to Fiji's outer islands. This roll-on/roll-off service is available on three vessels: *Ovalau II* and *Jubilee II* of Patterson Brothers Shipping, and *Princess Ashika* of North West Shipping Lines & Agencies. Car rentals for the voyage can be obtained through any of the agencies. Note that the Patterson Brothers vessels depart from Natovi landing (approximately a 1½-hour bus ride from the Suva post office), whereas the *Princess Ashika* departs from the Princess Wharf in Suva.

Patterson Brothers
The Patterson Brothers' *Ovalau II* departs Suva each Monday and Tuesday for Nawaikama (on the island of Gau), Koro, Savusavu and Taveuni, returning to Suva via the same ports each Thursday and Friday. Departure and arrival times are subject to change, so check with the office for information.

The *Ovalau II* has a capacity of 480 passengers, is fully air-conditioned and has three video TV sets, video games and a refreshment bar. The smaller *Jubilee II* can take up to 300 passengers. It is also air-conditioned, and has three video units and a refreshment bar. Patterson Brothers has an additional ferry, the *Romanda*, a WW II-vintage 'Fairmile' (former sub-chaser) which offers daily service (no vehicles) to Ovalau. One-way fares are:

Suva (Natovi)/Levuka   F$9
Suva (Natovi)/Labasa   F$18
Suva (Natovi)/Savusavu   F$20
Suva (Natovi)/Nabouwalu   F$18
Suva (Natovi)/Taveuni   F$20

The cost for shipping a car (and driver) to Ovalou, Vanua Levu and back to Viti Levu is F$90. Passengers are charged standard fares. For individuals without cars, Patterson Brothers provides transportation from the communities it serves to and from all its terminals. Those interested in further fare information plus car travel advice to the outer islands should contact Patterson Brothers Shipping at 315-644 in Suva.

The schedule for the *Jubilee II* is as follows:

Buresala/Natovi/Nabouwalu/Ellington (Monday, Thursday)

Buresala	dep	5.30 am
Natovi	arr	6.30 am
	dep	7 am
Nabouwalu	arr	10.30 am
	dep	11 am
Ellington	arr	2.30 pm

Ellington/Nabouwalu/Natovi/Buresala (Tuesday, Friday)

Ellington	dep	7 am
Nabouwalu	arr	10 am
	dep	11 am
Natovi	arr	2.30 pm
	dep	3 pm
Buresala	arr	4 pm

Buresala/Natovi/Buresala (Wednesday, Saturday)

Buresala	dep	5.30 am
Natovi	arr	6.30 am
	dep	3 pm
Nabouwalu	arr	4 pm

North West Shipping Lines

The *Princess Ashika* visits a few more ports of call than the Patterson Brothers'

vessels and has the advantage of departing directly from Suva instead of being a 1½-hour bus ride away in Natovi. Also, it stops right in Levuka Harbour instead of Buresala (a 45-minute bus ride from Levuka) on Ovalau. For people with vehicles this may not be a burden, but for ordinary passengers it is more convenient to be taken directly to your ports of call without having to take buses. The *Princess Ashika* visits Savusavu on Vanua Levu, Levuka on Ovalau, the island of Koro, and the island of Taveuni. The big disadvantage with North West Shipping Lines (and this is no small matter) is that the firm doesn't stick to its schedule as rigidly as Patterson Brothers, a shipping line which has been a fixture in Fiji for 50 years and can be counted on. Always double-check when booking with North West – they are known to cancel if there are not sufficient passengers.

The *Princess Ashika* is a fully air conditioned, 700-ton vessel carrying up to 500 passengers. It has a full-service restaurant, on-board video entertainment, multilingual hostesses and a lounge. Phone 385 388 or 385 360 in Suva; or 82 613. Fares and schedules are as follows:

One-way fares:

Suva/Taveuni	F$34
Suva/Koro	F$30
Suva/Kadavu	F$30
Suva/Levuka	F$10
Suva/Savusavu	F$28
Suva/Labasa	F$30

(via bus from Savusavu)

Suva/Levuka/Savusavu (Sunday)

Suva	dep	4 pm
Levuka	arr	8.30 pm
	dep	9.30 pm
Savusavu	arr	4.30 am
		(Monday)

Savusavu/Koro/Suva (Monday)

Savusavu	dep	6 am
Koro	arr	9.30 am
	dep	10.30 am
Suva	arr	5.30 pm

Suva/Savusavu (Tuesday)

| Suva | dep | 5 am |
| Savusavu | arr | 3 pm |

Savusavu/Suva (Wednesday)

| Savusavu | dep | 7 am |
| Suva | arr | 5 pm |

Suva/Savusavu/Taveuni (Thursday)

Suva	dep	5 am
Savusavu	arr	3 pm
	dep	5 pm
Taveuni	arr	6 am
		(Friday)

Taveuni/Savusavu/Levuka (Friday)

Taveuni	dep	11 am
Savusavu	arr	3 pm
	dep	5 pm
Levuka	arr	11 pm

Levuka/Suva (Saturday)

Levuka	dep	11.30 pm
Suva	arr	4.30 am
		(Sunday)

BY ROAD

Fiji has about 3300 km of roads, of which 1200 are bitumen sealed. Most of the paved highways are on Viti Levu, which has a 500-km road that circles the island. Most of this highway is paved, and although authorities perennially claim that the highway will be completed 'next year,' construction is a never-ending affair. Whenever a heavy hurricane or flood devastates a particular region, the road is inevitably washed out, setting back the schedule once again. The paved sections that do exist are splendidly engineered but drivers must contend with cattle, horses and goats that feed on the edge of the highway and may wander across at night. Motorists should also be aware of villagers who sometimes walk dangerously close to passing vehicles or sit in groups at the edges of roads that pass through communities. Likewise,

drivers have very little 'driver's education' and will do things like pass on blind curves or tailgate unnervingly close. The driver's motto should be 'Watch out for everything – human, beast or machine.'

To drive a rental vehicle visitors need only a valid driver's licence from their own country to qualify. North Americans, note that Fiji drives on the left side of the road. Travellers should also note that there are service stations near all major towns but in some of the rural areas they are practically non-existent. If you get caught on a back road with a nearly empty tank, it might be wise to ask in village shops, which frequently sell fuel from drums.

Many locals do have cars but the majority of the population depend on buses and trucks, which are the main means of transportation even for those in very remote areas. The buses, whose bodies are manufactured in Fiji, are noisy, smoke-belching beasts with open windows sealed from foul weather by means of a tarp which is communally rolled down at the appropriate time. Although time consuming, travel by bus can be rewarding for the visitor because it encourages mixing with the local population. On the outer islands where rental vehicles are scarce, visitors may find that local buses and taxis are the only form of transportation. Buses are very inexpensive (figure on approximately F$0.75 per 20 km), run regularly, and can be caught at roadside bus stands. In more rural areas they may be hailed like taxis.

Car Rental

Car rental agencies have sprung up like mushrooms over the past few years and every major hotel has a rental desk. Generally the larger agencies keep the cars in good shape, but it's always a good idea to give the prospective vehicle a spin around the block before you take it out in earnest. Even big-name agencies can have maintenance lapses and the cars may lack minor things like working brakes or pressure in the tyres. Rates vary a bit, but on the average, expect to pay at the least F$14 per day (in addition to a F$0.15-per-km charge) or around F$35 per day for unlimited mileage. Both UTC and Budget have four-wheel-drive Suzuki jeeps.

Motorcycle Rental

Wing Lee in Suva (tel 385 788) rents Kawasaki motorcycles. The cost is F$20 per day for a 250cc and F$11 for a 125cc or a 100cc. A deposit of F$80 is mandatory. Rates can be negotiated for long-term rentals. Budget Rentals in Suva (tel 315-899) or Nadi (tel 72 735) have four-wheel Suzuki off-road bikes for F$15 per day plus F$0.15 per km. Unfortunately there are no (two-wheel) motorcycle rentals on the western side.

Taxi

Generally, taxis are an inexpensive way to get around in Fiji. A crosstown fare in Suva, for example, averages around F$1.50. Many taxis in rural areas do not have meters, so it's wise to negotiate or at least ask the driver what the cost is.

Express Bus

There are three bus companies that offer express air-conditioned bus services between Suva and Nadi on the Queens Road and one firm that has services between Lautoka and Suva on the Kings Road. These are the most comfortable and speediest but not necessarily the most interesting buses to take.

Queens Coach

Departs Nadi Airport at 7.30 am and proceeds to Regent Hotel, Nadi Hotel, Fijian Hotel, the town of Sigatoka, Reef Hotel, Naviti Hotel, Hyatt Regency, Pacific Harbour and Orchid Island, arriving at the Tradewinds Hotel outside Suva at noon. On the return leg it departs the Tradewinds at 5 pm (stopping at the same points as above) and arrives at Nadi Airport at 9 pm. Suva-Nadi or Nadi-Suva fare is F$10. Phone 313543 in Suva and 72889 in Nadi.

Fiji Express

Departs Nadi Airport at 9 am and 12 noon, stopping at the Regent Hotel, Nadi Hotel, Fijian Hotel, Reef Hotel, Naviti Resort, Paradise Point, Hyatt Regency, Pacific Harbour, Tradewinds and downtown Suva. Arrival times are 2.30 pm and 5.30 pm respectively. On the other side of the island there are two coaches also leaving from Suva at 9 am and noon, also arriving in Nadi at 2.30 pm and 5.30 pm. This firm has connecting service to Lautoka (on the western side of the island) as well. Suva-Nadi or Nadi-Suva fare is F$15. Phone 72821 in Nadi and 25637 in Suva.

Pacific Transport

Pacific Transport Ltd has one air-conditioned express leaving Lautoka at 10 am, arriving at Nadi Airport at 10.45 am and making other stops in Nadi Town, Sigatoka and Deuba, arriving in Suva at 4 pm. Its counterpart also leaves Suva at 10 am, making all the same stops and arriving at Nadi Airport at 3.45 pm and Lautoka at 4.15 pm.

This bus company, which caters much more to local traffic, has three other (non-air-conditioned) express buses leaving from both sides of the island (Suva and Lautoka) and four other 'daily' buses (also leaving from both sides of the island). The daily buses, which stop at every village along the route, take an additional two hours to make the journey. Fare from Nadi Airport to Suva is only F$5.90. The traveller taking buses from one side of the island to the other with time on his/her hands need not worry about catching a bus at any time of the day because there are always buses running on the hour (usually every 50 minutes).

If in doubt as to where to catch a bus, the best bet is simply to ask. If you are in a remote area it's always easy to flag down a bus from the side of the road. For more information regarding Pacific Transport call 25425 in Suva; or call 70044 or 72715 in Nadi.

Sunbeam Transport
Sunbeam is the only bus company with express service on the northerly Kings Road. Daily express buses from Lautoka to Suva leave at 6.30 am and 4.30 pm, with three other local buses departing at various other times. Express service from Suva to Lautoka is at 6.45 am and 5.15 pm, with two other local buses in the mornings. Express stops include Ba, Tavua, Vaileka, Korovou and Nausori. Fare is F$7.50 Lautoka-Suva. For information call 24 229 or 22 911 in Suva; or 62 822 or 60 581 in Lautoka.

The Fiji Archipelago

Fiji is known in the Fijian language as *Viti*. The present name came from the Tongans, who prior to the mid-18th century called the island group *Fiji* (now *Fisi*). According to linguist Albert Schutz, early use of the name 'Fiji' by Captain Bligh and the Reverend John Davies probably reflects this Tongan influence. Some of the early spellings were 'Fejee' and 'Feejee,' which persisted well into the 19th century.

Geographically speaking, the two major features of the Fiji group are Viti Levu, the largest island, with 70% of the population; and, to the north-east, Vanua Levu, the second largest island. Vanua Levu is also a centre of population, although more sparsely settled than Viti Levu. To the south-east of Viti Levu and Vanua Levu, the majority of Fiji's other islands are scattered over 500,000 square km of ocean. Among these islands are the Lomaiviti group, which includes Ovalau, where Fiji's original capital of Levuka is located; Kadavu, located south of Viti Levu and a bastion of traditional culture; and the Lau group, whose history and culture were very influenced by the close proximity of Tonga.

Politically the archipelago is divided into four areas or 'divisions' – the Northern Division which is composed of Vanua Levu and the neighbouring islands of Taveuni, Rabi and Qamea; the Western Division which consists of the western half of the main island of Viti Levu, including the Yasawa Islands to the north-west and Vatulele to the south; the Central Division made up of the eastern half of Viti Levu; and the Eastern Division, composed of the Lau group, Kadavu and the Lomaiviti group.

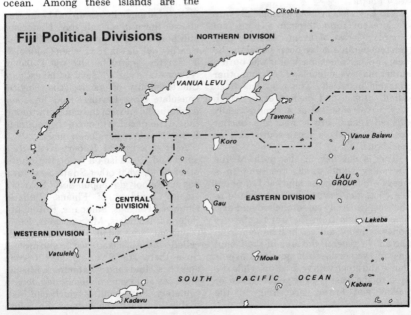

83

Viti Levu

Viti Levu, which translates as 'Great Fiji,' is the largest and oldest island in the archipelago. Roughly oval in shape, it measures 146 km long and 106 km wide and has an area of 10,389 square km. When compared to other Pacific islands, it is exceeded in size only by New Caledonia and Hawaii. With a population of approximately 518,000, it is also the most populous island in Fiji.

Commensurate with the island's size is its importance. Viti Levu's rich river valleys support the country's densest population centres. Extensive sugar lands lie on its western and northern coasts. Gold mines, dairy farms, light manufacturing and the most important industry, tourism, contribute to its wealth. In addition, the island is the main centre of air and sea communications in the southwest Pacific.

Viti Levu has evolved geologically into its present form through a long and complex series of events. During protracted periods it lay deep beneath the sea; at other times much of it was buried under massive amounts of lava and other volcanic materials. The land has been tilted, broken and pushed every which way, yet it emerged as a symmetrically shaped island with a mountain barrier forming roughly a north-south axis or backbone.

The island lies in the path of the prevailing trade winds, resulting in a heavy rainfall over the windward slopes of the east, and leaving the countryside to the west generally sun-drenched and dry. The transition from the wet to the dry zones is abrupt, and can best be seen from the air. In general, the area of the island east of the north-south mountain axis is dense and green with vegetation, while the area to the west is light yellow-green or yellow and brown, according to the season.

SUVA

Suva can lay certain claim to being the largest and perhaps the most livable city in the South Pacific outside of New Zealand or Australia. The capital of Fiji since 1883, it is set on 15 square km of peninsula adjacent to one of the finest naturally protected harbours in the South Seas. It is home for about 76,000 people, with another 30,000 living in the fast-developing corridor along the 25-km stretch from the city limits to the airport at Nausori.

Perhaps the biggest drawback to the town is its weather, which is wet and often muggy. The nicest way to describe Suva is as a changeable town that gleams in the sunlight and turns metallic grey in the rain. And rain is not an uncommon occurrence in the capital of Fiji. An average of 3000 mm of precipitation (120 inches) fall annually and up to 347 mm can shower down in a single day. Historians still ponder the minor miracle of the fair weather one day in 1861 when Colonel W T Smythe, instructed by the Duke of Newcastle, came to Suva to investigate the feasibility of moving the English consulate from Levuka. Had he come during in the midst of the usual downpour, the fateful decision to move the capital to Suva may never have been made.

As Fiji journalist Robert Keith-Reid aptly said, 'Suva isn't a jewel. But on the other hand, what other South Seas town has such a polyglot population?' Suva is a steamy cauldron of Fijians, Indians, Chinese, Tongans, Samoans, Rotumans, Solomon Islanders, Micronesians, Europeans and 'fruit salad' as they are locally called – those of mixed race. In and around Suva there are a variety of Christian churches, Hindu and Sikh temples, Muslim mosques and even an abandoned Jewish cemetery. Fiji's capital, which can justifiably be called the hub of the South

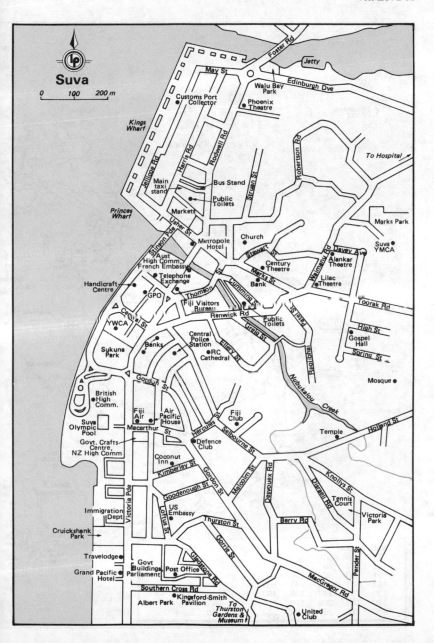

Suva

0   100   200 m

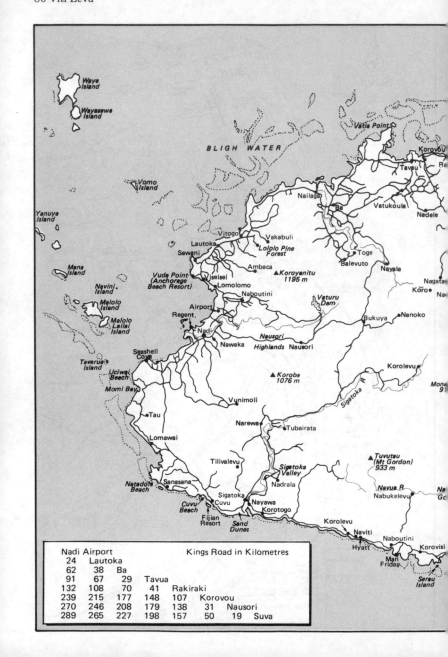

Nadi Airport							Kings Road in Kilometres
24	Lautoka						
62	38	Ba					
91	67	29	Tavua				
132	108	70	41	Rakiraki			
239	215	177	148	107	Korovou		
270	246	208	179	138	31	Nausori	
289	265	227	198	157	50	19	Suva

Viti Levu

0   10 km

Suva					Queens Road in Kilometres		
49	Pacific Harbour						
96	47	Korolevu					
120	71	24	Korotogo				
127	78	31	7	Sigatoka			
183	139	92	68	61	Nadi Town		
197	148	101	77	70	9	Nadi Airport	
221	172	125	101	94	33	24	Lautoka

Pacific, has a modern array of communications facilities and has attracted a host of international bureaus and regional institutions. These include half a dozen United Nations agencies; embassies from China, the USA and France; the South Pacific Bureau for Economic Cooperation; and the University of the South Pacific.

Early Suva

Before Suva became the centre of European activity in Fiji, it was a typical village, embroiled in the political squabbles and intrigues of the day which often resulted in attacks by rival tribes. The European settlement of this waterfront community was prompted by a series of events that began during a celebration of America's Independence Day on 4 July 1848. The first was a fire in a house belonging to entrepreneur John Brown Williams, United States commercial agent in Fiji. While the fire burned, many of Williams' possessions were 'liberated' from the burning structure by villagers, who saw no reason to give them back. Consul Williams, as he was called, took full advantage of the situation and inflated his 1848 loss of goods looted by the Fijians from approximately £200 (as some have estimated) into nearly £10,000 at the time of his death.

The responsibility for these actions was placed upon Chief Cakobau, who at the time was the self-styled 'Tui Viti' or King of Fiji. Having failed to eliminate the debt by an attempt to cede Fiji to Britain (which took some nerve because Chief Cakobau really didn't have dominion over the entire country), he quickly accepted the offer of the newly formed Polynesia Company to pay the amount.

The agreement was that the Polynesia Company would pay back the money in exchange for 200,000 acres of land and trading and banking rights in Fiji. About 23,000 acres of the total were in the Suva area. The price worked out to about a shilling an acre – not a bad deal even in those days.

Polynesia Company Settlement

After acquisition by the Polynesia Company, a boatload of Australian settlers arrived in Suva in 1870 to plant cotton and later sugar. Early settlers camped on the beach until the land, densely covered with vegetation, was cleared for their native-style huts. One settler described the ordeal:

Our women folk bore themselves bravely, and lived up to the traditions of our race, but it was dreadfully trying to them and the children. They were devoured by mosquitoes, terrified by the hordes of fierce land crabs, and drenched with rain when the fine weather broke up. Most of us had come totally unequipped with mosquito curtains, and I shall never forget how those fell insects punished us ... I tried everything I could to dodge the little beasts.

Ironically, the efforts that went into cultivation were in vain because the land itself was not suited to the crops. The agricultural venture in Suva failed and the planters were ruined. However miserable things were for the fledgling community, land speculators knew that if Suva could be made the new capital, business could be coaxed there, real-estate values would soar, and they would be rich. The old capital, Levuka, which had long been the metropolis of the Pacific, was a brawling, prosperous town but its days as capital were numbered. Although it was a garden spot, the old capital was hemmed in by 600-metre cliffs which left no room to expand. It became apparent that a new capital was needed.

In the meantime, land in Suva was purchased by two major parties who did their best to promote it as an ideal spot for a new capital by giving the government ample real estate to build their offices. Thus, in spite of the wet climate, the local government had the proper incentives to establish the new capital in Suva, and in 1882 they did just that.

The New Capital

The plan of modern Suva is credited to

Colonel F E Pratt of the Royal Engineers, appointed in 1875 as Surveyor-General and Director of Works; and to his assistants W Stephens and Colonel R W Stewart. Despite well-intentioned plans for the capital, Suva's early days saw only gradual improvement – roads were poor, water supply was tenuous at best, and not all construction adhered to the city plan. Gradually these deficiencies gave way as the town grew. A few years past the turn of the century Suva was actually a tourist attraction in its own right. The editor of *The Commercial Directory & Tourists' Guide to the South Pacific Islands* observed:

Why Fiji is visited by such a small number of tourists is a puzzle to the writer, for there is not a more interesting or enjoyable trip on the globe. The climate is particularly healthy, and the white settlers being mostly from Australia, vie with each other in extending hospitality to visitors, while the natives, particularly those who live away from the large centres of European population, always extend a cordial welcome to the *Turanga Papalangi* (white gentleman), or the *Marama Papalangi* (white lady). Suva is the capital of the colony, and situated on the shores of a fine reef-protected bay of the same name, whose opposite shore is backed by imposing looking ranges of verdure-clad mountains, rising peak after peak until an altitude of probably 4000 feet is attained – they look truly grand, particularly at sunset or during an approaching storm (a frequent occurrence), or better still when the storm has passed and the white clouds cover their feet, and the picturesque-looking peaks ... stand boldly out against the dark-blue horizon, 'tis really a sight to be remembered.

Some things never change.

Information

For information contact the Fiji Visitors Bureau office (tel 22 867) on Thomson St. Like the FVB, the banks, the post office and the airline bureaus are centrally located. Maps can be purchased at the Lands & Survey Office in the Government Buildings complex, at the government bookstore opposite the Fiji Visitors Bureau, or at other bookstores.

Important Numbers

CWM Hospital/Ambulance
    tel 313 444
Police
    tel 311 222
Immigration Office
    tel 211 640
Fiji Customs
    tel 22 831
Early morning wake-up calls
    tel 010
Directory Enquiries
    tel 011
Overseas Calls
    tel 012

Diplomatic Offices

Australia
    Dominion House, 8th Floor, Suva (tel 313844 office or 312564)
Belgium
    Munro-Leys and Co, Air Pacific House, Suva (tel 23091)
China (People's Republic)
    Queen Elizabeth Dr, Suva (tel 22425)
Denmark
    Mr A Dickson, Air Pacific House, 7th Floor, Suva (tel 22638 office or 383142)
Finland
    Mr Swain Christian, Shell Fiji Ltd, Prouds Building, Suva (tel 313933)
France
    Dominion House, 1st Floor, Suva (tel 312925)
India
    Mr Chitelenchery Ravindranathan, Fiji Development Bank, 2nd Floor, Suva (tel 312255 office or 27595, 383372)
Italy
    Mr R W Warner, Hunts Travel Service, Dominion House, 2nd Floor, Suva (tel 25463)
Japan
    Mr Ken Ikebe, Dominion House, 2nd Floor, Suva (tel 25631)
Korea
    Vanua House, 8th Floor, Suva (tel 311977)
Nauru
    Ratu Sukuna House, 7th Floor (tel 313566)
Netherlands
    Mr R J Woodman, Stinson Building, Tofua St, Walu Bay, Suva (tel 312722)

New Zealand
Mr Lindsay Watt, Ratu Sukuna House, 8th Floor, Suva (tel 311422)
Norway
Sir Robert L Monro, Air Pacific House, 3rd Floor, Suva (tel 23091)
Pakistan
Mr Rahim Zullah, 17 Nukuwatu St, Lami (tel 361388)
Papua New Guinea
Mr Naime Doko, Ratu Sukuna House, Suva (tel 25420)
Philippines
Mr Abdul Lateef, Honson Building, Suva (tel 312344)
Sweden
Mr Aminiasi Katoninvaliku, Ratu Sukuna House, Suva (tel 312644)
Tuvalu
Mr Kamuta Latasi, National Bank of Fiji Building, 1st Floor, Suva (tel 22697 office or 27430)
UK
Mr Roger Barltrop, Civic Centre, Suva (tel 311033)
USA
Loftus St, Suva (tel 23031)
West Germany
Mr Gerald Barrack, Burns Philp (South Seas Ltd), Suva (tel 31177 office or 25161)

Airlines
Air New Zealand
Queensland Insurance Centre, Victoria Parade (tel 313 100 or 312 444)
Air Pacific
CML Building, Victoria Parade (tel 24 624)
Canadian Pacific Air
Thomson St (tel 311 844)
Continental Airlines
Victoria Parade (tel 313 088)
Fiji Air
Victoria Parade (tel 22 666)
Japan Air Lines
CML Building (Air Pacific Office) (tel 24 624)
Qantas
CML Building, Victoria Parade (tel 313 888)
Air Nauru
Victoria Parade (tel 313 731)

Pacific Crown Aviation (Helicopter Charters)
Lami Airport, (tel 361 532 or 361 422)

Pharmacies/Chemists
A J Swann & Co
6 Union Travel Plaza, Thomson St (tel 23 743)
Central Pharmacy
109 Cumming St (tel 23 842)
City Pharmacy
62 Cumming St (tel 26 118)
Gordon Street Pharmacy
96 Gordon St (tel 313 131)
Harbour Pharmacy
15 Harbour Centre, Thomson St (tel 312 830)
Madison Pharmacy
45 Cumming St (tel 313 370)
Medix Pharmacy
167 Renwick Rd (tel 23 312)
Mouats Pharmacy
Epworth House, corner of Nina and Stewart Sts (tel 22 363)
Suva Pharmacy
21 Terry Walk (tel 22 550)

Health Aside from the *Colonial War Memorial Hospital*, of which there has been a plethora of health-care horror stories, there are the *Gordon Street Medical Centre* (Gordon and Thurston Sts) and the *Bayly Clinic* (187 Rodwell Rd, tel 315 888) for the financially embarrassed. The most highly recommended place is *Dr Mitchell's Medical Clinic* at 96 Gordon St (tel 313 131), which is popular with the expatriate community. If in need of a recommendation, call your embassy or high commissioner's office.

Things to Do & See
Suva is a walker's town; most of it can be seen in one day with a sturdy pair of shoes and a healthy constitution. You need not be an Olympic athlete to take a walking tour, but the heat—especially for those not used to it—can make a stroll around Suva seem arduous. Visitors to Suva and to Fiji

in general should realise that people move slowly for a good reason in this tropical clime – less energy is drained from the body, and it makes sense not to sweat more than is necessary. Aside from a good pair of shoes, an umbrella or at least a hat will shade you from the sun and the rain.

Victoria Parade Victoria Parade is the 'main drag,' extending roughly from the post office to Thurston Gardens. It is really the heart of Suva. On it or nearby are most of the finest shops, the airline ticket offices, banks, travel agencies, the best hotel in town (Travelodge), the library, town hall, telegraph office, two of the most popular night clubs and the classic Grand Pacific Hotel. In the old days Victoria Parade was a muddy, one-sided street separated from the sea by a row of rain trees. Some of the rain trees are still there, although recent hurricanes have taken their toll on the old timers.

Suva Municipal Market Municipal markets along the style of Suva's can be found in Papeete (Tahiti), Apia, and all the larger communities in Fiji and the rest of the South Pacific. The Polynesian, Chinese, Indian and Fijian vendors hawk fish, meat, vegetables, fruit, coconut oil and nearly everything else that a Fijian household might need. Although some vendors are farmers belonging to cooperatives, most are middlemen who receive produce from outlying villages and sell it for a profit to the townspeople. The market provides a colourful and fascinating array of culture. Some sections deal entirely with yaqona or kava root (both whole and ground). Other merchants sell Indian spices exclusively, display freshly caught shellfish, sell tomatoes or offer bundles of *dalo* (taro root).

There is also a 'yaqona saloon' or room in the centre of the market dedicated solely to kava tipplers. As you walk by someone may call over, urging you to have a bowl. Should you take them up on it, for a few cents buy a round for the house, which is the customary reciprocal thing to do. You will no doubt see many strange or exotic fruits and vegetables and should not hesitate to ask what they are. Fijians always have time to talk to a visitor and appreciate the interest shown. Perhaps you might want to sample a passion fruit or purchase an avocado for the hotel room; here is where to buy them. Naturally any fruit should be washed thoroughly before eating.

Handicrafts Market Behind the post office, facing the sea on Stinson Parade, is the handicrafts centre. Do not confuse this with the government handicrafts shop in the Ratu Sukuna House on Carnarvon St. Unlike the municipal market which caters to locals, the handicrafts market is almost exclusively for visitors. The upshot is that you will be touted continuously. The prices can be cheaper here than at the souvenir shops, but prepare to bargain hard. Items sold are the usual tourist fare: cannibal forks, *tanoa* (kava bowls), carvings, *masi* (Fijian-style bark cloth), *gatu* (Tongan-style tapa cloth), sea shells and necklaces. The market is particularly active during ship days.

Visitors strolling the handicraft market area and Suva in general should beware of unusually friendly natives (usually carrying canvas bags) who offer 'swords' with your name carved on them. Sometimes the salesperson will ask your name and before you know it you are not-so-subtly being coerced into buying the custom-made 'artefact.' If you really want the souvenir, the going rate is around F$5 but these swords are by no means genuine Fijian woodcarvings. More accurately, they are someone's clever scam.

Cumming St Cumming St is known for its fine restaurants and duty-free shops. It is crowded and narrow, reminiscent of a Paris or London back street. Reclaimed from a swamp, it was developed as a commercial area and was called 'All

Nations Street' – a place where in the 1920s curry houses, yaqona saloons and houses of ill repute flourished. It also was the original home of the Municipal Market. Perhaps being the Sodom and Gomorrah that it was, the area was consumed by fire in 1923 and many of the structures were destroyed. During WW II, the tailors, barbers and café owners who did business on the street became sellers of artefacts and curios to meet the demand of military personnel with cash to spend. The character of the neighbourhood changed once again in the 1960s when import duties were lowered and entrepreneurs opened up duty-free shops. Cumming St retains this character today.

Toorak Toorak is a residential section built on a mildly sloping hillside that affords a fine view of the city. There are two possible origins of the name. The first and most likely is that since the majority of Suva's early settlers hailed from Melbourne, they named the neighbourhood after that city's most fashionable district. The second possibility is that because *toorak* translates as 'where the chief is' in one of Australia's aboriginal languages, the area was called that because its landowner, C A Huon, was regarded as the chief of the estate.

In its early days the neighbourhood was considered one of the finest in town, and two families – the Joskes and the Huons (both which have streets named after them) – fought bitterly over the property rights. Today Toorak has no pretensions about grandeur, but retains touches of its elegant trappings. These are found in massive retaining walls and moulded concrete fences that once surrounded some of the finest homes in Suva – a far cry from the modest dwellings they enclose today. One example of this period is the structure built by Dr Hamilton Beattie on the corner of Toorak Rd and Suva St. Designed with a Greco-Roman villa in mind, it has freestanding columns in bas-relief and swastikas (for good luck) over the entrance. The home is now divided into flats, and the estate, once adorned with fountains and a garden, is covered by wooden shacks.

Today Toorak is a microcosm of modern Fiji, a scrappy multi-racial neighbourhood full of children and the occasional bootleg beer distributor.

The Triangle The triangle, near the beginning of Victoria Parade, is what Albert Schutz in his fine booklet *Suva – A History & Guide* calls 'the true centre of Suva.' A century ago it was a small lagoon fed by a creek coming down Pratt St; today it is a miniature park usually occupied by several locals sitting on a bench at the foot of an *ivi* tree. At the centre of this triangular park is a concrete historical marker with four inscriptions. The landmark has a special distinction in that three of the four inscriptions set aside for posterity are incorrect:

'Suva Proclaimed Capital in 1882.' Not quite true. The home government actually approved the move from Levuka to Suva in 1877 and the action was announced by *The London Times* in August of that year. The government's official move from Levuka was made in 1882.

'Cross and Cargill First Missionaries arrived 14th October 1835.' Not quite. According to their diaries, the correct date was 12 October.

'Public Land Sales on this spot 1880.' Wrong location. Apparently the land sales did occur underneath an ivi tree but not this one. In reality the sales were a bit further down the road, near the present-day locale of Morris, Hedstrom and Company's store.

'British Crown Colony 10th October 1874.' Got this one right.

Old Town Hall & Swimming Pool The Old Town Hall, constructed just after the turn of the century, is one of the finest examples of Victorian architecture. Not only did it serve the duties of government, it was also a centre for the performing arts and a host to concerts, vaudeville acts and amateur shows. In the good old days the upper floor was used as a museum while the governmental offices were on the ground level. Today the hall is still used for concerts and social activities. The building, which recently housed an unsuccessful aquarium, is undergoing yet another incarnation; at the time of this writing it's not clear what it will be. There is, however, an excellent, inexpensive eatery operating out of the building, and there are shaded benches on which to sit and sip a Coke or nibble on curried chicken. In the evenings the area in front of the town hall is a rendezvous point for Lucky Eddie's, located on the opposite side of the street.

Behind the town hall is a very fine Olympic-sized pool open to the public. Admission is F$0.50.

Suva City Library Next door to the town hall is the Suva City Library, built in 1909. It is a noteworthy landmark in that the money to construct the edifice (£1000) was donated by the American steel magnate, Andrew Carnegie. Carnegie provided similar donations to other libraries around the world. I have found the librarians a very friendly bunch and the long-term visitor might find it worthwhile to take out a library card. The library recently received a fresh coat of paint.

Naiqaqi About a hundred metres down from the library, on the landward side of the street is an area called 'Naiqaqi,' which translates as 'the crusher.' This vicinity, which is now occupied by the Native Land Trust Board (NLTB) building and the Fiji Broadcasting Commission building, was once the site of Fiji's first sugar mill, built in 1873. Sugar grows quite well in Fiji but not in the Suva area, where the topsoil is thin and 'the crusher' was never a successful business venture. The 1½ metre diameter gear displayed near the Carnarvon and Loftus Sts corner is a remnant of this futile exercise.

Government Buildings The massive Government Buildings are one of the most prominent sites in Suva, but prior to 1935 the area was a swampy creek bed. Known as part of the greater Naiqaqi district, the area mostly contained tumbledown shacks and many of the neighbourhood's women plied the world's oldest trade.

To support the Government Buildings, more than five km of reinforced concrete pilings were rooted deep in the creek bed. The foundation stone was laid in 1937 and the building was completed in 1939. The new wing was completed in 1967. There are two statues gracing the grounds – one of Chief Cakobau and the other of Ratu Sir Lala Sukuna.

The Government Buildings may be of more than passing interest to the visitor. Here the Department of Lands & Survey office sells excellent topographic maps and city plans to the public. In the new wing is the Department of Information; it provides pamphlets such as 'Fiji Today,' which offers an overview of the country, statistics and general background information. Nearby, in a barrack-like annex, is the office of the Fiji Dictionary Project.

Albert Park The area that comprises Albert Park was part of the original land grant given by the Polynesia Company to the government as an inducement to move the capital to Suva. Named after the royal consort to Queen Victoria, it is and always has been a cricket ground, tennis courts and general recreational park.

The pavilion is named after Charles Kingsford Smith, who in 1928 became the first aviator to cross the Pacific. Smith began the journey in Oakland, California and refuelled in Kauai. He flew on to Suva without ever having seen the proposed landing strip, Albert Park, nor realising that a row of palm trees stretched across the middle of his runway, where the pavilion now stands. Fortunately, before Smith arrived the Suva radio station operator thought it might be a good idea to cut down the trees, and persuaded the

continued page 96

Artefacts

In recent years some of old Fiji's finest artefacts have been repatriated and are now on display in the Fiji Museum, located in Thurston Gardens in Suva. One of the largest collections of Fijian art outside Fiji became available when English collector James Hooper died in 1971 and his collection was sold in a London auction in 1979. Over 60 of Hooper's artefacts were returned to Fiji when Mobil Oil Australia purchased a selection on behalf of the Fiji Museum. The following include some of the old Hooper Collection and a smattering of other representative Fijian art.

Golden Cowrie – buli kula

One of the finest pieces in the Hooper Collection is the *buli kula* or golden cowrie high chief's pendant which is attached to a neck cord of plaited black fibres and embellished with light *voivoi* (pandanus) ties. To this day the *buli kula* is the most esteemed of all ornaments, prized for its beauty and rarity. In the days of sailing ships, sea captains would often ask chiefs for the golden cowries as souvenirs but were nearly always refused them or told that there were none to be had.

Like so many of the finest Fijian artefacts, this pendant was collected and preserved by a Methodist missionary in the 19th century. Missionaries became the recipients of such items because they stayed long enough to win the respect of the chiefs, or were given the artefacts by converts for the purpose of selling them to raise money for the church.

War Club – vunikau bulibuli

This *vunikau bulibuli* would be a typical rootstock club if it were not for the ivory inlaid studs and stars on the business end of the weapon. The inlay work, a Tongan motif, was most likely crafted by a Tongan artisan residing in Fiji, whose primary task was to build a war canoe. In former times it was not unusual for Tongan chiefs to send over boatbuilders to Fiji for years at a time in order to have canoes built.

Making a club involved the work of two men, one to uproot a sapling and season it, and another to do the carving or, in this case the inlay work. This explains why such a classically Fijian weapon bore the earmark of a Tongan. In warfare Fijians seemed to prefer heavy weapons for the purpose of crushing skulls and this club (which weighs six kg) is no exception.

The Old Lady of Kauvadra – bui ni Kauvadra

Although not part of the Hooper Collection, the *bui ni Kauvadra* is a recent museum acquisition of great importance. She is a key figure in Fijian mythology – the grandmother of all gods and goddesses. Her uniqueness is that she is a human figure, a rarity in Fijian art.

Her noticeable lack of arms is due to some mythical battle that time has forgotten. The hooks near her feet were probably used to hang offerings and the tattooing on her groin was common among Fijian women prior to the coming of the missionaries. Likewise, both her ears are slit to accept earlobe plugs. Her skirt, which once fell below her waist, has disintegrated with time, as has the human hair which once covered her head and pubic area.

Priest's Yaqona Dish – dave ni yaqona

The *dave ni yaqona*, carved in the form of a human figure, is one of several still in existence. The ceremonial yaqona (kava) dish was used exclusively in Fijian temples and only by the priests. Unlike the normal kava drinking ritual, where the brew would be drunk from coconut halves with both hands, the priests placed the dave ni yaqona on the floor of the temple and sucked the contents out of the dish without touching it.

Although Fijians have long since stopped practicing their ancient religion (at least most Fijians), kava drinking remains an important social activity in modern Fijian culture. Like the use of tabua, it is a custom likely to continue.

Both the *bui ni Kauvadra* and the *dave ni yaqona* were collected by the missionary R B Lyth prior to 1854 and donated to the museum by the London-based Methodist Missionary Society.

governor (against the wishes of the city authorities) to raze them and level the field. Airplanes were a bit of a rarity in those days and nobody ever thought the aviator need be warned that the field was actually below the level of the street. *The Southern Cross* had no brakes and when the plane landed on 6 June, Kingsford Smith expertly stopped the twin-engined Fokker within a few metres of the field by swinging it almost at right angles before it stopped.

Grand Pacific Hotel The shoreline adjacent to the Grand Pacific Hotel (or GPH as it ir called by locals) was once a landing spot for commoners from the nearby village. It was called *Vu-ni-vesi* after a group of *vesi* trees that grew there. The first hotel built on this spot, The Hotel Suva, was little more than a shack but the GPH, which opened in 1914, was to 'set the standard for the entire Pacific,' according to Al Schutz' *Suva – A History & Guide.*

Constructed by the Union Steamship Company as a base for New Zealand and Canadian shipping services in the north and south Pacific, the hotel's design mirrored the first-class accommodation found on ships of the day. Like ship-board cabins, the bedrooms opened onto wide decks on one side. On the other, they provided entry to a balcony that overlooked the main lounge. Marine-type plumbing and salt-water baths added to the nautical air of the hotel.

Today the glamour that this colonial landmark once enjoyed has faded, but this elegant, white-porticoed building still offers good accommodation at a modest price. Inside is a bar with ceiling fans and wicker chairs that is at least worth checking out.

Thurston Gardens These gardens contain a large collection of flora from throughout the South Pacific. Named after the amateur botanist and founder, Sir John Bates Thurston, the present site was opened in 1913. The gardens are well kept

and almost always uncrowded. Located on Victoria Parade, they are also an entrance to the Fiji Museum.

Fiji Museum Founded in 1904, the original site of the museum was in the old town hall. After being moved to several locations, the present building was constructed on the grounds of Thurston Gardens in 1954. Despite the multitudes of artefacts that left Fiji in the hands of missionaries and sailors, the museum has the finest collection of Fijian relics in the world. Among the exhibits are collections of war clubs, ivory necklaces, cannibal forks, spears, bowls, pottery, tools, cooking utensils, combs and a replica of a huge *drua* – an ancient, double-hulled canoe. One of the war clubs – which was actually used in battle – has several notches chiselled in it, each representing an enemy slain in battle. The rear of the museum is dedicated to the arrival of the European and American sailing vessels, highlighting the beche-de-mer, whaling and sandalwood eras. There is also an exhibit illustrating the saga of the Indian indenture period and the infamous blackbirding trade that brought Micronesians and Melanesians to Fiji. In addition, you'll see actual relics from the famous *Bounty*.

Aside from collecting and chronicling Fijian artefacts, the museum is also a research and educational institution. The staff, led by Museum Director Fergus Clunie, engage in archaeological research, the preservation of Fiji's oral tradition, and publication of material on language and culture. Despite the museum's good works, lack of space to showcase the exhibits and chronic lack of funding have always been problems. The museum is open daily from 8.30 am to 4.30 pm, excluding Saturday. Admission is F$0.50 Monday through Friday but free on Sunday. Anyone visiting Suva should not miss the museum.

Government House The first government house was constructed in 1882 as a

Top: Victoria Parade, Suva, Viti Levu (RK)
Left: *Bure Kalu*, old temple at Pacific Harbour near Suva, Viti Levu (FVB)
Right: Sacred Heart Cathedral, Suva, Vitu Levu (FVB)

Top: Grand Pacific Hotel, Suva, Viti Levu (FVB)
Bottom: Regal Cinema, Suva, Viti Levu (FVB)

residence of then Governor Des Voeux. This burned to the ground after being struck by lightning in 1921 and the current building was erected in 1928. Today it is occupied by the Governor General and guarded by two sturdy soldiers clad in the traditional *sulu*. The government house is not open to the public but changing of the guard can be seen on the first Tuesday of every month at 11 am. The entrance is directly on Queen Elizabeth Drive.

University of the South Pacific Established in 1968 on an area that was once a New Zealand seaplane base, USP is a regional institution, jointly operated by 11 South Pacific countries. In attendance are about 2300 full-time students from every South Pacific country except the French-speaking colonies; the majority of the students are from Fiji. The main campus, located off Laucala Bay Rd, has an excellent library and can be reached by the Vatuwaqa bus.

Beaches Near Suva Sorry folks, there aren't too many beaches on this side of the island and there really isn't one near the city limits. The closest beach is in the Deuba/Pacific Harbour Resort area opposite the Coral Coast Christian Camp, a 45-minute automobile drive from the capital. Unless you have a car it really is a long haul via bus.

Coral Sea Cruise The Coral Sea cruise is a pleasant half day (9.30 am to 1.15 pm) or full day (9.30 am to 3.30 pm) trip aboard a motor launch with glass-bottom panels. The launch visits Suva Harbour's barrier reef and tiny Nukulau Island. Divers accompanying the vessel bring coral and other specimens aboard for your inspection and you can swim, beachcomb or bake in the sun (assuming the sun is shining!). Price of cruise includes fresh fruit, tea, luncheon, taste of coconut juice, and transfer to Suva Jetty from any local hotel. Price is F$24. Phone 361 258 for more information.

Recreational Organisations *The Rucksack Club*, made up mostly of expats, offers weekly hikes and/or excursions to the other islands and the interior of Viti Levu. These expeditions are well organised and inexpensive. The club provides temporary memberships for visitors (at F$2 for two months), which should be taken advantage of if you are going to be in the Suva area. Phone 385 917 or write PO Box 2394, Government Buildings, Suva, for more information. *Fiji Shell Club*, PO Box 5031, offers excursions to outlying areas for serious shell collectors. They meet on the first Tuesday of the month at Suva Grammar School. Call Margaret Patel at the Fiji National Archives (tel 24031) for more information.

Places to Stay
The hotels listed below are considered good value for their price range; the ones with asterisks are my choices as best in their class. Hotel reservations can be made through your travel agent. For the best hotel in town, the Travelodge, this is certainly a good idea. Most of the other hotels on the 'Suva side' do not necessitate a reservation, but should you desire one, they can be telexed. Most hotel prices are 'fixed' but some have so-called 'local' rates, especially if the premises are empty or if you are considering staying awhile. Do not even think about negotiating for prices in the more popular areas on the western side of Viti Levu.

Places to Stay – bottom end
Coconut Inn (tel 23 902 manager or 383 911 guests) is the rock-bottom, bargain-basement spot for backpackers. Accommodation is funky dormitory style (men and women separated). There is hot and cold water, cooking and washing facilities, and a locker/storage room. This is an excellent place to ferret out information from other travellers. Price is F$4 per night for bunks. The Coconut Inn is on Kimberly St two blocks from Victoria Parade.

One of Suva's oldest hotels is located on Usher St – *Hotel Metropole* (tel 24 019 or 24 010). At first glance, the rowdy public bar on the ground floor does not make it the most appealing accommodation but the 195 rooms, located above the fray, are clean, the location is excellent and in all it's quite adequate. Rates are F$9.45 for a single and F$15.75 for a twin. There are communal baths but each room has a wash basin.

Located on 5 Princes Rd, *Tanoa House* (tel 381 575) is one of the premier, no-frills budget accommodation places in Suva. It's located in an old colonial building, 10 minutes' bus ride from the centre of town. Amenities include dining room and bar. Rates begin at F$10 single, F$15 double and F$18 triple. The food is good and extremely reasonably priced – F$2 for a full breakfast, F$3 for lunch and F$4 for dinner. To get there take the Samabula bus at the market and ask the driver to let you off at Tanoa House (near the Fiji Institute of Technology).

South Seas Private Hotel (tel 22 195) is also backpacker accommodation. It is found on Williamson Rd behind Albert Park and it has 34 rooms, hot and cold water, laundry facilities and a communal kitchen. The rate is F$4.50 per night, single or double rooms.

The *YWCA Hostel* (tel 25 441), located adjacent to Ratu Sukuna Park, is an excellent place to stay if you are a single woman with little money in your pocket. It has hot and cold water, ceiling fans, laundry facilities and a good, inexpensive cafeteria that is open to the public. The hostel is a great place to sample simple, local cuisine, whether you are a guest or not; the cafeteria is open to the public. The rate is F$8 per person.

Places to Stay – middle

The *Southern Cross Hotel* (tel 22 651) is known by locals for its entertainment in the lounge – a toned-down nightclub where one gets revved up before going on to the next nightclub. The 35-room hotel

is also a perfectly adequate place to stay. Prices start at F$40 for a single and F$45 for a double. The hotel is located on Gordon St, a five-minute walk to Victoria Parade.

On Robertson Rd, a three-minute walk to downtown Suva, *Tropic Towers Apartment Hotel* (tel 25 819 or 313 855) is a 30-room air-conditioned apartment complex. Modestly furnished rooms sleep two to five persons, include self-contained cooking units, refrigerator and laundry facilities, and are inexpensive. Generally the hotel is full of family groups from Australia and New Zealand. Prices begin at F$22 for a single and F$30 for a twin.

A good place to moor a yacht is *Tradewinds* (tel 361 166), located on the water in Lami (five km out of Suva). On the weekends it's a good place to hear local bands. Unfortunately, as a hotel it has become rather run down and is comparatively isolated from Suva. For the money, F$45 single, there are better places to stay in town.

Capricorn Apartment (tel 314 799) at 7 Fort St is another quite adequate apartment complex with self-contained units for the do-it-yourself visitor. Amenities include pool, air-conditioning, general store, baby-sitting and dial-a-meal-service. Prices are F$30 for a single and F$38 for a double.

The *Townhouse Apartment Hotel* (tel 22 661) at 3 Forster St, two blocks off Victoria Parade, has one of the best views in Suva and is a highly recommended hotel with an apartment-building feel. There are 28 self-contained units (many with a fine view of the city) which have cooking facilities, restaurant, garage space, baby-sitting service and an excellent location: The roof-top bar is one of the undiscovered, quiet places at which to drink in an otherwise boisterous town. Single units begin at F$28 and doubles at F$32.

A 10-minute walk from downtown is the *Suva Peninsula Hotel* (tel 313 711), on the corner of Pender St and McGregor Rd. It has a restaurant, pool and a rather sleazy bar. Rates are F$28 for a single and F$34 for a double.

The *Grand Pacific Hotel* (tel 23 011) is a national landmark. You get the feeling that the spirit of Somerset Maugham may walk its halls. Though well maintained and somewhat dowdy, this relic of the empire is still a good place to stay for the budget traveller. The GPH was opened in 1914 and according to one historian was the trend-setting hotel in its day. It has quite a few amenities, including air-conditioning, a pool, a bar and a large floor-level lounge with wicker chairs. It is centrally located on Victoria Parade. The GPH has 72 rooms; prices begin at F$40 for a single and F$48 for a double. There are also seven non-air-conditioned rooms with overhead fans available for F$22 single and F$30 double.

Located on Gordon St, *Sunset Apartment* (tel 23 021) is about a 10-minute walk from downtown. It has 11 self-contained two-bedroom units and air-conditioning. Rates for singles begin at F$20 and doubles at F$26.

The President Hotel (tel 361 033) is a 10-minute drive from Suva, between the capital and the suburb of Lami. Formerly the Isa Lei, it has slid into less-than-wonderful shape over the last few years but is undergoing renovation. The hotel has 42 rooms with air-conditioning, refrigerators and private terraces with fine views of the harbour. Rates begin at approximately F$30 single and F$35 double.

Places to Stay – top end
The *Suva Travelodge* (tel 314 600) is the top-rated hotel in Suva. It has recently undergone a F$750,000 renovation that clearly shows in the redesigned lobby, bar, gift shop and entrance (which sports the only revolving door in Fiji). The hotel's 132 rooms have also been upgraded and there are convention facilities for about 100 people. Other amenities include piano bar, coffee shop, hair salon and tour desk in the foyer. The restaurant's food is

more expensive (F$5-12 for entrees) compared to what you can get in Suva, but it's good. Located on Victoria Parade, facing Suva Harbour, the location is good – within walking distance of all the banks and nightclubs you'll ever need. A single begins at F$72 and a double at F$82.

The *Suva Courtesy Inn* (tel 312 300) has the distinction of being the second-best hotel in Suva. Located on Gordon St, two minutes' walk from Victoria Parade, it has all the amenities including a pool, 24-hour room service, fine restaurant and 56 rooms – some with an excellent panorama of Suva Harbour, and all with air-conditioning. In the evenings the lounge features a cool jazz combo – a good place for a quiet drink. Rates are F$56 for a single and F$60 for a double.

Toberua Island Resort (tel 49 177) is actually off the coast, near Suva. Hoteliers consider it the finest island resort in Fiji, and Harper's Hideaway Report rates it as one of the top 12 small island resorts in the world. Host Michael Dennis oversees every aspect of his tiny paradise and there is plenty of snorkelling and day trips to uninhabited islands. I can say from personal experience that this is a jewel of a resort and I highly recommend it for honeymooners or any other category of couples. The cuisine is fine and there are 14 *bures*. Price for a single is F$105; for a double it's F$125.

Pacific Harbour International Resort (tel 45 022) is actually not in Suva. It is Fiji's only master planned community, a combined resort and residential complex located about 50 km from the capital. Pacific Harbour covers 500 hectares and has it all, including an 18-hole Robert Trent Jones-designed golf course (the best in Fiji), an oceanside pool, game fishing/charter boat, two restaurants (including the fine Japanese Sakura House), an 84-room hotel and 180 villas. On the premises there is an excellent disco, a horse-betting outlet for Aussie races, car rental service from Avis and Budget, a Bank of New Zealand branch, a post office, a bottle shop and a host of boutiques.

Pacific Harbour is also the home of the Cultural Centre and Marketplace which spotlights the renowned Dance Theatre of Fiji, a troupe that travels around the world regularly and is famous for its innovative choreography. Admission for dance theatre is F$6. The Cultural Centre also features firewalking exhibitions (F$6) and a Disneyland-style trip back into time. This entails a boat trip around the centre of a man-made lake. Visitors stop briefly at various 'ports' to watch Fijian actors demonstrate ancient rituals. The cost is F$7 for adults and F$3.50 for children and is kind of a fun thing to do. (The trip is fully detailed in the 'Around Suva' section.) Hotel rates begin at F$59 single and F$65 double. Many of the villas are privately owned by individuals from Hong Kong, the UK and Australia, but others can be rented beginning at F$87-100 per day for up to four persons, which is certainly reasonable. The units have fully equipped kitchens and two to four bedrooms; some even have private pools. Green fees for the golf course are cheap – F$8 for 18 holes. Pacific Harbour has regular bus service from Suva (see Getting Around section) and has its own airstrip which offers service from Nadi via Sunflower Airlines.

Aside from land-based activities, Pacific Harbour has charters-only, big-game fishing aboard the MV Marau, which holds up to 10 passengers. Game fish include marlin, sailfish, wahoo, mackerel, tuna and barracuda. Phone 45 347 for more information. Diving excursions to Beqa are organised through Scùbahire, which has a boat at Pacific Harbour.

In a nutshell, Pacific Harbour has a lot of things going for it as a 'bedroom ' community of Suva and is a popular getaway spot for well-heeled locals. However, it is in the middle of nowhere; Pacific Harbour is 'it' as far as Deuba is concerned. Secondly, the weather is similar to Suva's, which may discourage people from spending a lot of time here.

Places to Eat

Although the quality of restaurants in Suva could never reach the level of Tahiti's French-influenced ones, it has flowered in just the past few years. Fine food is available, most of it very inexpensive. Price for an average meal for two at a halfway decent restaurant, not including alcohol, ranges from $F10-16. Variety is also good. The basic fare is 'European,' Indian, Chinese, Fijian or combinations thereof. Most of the restaurants are located in downtown Suva within minutes of each other. Wine selection is limited mostly to Australian varieties but Italian wines are now being imported.

Prices quoted below are sans alcohol. Asterisk denotes my favourites:

Snack Bars, Cafés & Cheap Eats * *The Suva Wharf* is not the name of a fancy restaurant but the actual wharf itself, where there are about 20 vendors selling basic Fijian food like fish in coconut milk, chop suey, curry, dalo, etc at the most rock-bottom prices in town – not over F$1. Many locals eat here for lunch. To get to the area, go through the entrance to the wharf (near the public market) and continue walking until the very end. This is one of the few places in town where you can get traditional Fijian fare.

The *YWCA, adjacent to Sukuna Park, is also inexpensive and is the other place that features homestyle Fijian fare. Food is served cafeteria-style and lunch can be had for about F$2. Plain and wholesome food.

You will pass *Pizza Hut* at Victoria Parade many times, but do not enter if you know what good pizza is. Average price F$5.

The *Curry Place* on Pratt St is a luncheonette with several varieties of curry, including vegetarian, goat, beef and chicken. Nothing fancy but consistently good food. The small booths are a nice touch. Price ranges from $F2-3.

Jude's, Shop No 3, Vanua House, is a

small luncheonette smack in the middle of downtown Suva. They specialise in sandwiches. You stand in a cafeteria-style line, choose what type of sandwich you want, what type of bread, what type of condiments, etc and they make it on the spot. Sounds typical of any deli in the world but it's the only one of its kind in Suva. Price of sandwiches is F$1.50-2. Jude's is also the only place in Suva where you can get espresso coffee.

The *Anchor Inn in Old Town Hall is under new management and has improved 100%. Service is cafeteria style; luncheon, the only meal, features excellent curries as well as Fijian and Chinese dishes. Pleasant surroundings either on a terrace or on picnic-style benches facing Victoria Parade. Prices average only F$2.50 for a full lunch.

*Hari Krishna Restaurant on Pratt St is vegetarian only, and is run by adherents of the Hari Krishna sect. The best vegetarian food in town is served in a variety of exotic ways. The café is very clean but small; get there early for lunch. Prices average only about F$2.50 for a complete meal. Also, they have the best A-1 ice cream in town for under F$.50 a cone. Even if you do not crave vegetarian food, try the ice cream.

*Old Mill Cottage Café/Restaurant, Carnarvon St, is a stone's throw from the American Embassy and is run by the same folks who own the Coconut Inn. The converted home with bench-style seating is very popular with government office workers because of its proximity to the Fiji Government Buildings. Innovative cookery includes Chinese dishes, curries and Fijian food like taro and palusami with lolo (coconut cream.) Very fine food and clean surroundings; among the best of the lunch-time eateries. Prices are F$2.50-3.

Cheaper Restaurants *Lantern Palace at 10 Pratt St is a relatively new restaurant and without a doubt serves the best Chinese food in town. Expect to spend F$6-8 per person.

*Samraat, upstairs at 10 Ellery St, serves excellent, reasonably priced Indian food – perhaps the best in town. Lots of exotic fare and great curries with the country western sounds of Jim Reeves twanging on the speakers. An average meal costs about F$6.

Just around the corner from the Fiji Visitors Bureau is Bamboo Terrace, with a complete, inexpensive buffet (under F$3) – one of the best lunch deals in town. You can sit on a balcony overlooking the street and it is quite pleasant.

For decent Chinese food there's Wan-Q, 25 Cumming St. Prices range from F$5-7.

You can bet your sombrero that Traps, Victoria Parade, is one of the few Mexican restaurants in the South Pacific. Food is not the same as you'd get in Mexico City but it's actually quite good. Entrees include tacos, enchiladas, chile con carne and burgers. Price averages F$5-7 per person.

*The Java Room at 46 Gordon St is owned and operated by former Fiji Times journalist and music critic Bharat Jamnadas. It is the only restaurant that offers Indonesian, Vietnamese and other South-East Asian dishes. Bharat is an entrepreneur who goes beyond the normal restaurateur because he is an experimenter, combining tried-and-true recipes with his own subtle concoctions. I rate the Java Room among the best eateries in Suva. Prices are very reasonable; the average main course ranges from F$4-6.

The *Castle Restaurant, on Fenton St in the Lami Shopping Centre, is a 10-minute drive from Suva. This modest Chinese eatery ties with the Lantern Palace as the best Chinese restaurant in the Suva area, the reason being that it is owned by the same people. If you're in the mood for Chinese food, it's worth the drive. Main courses are priced around F$4-5.

Expensive Restaurants Le Normandie, 36 Cumming St, serves good French food that is certainly the best you can expect outside of a French colony. Run by a French expatriate couple, price is about F$12-15 per person. As part of the atmosphere, the Fijian waitresses dress as French peasants and wear nametags saying 'Claire' or 'Solange!'

At 16 Bau St, *Scott's* has a very nice Continental atmosphere complete with antiques but is pretentious and overpriced. Food is OK but no meal in Suva is worth paying F$40 for, which is about the average cost here.

Sakura House in Pacific Harbour is a 45-minute drive from Suva, but if you crave excellent Japanese food this is the place to go. Meals average F$12-18.

Steak and seafood are consistently very good at the *Red Lion*, Victoria Parade. The restaurant is plush by Fijian standards. Meals average around F$10 per person. Entrees include pepper steak, teriyaki steak, burgers, *walu* and seafood crepes. The staff wear quaint uniforms.

The *Galley Restaurant*, Suva's only floating restaurant, is also the newest eatery on the scene. Originally a vessel from the Blue Lagoon fleet, it was featured in the latest version of the film starring Brooke Shields. The Galley is primarily a seafood restaurant – the only one in Suva. Specialties are authentic Fijian dishes such as fish and *lolo* (coconut cream), prawns, lobster, turtle and clams. They also feature a special Fiji-style bouillabaisse. Prices are in the F$4.50-18 range and reports have been good. They also have a wine list (mostly Australian) which is fairly extensive for Fiji. The Galley is the only place in Suva that serves a Sunday brunch; this includes hotcakes, omelettes and the works. Price is F$3.50 per person. Owner Tiko Eastgate, a local, says it's advisable to make reservations (tel 313 626). Below the restaurant is the *Engine Room*, a posh disco that costs F$1.50 on weekdays and F$3 on weekend nights. The restaurant/disco is anchored in Suva Harbour across from Sukuna Park, a two-minute walk from Victoria Parade in downtown Suva.

The *Suva Travelodge* is comparatively expensive but it's the only place in town serving meals until midnight and thus is worth knowing about. Prices are in the F$5-25 range.

Entertainment

Suva has plenty of nightlife for the interested. Clubs range from seedy dives to posher, more reputable discos. Nightclubbing is a popular recreation for urban, single Fijians and is socially quite acceptable – many charitable and social organisations use the clubs as places to hold fund-raising dances.

Lucky Eddie's is a nocturnal institution in Fiji. It is modern, tacky, loud, safe from violent behaviour and very popular with tourists. Entertainment alternates between live bands and disco, depending on the night. Adjacent to Lucky Eddie's is *Rockefeller's*, a sort of upscale annex under the same ownership and entered via Lucky Eddie's. Rockefeller's is more expensive and ritzier in decor with plush seats, a fancier bar and wood panelling. Music here has a slightly lower decibel rating but like Lucky Eddie's is mostly rock or disco. Admission is about F$3 on a weekend night. The club is located on Victoria Parade, opposite the Old Town Hall.

Golden Dragon was once the top nightclub in Suva and is perhaps a half a cut below Lucky Eddie's in prestige. However, on a weekend night the familiar cry 'We go to Dragon!' can still be heard. The Dragon is also a booming disco, with no shortage of singles seeking companions. It's located on Victoria Parade, opposite the Fiji Development Bank. Admission is about F$3 on weekends.

Tradewinds in Lami and the *President* (on the way to Lami) are popular with visitors and locals on the weekends, often having good bands. Half a notch down the ladder is *Chequers* (on Waimanu Rd) and *Flamingo* (on Victoria Parade), both rather tacky and full of youthful imbibers on the make.

Though affluent Fijians turn up their noses at the *Bali Hai*, this working-class dive is my favourite night spot. Bali Hai has no pretensions about being upper crust and can be a bit rough, although I have never seen 'Europeans' get into trouble. No disco here – live Fijian music is the order of the day. Admission is about F$2 on weekends. The club is across from the bus stand near the Phoenix Theatre.

The *Engine Room* is a floating disco, located below the Galley Restaurant which is anchored opposite Sukuna Park on Suva Bay. It is posh, expensive by Suva standards (F$3) and very chic.

Located in the hotel of the same name, the *Southern Cross* is the most civilised club in town. Music is half western pop tunes and half Fijian pop. The band is live, but the action is tame compared to that in the other nightspots, perhaps because the crowd is a bit older and well heeled. It is also popular with 'Europeans' and on a weekend is usually the final stop before heading towards Lucky Eddie's or 'Dragon.' The Southern Cross closes its doors around midnight and admission is usually free.

Private Clubs Many of the private clubs are great places to meet people and have excellent recreational facilities as well. Although private, most will make allowances for visitors through local friends or if you simply call the club secretary.

Originally a spit-and-polish bastion of the empire, the *Defence Club* is still very much an 'old boys' type of environment minus the racial exclusivity. Plenty of magazines to admire in the reading room, an attractive bar and an all-male environment. The address is 57 Gordon St (tel 22 131).

The *Royal Suva Yacht Club* (tel 23 666) offers facilities for yachts – bathrooms and toilets are ashore. Great social scene on the weekend. Daily rates are F$8 per day per yacht with one person aboard, F$12 per day for yachts with more than one crew member.

Another fine place to meet people is the *United Club*, especially during their weekend dances. It's on Williamson Rd (tel 22 478).

Getting Around

Airport Transport Fiji's international airport is not at Suva, it's at Nadi, on the other side of the island. From Suva there are two alternatives to getting to the domestic airport in Nausori, about 20 minutes away – regular taxi or small buses from the CML Building (near the Air Pacific office). A taxi will cost up to F$12, while fare for the bus is F$1. Schedule for the buses is Monday through Friday at 6.30 am, 7.30 am, 9 am, 10 am, 11.30 am, 12.30 pm, 1.30 pm, 2.30 pm and 5 pm. Schedules differ slightly on weekend afternoons, so call 312185 for further information. Get to the CML building 15 minutes ahead of departure time. The bus does have the slight disadvantage of having no scheduled runs for early morning flights, in which case you have to take the taxi. If you enquire at a hotel about the CML bus and no one seems to know about it, don't believe them. (They are probably getting a percentage of the taxi driver's fare.)

Bus The real economy-minded visitor can ride the buses – noisy and smoke belching but charming and dirt cheap. A fare across town costs no more than F$0.25. Buses depart from the terminal next to the market.

Taxi Taxis are super abundant and cheap. At the most, a fare around Suva or its environs will be about F$1.50 or less, and certainly not over F$2. Taxis in Fiji have what's called a 'return fare' system, meaning that after a cab has dropped off a fare and is returning to its stand, the price for the fare is only F$0.30 as long as the driver does not go out of his way. At this point a taxi will stop to pick up all the passengers it can, to make up the loss. Most Suva taxis have meters that work but this is not the case in rural areas. Always make sure of the price or at least the approximate price when boarding a taxi with no meter.

Car Rental

Avis
  Corner of Thomson & Usher Sts, tel 313 833
Budget
  123 Foster Rd, tel 315 899
Dollar Rent-A-Car
  tel 313 131
Hertz (Lami)
  tel 361 899
Dominion Rentals
  Pratt St, tel 25 977
United Touring
  tel 25 637

Yachting Boats can be moored either at the Royal Suva Yacht Club on the edge of Suva (tel 24 848), or at the Tradewinds Hotel (tel 36 166), a 10-minute drive outside of town. Cost for mooring, hot showers and use of all facilities at the Club (which is a big social organisation in town) is F$12 per week for vessel and entire crew. Admiralty marine charts can be purchased at Carpenters Shipping, 1st Floor, Harbour Centre Building, Thomson St (across from Morris Hedstrom).

AROUND SUVA
Orchid Island

The visitor who arrives in Suva with little time on his/her hands and wants to take an excursion may be faced with the choice of visiting Pacific Harbour or Orchid Island. Both are worth seeing, and although both are 'cultural' in nature, they have different slants.

Orchid Island, located 10 km from Suva, is small in scale compared to Pacific Harbour and is the closer of the two attractions. It is an island in the sense that it is built in the midst of a mangrove swamp, prone to flooding during calamitous weather. Operated by the very personable Gwynn Watkins, a former forestry official with the colonial government, Orchid Island is basically a museum/ zoo with introductory exhibits on Fijian history, culture and flora and fauna. In addition to the museum-like exhibits, there is a replica of an old Fijian village that includes a *bure kalou* (ancient temple) and a chief's house. Local villagers dressed in traditional garb demonstrate handicrafts such as tapa-making, pottery and basket-weaving. Orchid Island is the closest thing Fiji has to a zoo; besides being home to turtles, mongooses, parrots and other birds, it is the only place where you can see Fiji's recently discovered species, the crested iguana. You can also learn about Fiji's agriculture, geology and natural resources (such as timber). Naturally, there is a handicrafts shop.

Besides the natural sciences, owner Gwynn Watkins is fascinated with the heritage of Fiji's ancient religion and its supernatural manifestations. Orchid Island has a kind of 'Ripley's Believe It or Not' element that may be intriguing for some and entertaining for others. Watkins claims that the Fijian temple on Orchid Island, the first to be constructed since the heathen days, has been resettled by the local *vu* or ancestral spirits. It is his contention that sceptics will have difficulty taking a decent photo of the old temple without mysterious fogging of the film or some other strange occurrence. His proof is the countless times this has occurred in the past. He also has photos that have captured on film the essence of these spirits.

In a nutshell, Orchid Island is an intimate, family-run sideshow that is fun and genuinely attempts to educate the visitor about Fiji. It is open seven days a week and costs F$9 for adults, F$4.50 for children. Transportation is available from the Southern Cross, Courtesy Inn, Peninsula Hotel, Grand Pacific Hotel, Tradewinds Hotel and the bus stop in front of the Morris Hedstrom store in Suva. You can drive there in 15 minutes (going in the direction of Nadi). The tour begins at 10.30 am and lasts about three hours. Phone 23 227 for more information.

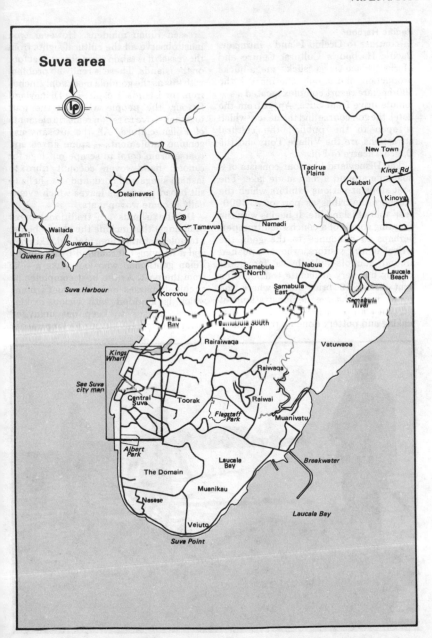

Pacific Harbour

In contrast to Orchid Island's intimacy, Pacific Harbour's Cultural Centre and Market Place is a slick, mega-bucks production, and is only one facet of the 500-hectare resort complex located a 45-minute drive from Suva. Apart from the hotel, the golf course and the beach (which is open to the public), the cultural attractions are the Village Tour and the Dance Theatre of Fiji.

The Disneyland-like tour consists of a boat ride around a man-made lake. The boat stops at various exhibits which the brochure describes as part of a '3000-year' tour of island life. It begins with the haunting sound of a conch shell trumpet, perhaps to announce to the gods the arrival of the visitors, who are pushed around gondola-style by a ferocious-looking but very articulate warrior. The boat makes 10 brief stops where the guests may observe demonstrations of old-time crafts such as mat-weaving, tapa-making and pottery done by traditionally

dressed Fijian maidens. However, you must observe all the cultural sights from the vessel; it is taboo for visitors to set foot on the islands. There is really no problem with this as the gondola moors only inches from the islands. Despite the Disneyland flavour, the people who put the tour together strive to retain realistic elements of Fijian culture. All the artisans use genuine implements – stone adzes and coarse brain coral to scrape out logs for canoes; hand-woven coconut fibre to fashion slings and cord; and sea shells to slit broad pandanus leaves which eventually become woven mats.

On the islands are traditional *bures* (buildings) that include the chief's home, a temple, a storage area for food, a kitchen and a weaving hut manned by an elderly Fijian gentleman who looks like a relic from the past. As the boat completes its circuit, it passes near the chief's home which is studded with vicious-looking wooden spikes to keep out uninvited guests and equally vicious-looking warrior

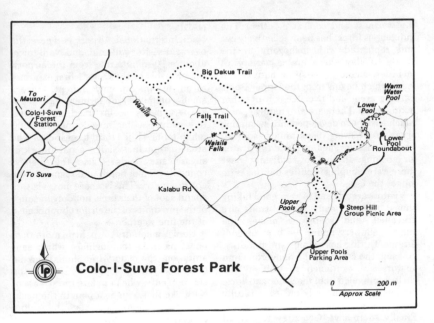

Colo-I-Suva Forest Park

To Mausori
Colo-I-Suva Forest Station

To Suva

Waisila Ck

Big Dakus Trail

Falls Trail

Waisila Falls

Kalabu Rd

Upper Pools

Warm Water Pool

Lower Pool

Lower Pool Roundabout

Steep Hill Group Picnic Area

Upper Pools Parking Area

0   200 m
Approx Scale

guards armed with war clubs. Part of the tour includes a blood-curdling mock battle between opposing warriors that makes you glad you weren't around in those days

The hour-long tour operates daily except Sunday and costs F$7 for adults and F$3.50 for children. Bookings can be made through any hotel or travel agent.

The Dance Theatre of Fiji and the firewalkers from the island of Beqa are the other daily cultural attractions at Pacific Harbour. The Dance Theatre, led by a soft-spoken chief by the name of Manoa Rasigatale, is committed to reviving the ancient legends and dances with original choreographed *mekes* (performances). Though the steps may not be completely traditional, the performances are true to Fiji in spirit right down to the hand-carved war clubs.

The firewalking show is one of those things you've always wanted to see and may as well experience at Pacific Harbour. The advantage here is that during the show an announcer explains the steps leading up to the firewalking to help the visitor understand what is going on. Although it seems crass (something akin to a blow-by-blow description of High Mass to non-Catholics), it is effective. Cost for the Dance Theatre performances (which are outdoors) and the firewalking exhibitions are F$3 for children and F$6 for adults.

Colo-i-Suva Forest Park

This is a lovely recreational area and nature reserve located 18 km from Suva past the suburb of Tamavua on Princess Rd. The park, which is highlighted by waterfalls, rushing streams and misty canyons, occupies the entire upper drainage of Waisila Creek, once lowland tropical forest. Colo-i-Suva is between 120 and 200 metres above sea level and is therefore cooler and slightly wetter than Suva. (The mean annual temperature in the park is 24°C, which varies an average of only 2°C between February and July, the warmest and coolest months.) The indigenous forest has been selectively cut and replanted with mahogany in the 1950s. Today there are a variety of facilities, including a 0.5-km nature trail loop (which begins from the Upper Pools parking area) and over 3.6 km of other hiking trails. There are also natural pools which have been developed into swimming areas, a rope swing, picnic tables – some of which have *bure* shelters – and fire grates for cooking. In the not-so-distant past there were camping facilities but this is no longer the case.

Visitors are advised to wear good hiking shoes because many of the trails are gravelled, and soapstone makes the surface slippery under the best of conditions. During heavy rains and flooding, crossing the creek can be dangerous and visitors are cautioned to wait in the shelters provided until the water subsides. Swimmers are also advised to carefully gauge the depth of pools before diving. Finally, there have been a few reports of rip-offs in this secluded area and hikers should be aware of this problem. Any questions about the park should be directed to the Forestry Station, Colo-i-Suva (tel 221 149 or 22 777).

Transportation to Colo-i-Suva is easy. Take the Sawani bus from the Suva terminal (about F$0.50) and walk from the bus stop to the clearly marked entrance. Begin your hike on the Waisila Falls Trail. Camera buffs should bring along high-speed film because even on a cloudless day the thick forest allows little light through.

Government Pottery Works

The pottery works are located in the Suva suburb of Nasinu, a 15-minute bus ride out of town. Visitors can watch pottery being made and can purchase reproductions of artefacts, dishes and Fijian-style clayware. Take the Nasinu bus and ask the driver to let you off at Valelevu, near the health centre. The pottery works are located behind the centre.

NADI

Nadi International Airport is where the overseas visitor will land, and Nadi town, about a 10-minute ride from the airport, will probably be the visitor's first exposure to an 'urban' Fiji environment. Once a small community of farmers and shopkeepers, it has mushroomed into a duty-free gadget-selling megalopolis of 9000 inhabitants – Fiji's third largest city. The area surrounding Nadi – a patchwork of sugar cane fields – has the highest concentration of hotels and resorts in the entire country. This is where most visitors spend a lot of their time, not only because of the proximity of the airport but because of the fine weather.

Nadi is a hot, dry town, little more than one long main thoroughfare which separates one row of duty-free shops from the other row on the opposite side of the street. Touts, who populate the streets of Nadi like flies, can be a pain in the neck. Just ignore them. If you have the feeling that Nadi lives almost exclusively off the tourist trade, you are right. Except for shoppers, Nadi has little for the visitor except perhaps the local outdoor market, which as in every town is adjacent to the bus station.

Despite Nadi's somewhat vacuous nature, the rolling, verdant countryside surrounding this western town is bucolic; the white sand beaches are unpopulated and gorgeous; and the mountainous region (known as the Nausori Highlands) to the east is nothing short of spectacular. Seeing the cane country is easy – just hop on a local bus or take any of the local tours. Seeing the Nausori Highlands is more difficult. Roads can be rough and/or muddy and car rental agencies wouldn't be happy if they knew you had plans to explore the boondocks. There are rentals of four-wheel-drive vehicles through UTC and Budget Rentals, and one company, Rosie Tours, offers a tour of this marvellous area.

Having a large Indian population, Nadi is a religious centre for Muslims and

Hindus. There are two mosques: the Nadi Mosque, near the Nadi Muslim Primary school in Navakai; and the Amadiya Mosque on the Nadi College Grounds. The major place of worship for Hindus is the Nadi Kalima Temple near the Nadi Bridge.

Things to Do & See

Newtown Beach This beach is located about six km north of Nadi Airport. The Newtown bus will get you there directly, or you can take any other local bus heading south from Nadi and walk the two km from the main highway to the beach. The fare will be around F$0.50.

Waqadra Garden Tour Located 2.5 km out of Nadi on Queen's Road, Waqadra Garden is a 70-year-old botanical paradise surrounding a plantation homestead. Flourishing within are varieties of bamboo, exora, teak, mahogany, raintrees, shower and bohina trees, hibiscus, frangipani, orchids, citrus, mango, bayrum, soursop and cashew trees as well as indigenous plants. You can either take the guided 'Greeters' tour for F$10 or drive there and pay the F$5 admission which includes tropical fruits and a drink. Phone 70 396 or 72 665 to arrange individual tours. Fiji handicrafts are also sold on the premises.

Airport Club For a minimal fee, swimmers and golfers may use the facilities at the Airport Club near Newtown Beach. It has an 18-hole course. Contact the clubhouse at 72 413.

Places to Stay

You will have more accommodation choices on this side of the island than anywhere else in Fiji. All prices are subject to 5% tax. Accommodation in the areas around Nadi and Lautoka can be divided into three general categories:

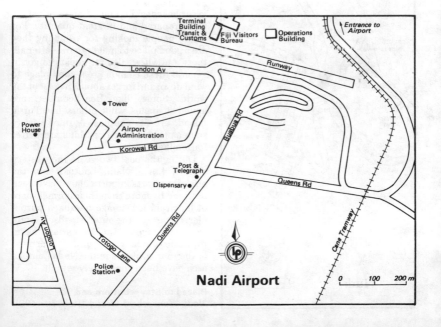

Nadi Airport

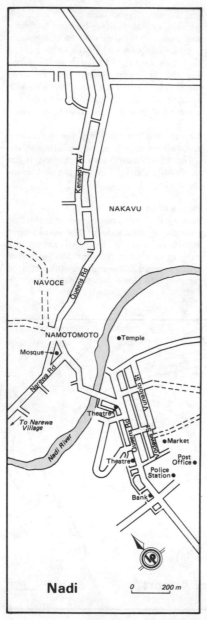

Nadi

0   200 m

Airport hotels – This type of accommodation ranges from first to economy class and is located close to the airport, often in the midst of canefields. All the amenities are usually available at these hotels, particularly at the good ones like the Mocambo or Travelodge, but they have the disadvantage of not being close to the beach.

Beachside resorts – These are opulent, self-contained units with water sports, tennis courts, boutiques, fine restaurants and, of course, excellent access to the beach. Many visitors who end up in these hotels (such as the Regent) never go too far from its confines.

Offshore islands – Off the coast of Lautoka are a group of tiny islands known as the Mamanucas where many island resorts are situated. Located an hour or two's sail from the coast, they offer accommodation ranging from moderate to luxurious. Their isolation provides a genuine 'South Pacific' ambience, excellent snorkelling, diving or deep-sea fishing and great beaches. Food is often buffet style, well prepared and in great quantity. For single people looking for company they are a good place to meet others – after all, there's nowhere else for guests to go. In general these islands are a good place to wind down and forget about the rest of the world. Some, like Beachcomber, are aimed at singles, while others, like Turtle Island, are for couples. A third variety such as Dick's Place or Mana are better for families.

During the past two years the western side of Fiji – Nadi, Lautoka and the offshore resorts in particular – have been battered by more than their normal share of hurricanes. Damage has been particularly severe on the outer islands. Despite the destructive toll the storms have taken, the positive side of the picture is that most of the tourist places in the Nadi/Lautoka area have been completely rebuilt.

Places to Stay – bottom end
Nadi Sunseekers Hotel (tel 70 400),

located just outside of Nadi town, has more of a dorm than hotel feel about it. With 21 rooms, it is one of the better inexpensive places with amenities like air-conditioning, pool, hot and cold water, and an extremely cheap restaurant. Prices begin at F$14 for singles and F$18 for doubles, and unlike many cheap hotels they do accept credit cards. Dorm facilities are also available for F$6 per night. Sunseekers is both quiet and clean.

Sandalwood Inn (tel 72 553) next door to the Dominion Hotel is also an excellent, cheap place to stay – very basic and clean. Available are hot and cold water, air-conditioning and pool. Credit cards are accepted. There are 23 rooms; rates start at F$16 single and F$24 double.

Seashell Cove Resort (tel 50 309) is one of the few places in Fiji with a campground and dorm facilities, so it's popular with the backpacking set. Amenities such as pool, hot and cold water, tennis, snorkelling and day trips to points of interest are offered. Aside from camping and dorm facilities, the resort also has 10 self-contained units. The rate is F$25 single and F$35 double. Dorm bunks are F$8 per night and camping is F$5. The resort is located a half hour's drive south of Nadi, about 500 metres from the beach. Public buses depart from the Nadi terminal Monday through Saturday at 4.45 pm.

Nadi Bay Hotel (tel 73319), located across the road and down the street (towards Nadi town) from the Dominion Hotel, is an antiseptically clean, modern hotel more in the fashion of an American 'motel' than anything I've ever seen in Fiji. It is newish in a tacky sort of way but has fine, self-contained facilities with kitchen, air-conditioning, bar, restaurant, pool and laundry. Prices begin at only F$6 for dorm, F$12 for single, F$15 for twin, and F$35 for family room. Tack on another F$5 per night if you want to use the stove and kitchen facilities. This is one of the bargains in the Nadi area and they honour credit cards. Just down the dirt road is Wailoaloa Beach, great for evening jogs.

Nadi Hotel (tel 70 000) is another quality, spartan hotel. The refurbished hotel is located in downtown Nadi and has 22 rooms (air-conditioning in some), hot and cold water, refrigerator, restaurant and bar.

Camping is available at the *Sunny Holiday Motel* (located midway between the Nadi Airport and Nadi town). The fee is F$3.50 per person per night. There is also camping at Sea Shell Cove (listed above). Of the two, Sea Shell Cove is recommended.

Places to Stay – middle
Dominion International (tel 72 255) has everything that the expensive hotels have except the stiff prices. Under new management that is serious about upgrading its image, the hotel is in the process of refurbishing its rooms and adding an all-weather tennis court and jogging track. The best thing about the hotel is the staff, who seem to go out of their way for the visitor and are among the friendliest I have found anywhere in Fiji. Located about 10 minutes from the airport, the hotel is a 10 minute jog from Wailoaloa Beach, which is usually deserted. The Dominion has 85 rooms, pool, airport transfer, restaurant, bar, gift shop and dancing. Prices are F$46 single and F$51 double.

A bit overpriced for its moderate class, *Tanoa Hotel* (tel 72 300) does have good service and accommodation. Located just a few minutes from the airport, the Tanoa has 132 rooms, bar, restaurant, gift shop, tennis, sauna, jogging track and pool. The band here is currently the best in the entire Nadi/Lautoka area. The place jumps on the weekends. Rates begin at F$48 single and F$58 double.

Skylodge Hotel (tel 72 200) with 48 rooms was one of the first airport hotels to be constructed in the area. It offers the option of self-contained units as well as the usual amenities like pool, restaurant and live music. The outdoor buffets are very good and the management is responsive to the needs of the visitor. The Skylodge is the most inexpensive and unpretentious of the middle-range airport hotels. Prices begin at F$28 single and F$33 double. Self-contained family units are F$50 per day.

Castaway Gateway (tel 72 444) is named so perhaps because it is literally at the doorstep of the airport. The clientele seems to be mostly young. Over the last year it has been completely revamped and in my estimation is as well run as any hotel in Fiji. It has a pool, gift shop, live music, outdoor bar and better-than-average hotel food. Of late the airport paging system has been 'wired' into the hotel's paging system so that imbibers will not miss their flights! Prices begin at F$52 single and $58 double.

Places to Stay – top end

Mocambo (tel 72 000) and its neighbour *Travelodge* (tel 72 227) share honours as the premium airport hotels. Mocambo with 132 rooms is slightly larger than the Travelodge (with 114 rooms), but in reality there is little difference in amenities (which include fine restaurants, gift shop, pool, etc) and price. Because of the frequency of hurricanes recently, both hotels have gone through millions of dollars' worth of renovation and improvement. There is no appreciable difference between the two. Both have tennis courts, and the Mocambo has a driving range. Both offer excellent accommodation, are extremely close to the airport, and are located in what was once cane fields. Both have some of the best dance bands in the Nadi area. Prices for the Mocambo begin at F$58 single and F$66 double. Rates at the Travelodge are F$69 single and F$79 double.

Regent of Fiji is the only upscale beach resort in the Nadi area and is considered by many to be the finest hotel in Fiji. It has 300 rooms, four bars, four restaurants and all the luxury you could want. Prices begin at F$110 per room for single or twin.

Amenities include boutique, general store (which stocks everything from newspapers to pharmaceuticals), hair salon and resident nurse on call. The nearby ocean provides access to water sports such as water skiiing, diving, sailing, paddleboats, hobie cats, windsurfing and snorkelling (which is complimentary). Water skiing, diving and snorkelling can be arranged at the tour desk. Also available are archery, a pitch-and-putt course and a pool. Tennis enthusiasts have the services of John Newcombe's Tennis Ranch (with six grass and four all-weather courts), which is right next door for professional instruction. In addition, the hotel provides the largest convention facilities in Fiji. The Regent is a headquarters for deep-sea fishing, too – South Seas Islands Cruises operates the 13-metre *Fleet Lady* and five other vessels for cruising and fishing trips.

Places to Eat

In Nadi most people tend to eat in their hotels. However, there are a few good 'no-frill' restaurants which serve less expensive fare than the hotels.

Maharaj, located in Namaka on the main highway 10 minutes from the airport towards Nadi town, gets a four-star rating. Not only is it one of the best restaurants in Nadi, it is one of the best in Fiji regardless of price. Excellent curries, Chinese food and seafood dishes range from F$3-6 for entrees.

Poon's is on Main St in downtown Nadi, upstairs in the Nadi Tower Building. I find its Chinese food consistently good. Prices range from F$3-6 for entrees. Worth visiting.

Curry Restaurant on Clay St in Nadi (not to be confused with the Indian Curry House on Main St) specialises (as you may have guessed) in curries and Indian food. If you have a weakness for this type of cuisine, this is where to go. Prices average around F$3.50 for an entree.

La Hacienda Pizza, located on the main drag between Nadi and the airport, is the Nadi area's only 24-hour pizza joint.

Top: Re-enactment of cession ceremony, Levuka, Ovalau (RK)
Bottom: Firewalking (FVB)

Top: Nadroga Mosque, Sigatoka, Viti Levu (FVB)
Left: Buildings in Ba, Viti Levu (RK)
Right: Palm trees (RK)

Pizza is excellent by Fiji standards, but true aficionados might quibble about the texture of the crust, which is too bread-like. Decor is stucco with Mexican/Spanish motif and tacky velveteen portraits of flamenco dancers on the walls. I think that the Scottish owner might be a little confused about pizza joints, which are supposed to be Italian. Try the marinara pizza if you like seafood. Prices range from F$5.50 to F$16 for a large pizza which will feed two to three people.

Entertainment

For avid nightclubbers the western side of Viti Levu will be rather quiet. The hotels provide most of the entertainment around here and generally there just isn't that much. The best dance band is at the Tanoa, but the live music at the *Mocambo* and *Travelodge* is also good. The action is on the weekends. The major hotels all have traditional dancing shows known as *mekes* and firewalking exhibitions which can easily be gleaned from the schedule in

Fiji Fantastic or *Fiji Beach Press*. There is one nightclub in Nadi, an air-conditioned dive known as the *Bamboo Palace* which is very local and can get on the rough-and-tumble side. There are also four cinemas. Check the *Fiji Sun* or *Fiji Times* for listings.

LAUTOKA

With a population of almost 30,000, Lautoka is Fiji's second largest city and its second most important port. From here most of the vessels sail not only for foreign ports but to the outer islands and the resort areas. Lautoka is also a quintessential sugar town, with reputedly one of the largest sugar mills in the southern hemisphere. The mill can be visited by tourists today. Although tourism is important to the region, sugar is still king here and the sugar industry is the largest single employer in the district.

Though only 19 km from Nadi, you get the feeling that Lautoka has existed quite a while without the tourist trade. In my

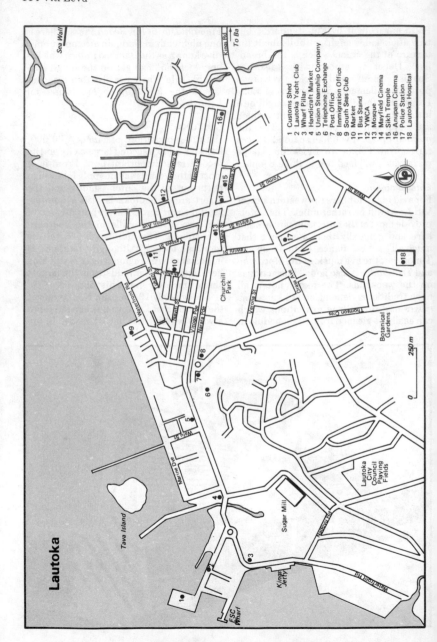

Lautoka

1 Customs Shed
2 Lautoka Yacht Club
3 Wharf Pillar
4 Handicraft Market
5 Union Steamship Company
6 Telephone Exchange
7 Post Office
8 Immigration Office
9 South Seas Club
10 Market
11 Bus Stand
12 YWCA
13 Mosque
14 Mayfield Cinema
15 Sikh Temple
16 Anupam Cinema
17 Police Station
18 Lautoka Hospital

opinion it is perhaps a bit friendlier than Nadi and a much better place to go duty-free shopping. The merchants seem much more relaxed and the touts aren't grasping at your arm, trying to pull you into their shops.

Tradition has it that within the bounds of today's Lautoka city limits there lived two tribes. One day a fight broke out between the tribes' chiefs at a spot known today as 'Farquahr's Point.' As one chief speared the other he screamed 'Lau-toka' which means 'spear-hit' or 'hit to win.' Thus Lautoka acquired a name.

The first sighting of the area was on the dawn of 7 May 1789 when Captain Bligh of the *HMS Bounty* sailed by in his launch with loyal crew members – those who had been tossed out as a result of the famous mutiny on the *Bounty*. Bligh made rough charts of the shores of Lautoka and sketched the mountains in the background.

At the end of the last century the Colonial Sugar Refining Company (CSR) decided to build a mill in Lautoka. Indian indentured labourers and Solomon Island workers were brought in to do the construction and in 1899 the work began. The mill began crushing in 1903 and still operates today.

Lautoka was proclaimed a city on 25 February 1977 and today is the headquarters for important government and statutory bodies such as the Fiji Electrical Authority, the Fiji Pine Commission and the National Marketing Authority. It is the administrative capital of the Western Division, which contains over 50% of the nation's population.

Things to Do & See

The Queens Road into Lautoka is lined with royal palms, and railroad tracks from the ubiquitous sugar train run adjacent to the highway towards the huge **sugar mill** looming in the distance. The business of Lautoka is and always was centred around sugar. By calling the Fiji Sugar Corporation (tel 60 800) you can arrange a tour of the mill. There is also the **Lautoka Golf Club**

(nine holes), tel 613 411. Green fees are under F$5.

Saweni Beach, located about six km north of Lautoka and two km off the main road, is the nicest beach near town. You can get there by jumping on any north-bound local bus at the terminal. Like all Fijian communities, Lautoka has a sizable **market** selling produce, yaqona and trinkets, but nothing terribly different from any of the others. Finally, if you're really bored there are four **cinemas**.

Places to Stay – bottom end

The Hare Krishna followers have their largest temple in the South Pacific in Lautoka and it doubles as a crash pad for whoever is homeless, indigent or maybe just curious. The *Hare Krishna Temple* is on Tavewa Avenue.

There are also two acceptable inexpensive hotels in Lautoka town, *Cathay* and *Seabreeze*. A good hotel is the *Lautoka Hotel* with rooms at F$35 single and $43 double; it's possibly the only hotel in Fiji with waterbeds. However, considering the choice of good accommodation between Lautoka and Nadi (located in less congested areas), there is no good reason at all to stay in Lautoka unless you are just curious or have met an attractive Lautokan.

*Saweni Beach Hotel (tel 61 777), located 11 km north of the airport, is one of two beachside hotels between Nadi and Lautoka. The F$40 units (single or double) are individual, whitewashed, cement block houses. They are clean and each has a small stove, refrigerator and utensils. A small local store is located nearby for provisions. There is a bar but no restaurant on the premises. When I visited the hotel, the Australian High Commissioner's family was there, so the place couldn't have been too bad. The resort also has dorm units for F$6 per night. Saweni Beach (which is a local hangout) is so-so as far as beaches go, has shaded picnic tables, and is just a few metres from the cottages. To get there take the Saweni Beach turnoff or the

Saweni bus which goes directly to the beach. If you can't get the exact bus, any local bus going north from Lautoka will drop you off on the main road, which is a two km walk from the hotel.

Anchorage Beach Resort (tel 62 099) is located on a gorgeous bluff on Vuda Point, the spot where tradition says the first Fijians landed. Anchorage is also located between Nadi and Lautoka and is the only other beachside resort in this area. It was battered quite severely during the last series of hurricanes to hit Fiji but should be revamped by the time this book is complete. The site of the hotel is one of the nicest imaginable, even if a 'tank farm' for fuel is located nearby. Below is a beach and reef – the snorkelling is mediocre. The resort has 10 rooms (single F$45, double F$50) and six units with kitchen facilities that sleep four for F$60. There is a restaurant on the premises with a menu that changes daily and ranges from F$6 to 12. Anchorage Resort also has a pool, offers free transport to and from the airport and will take you to the main road to catch the Beachcomber bus. To get there take the Vuda Point turnoff a few km and then take a left 1.5 km to the hotel.

Places to Eat

Even though Lautoka is Fiji's second largest city, its restaurants do not come close to Suva's in variety. There are, however, some fair, inexpensive eateries. For Chinese cuisine Eddie Hing's *Sea Coast Restaurant* on Naviti St is a good bet. Prices range from F$2-6. Indian food enthusiasts can try *Hot Snaxs* on Naviti St or *Asterix* on Yasawa St, which have curries, Chinese food and European dishes. Prices at both are under F$4.

Entertainment

Club 21 and *Galaxy Disco* on Naviti St are the local dives. They have plenty of action – sometimes in the form of fist fights. Tamer, but still seedy, is the Captain Cook lounge on the ground floor of the *Lautoka Hotel*. *Hunter's Inn* (near the Lautoka Hotel on Naviti St) has more of a tourist and local mix and visitors may consider it the most civilised nightspot in town.

OFFSHORE RESORTS

There are numerous resort islands off the coast from Nadi and Lautoka, all in the middle to top end price brackets. Although nightly costs are quoted below for these resorts the vast majority of people staying here will be on all-inclusive package tours.

Beachcomber

Beachcomber (tel 62 600) is the most popular island for the young and the unattached. It is a tiny speck of land (you can walk around it in 10 minutes) located a 45-minute boat ride off the Nadi coast. Here you'll find an informal atmosphere, plenty of good food served buffet-style, and optional dorm-style accommodation. Activities include snorkelling, excursions and dancing. Rates (which include all meals) begin at F$32 for dorm facilities, F$56 for single and F$80 for twin rooms. A *bure* is F$71 single, F$96 double. Great entertainment, live music and 27 rooms.

Musket Cove

Musket Cove (tel 72 371) shares Malololailai with Plantation Island Resort and also shares the same air service via Sunflower from Nadi. It is very informal and funky compared with its neighbour (and most of the other offshore resorts), but accommodation is more than adequate and the beach is second only to Mana's. There are 24 *bures* (many of which are being upgraded) with kitchenettes that include refrigerator, stove and utensils. Nearby is a general store for do-it-yourselfers, and there is also a bistro where lunch and dinner are served. Other amenities include a wonderful gift shop on the hill, pool, bar and Manasa's Dive Shop where you can dive fully equipped for only F$28 per day. The advantages at Musket Cove (compared to its neighbour) is that it's cheaper and more intimate, and all water sports and the price of air transportation are included in the tariff. You can also use the upscale facilities of neighbouring Plantation Island Resort. Musket Cove would be a good choice for a family as well as a single person. Rates begin at F$50 for a single and F$70 for a double. On the premises, luxury condominiums are also being constructed, which seem incongruous next to the budget accommodation. They are only the beginning of a modern complex that will include a golf course and an entire resort community. Rates for the condos, or 'villas' as they are called, begin at F$55 for a single and F$80 for a double.

Castaway

Castaway (tel 87 286), located just north of Malolo Island, has recently been renovated to the tune of US$1 million and caters to a younger crowd. However, it is more formal in tone and more luxurious than Beachcomber. Amenities include sauna, pool, fine cuisine and all water sports. Prices are F$76 single and F$82 double. Meals are separate – F$22.05 for the modified American plan (breakfast and dinner) and F$26.25 for the American plan (breakfast, lunch and dinner). The deep-sea fishing boat *Dauwai*, run by South Sea Island Cruises, also operates from Castaway. The charter boat carries six to eight people and goes up to 30 knots.

Plantation Island

Plantation Island (tel 72 333), like its neighbour, Musket Cove, is located on Malololailai, a gorgeous horseshoe-shaped island with a lovely bay. It is connected with Nadi via Sunflower Airlines and by launch service from the Regent Hotel. Since the last hurricane, it has risen out of the ashes like a phoenix to become among the finest offshore resorts in Fiji. The clientele is mostly young couples and singles. There are 90 rooms, many of them very attractive white-washed *bures* with

thatched roofs and elegant interiors. There are also very nice dorm facilities for F$12 per night. Rates for singles are F$78, doubles F$86 and triples F$102. The large *bures* which fit up to 10 people go for F$180 per night. The three-meal package is F$22 per day and the restaurant is good. The band is also excellent. Other amenities include pool and disco. The resort has a very complete water sports program that includes fishing, diving, water skiing, snorkelling and coral viewing, but the package for this costs an extra F$20 for a single or F$30 for a couple for the duration of your stay.

Tavarua

Tavarua, a 12-hectare island off Momi Bay, is Fiji's only surfing resort and one of the few in the South Pacific devoted solely to this sport. To get there you must first get to Sea Shell Cove (a 45-minute ride from the airport) and catch a launch. Amenities include 10 double bure units plus a kitchen and dining area. Most of the island's power comes from a solar unit, which according to the owner is the largest installation of its type in Fiji. Game-fishing, windsurfing and diving can also be arranged. In case of accident, there's a special transfer system to medical facilities on the mainland. Daily rate is F$100 (including meals, transfers, drinks and other activities). For further information write to Tavarua Resort, Tavarua Island, Fiji or contact Aquarius Tours in Torrance, California, USA at 213 379 0056.

Mana

A family– and couple-oriented resort, *Mana* (tel 61 455) has more of a formal 'hotel' feeling about it. It is the largest offshore resort (120 hectares) and has 120 *bures*. Amenities include pool, refrigerators, radio, general store, resident nurse, restaurant, tennis, snorkelling, water skiing, sailing and water scooters. Rates begin at F$70 single and F$75 for a double. The beach here is the best in the Mamanuca group.

Club Naitasi
Club Naitasi (tel 72 266), located on Malolo Island (the largest in the Mamanuca Group), is nestled at the base of a hill and is just metres from a fine little white sand beach. It has 38 *bures* and deluxe two-bedroomed villas. It is definitely upmarket in atmosphere, family– and couple-oriented, and has comfortable, well-constructed rooms. Those desiring a cozy, quiet resort will not be disappointed here. Amenities include pool, cooking facilities for guests, an excellent restaurant, a mini tennis court, diving, snorkelling and water skiing. Water sports cost an additional F$20 per person for the duration of your visit. Accommodation begins at F$66 single and F$82 double. There are also luxury two-bedroom villas for F$120. Speedboat transfers from Malololailai to Naitasi or Castaway are F$5 one way, and seaplane transportation is available from Nadi Airport.

Treasure Island
Treasure Island (tel 61 599) is owned by Islands in the Sun, the same people who do such a good job on Beachcomber. Because of the recent hurricanes the resort has undergone F$1 million in renovations. Like Beachcomber, it is a tiny island, but more formal, more luxurious and more family oriented. There are 68 *bure* units with refrigerator and ceiling fans. Plenty of snorkelling, fishing and excursions on the water. Singles begin at F$76 and doubles at F$82. A meal package can be arranged for F$24 per day for adults and F$12 per day for children.

Turtle Island
Turtle Island (tel 72 921) bills itself as a super-exclusive resort and has received rave reviews in the American press. For the substantial amount you pay to stay there, it should have. Owned by an American, Richard Evanson, who struck it big in the cable television market, the island was the location for the filming of *Blue Lagoon* and is the only resort in the Yasawa chain. To get there you must take a 25-minute airplane flight on (naturally) Turtle Airways which costs F$170. Food and wine are reportedly excellent and guests are free to use sailboat, canoe, windsurfers and horses at their leisure. There are just 12 units on the 200-hectare island. Only couples are allowed on the island. The cost for a double is F$398.

Matamanoa
Matamanoa (tel 60511) is the newest of the area's offshore resorts. A two-hour boat ride from the Regent Hotel, it offers water skiing, snorkelling, windsurfing, a bush trek, and picnicking on three nearby uninhabited islands. The 20 *bures* are F$68 single and F$72 double. Other amenities include pool, restaurant and bar/lounge.

SIGATOKA & THE CORAL COAST
Located at the mouth of the Sigatoka River (Fiji's second longest river), Sigatoka town lies in close proximity to rich farmland and some of Fiji's finest hotels. The 136-km-long Sigatoka River flows through what is known as Fiji's 'Salad Bowl', a river valley that offers some of the most scenic landscapes in the country. With a population of about 2000 the town is hardly a metropolis, but instead provides the visitor with a combination of tourist facilities and a genuine 'local' farm-town atmosphere. Sigatoka might be called the 'gateway to the Coral Coast,' an area that contains many resorts and stretches from the township approximately 70 km down the coastline in an easterly direction.

Sigatoka is a quiet community marked by a gorgeous mosque and a lengthy bridge that crosses the river. The municipal market on the edge of town is worth visiting just to see the abundance of regional produce and a sizeable handicraft selection. Duty-free stores are abundant here and it's much more pleasant to conduct business with the small-town merchants than with those in Nadi. Outside of town there is the river valley

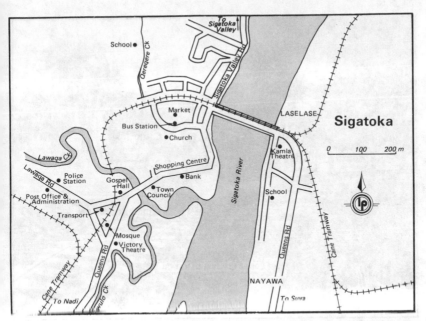

road for motorists or an approximately two-hour boat cruise up the river. The launch stops at a village to let you observe the yaqona ceremony and see a *meke* (traditional dance performance). Cost for the trip is F$10. Two km north of town are the sand dunes near Kulukulu Village – another attraction well worth visiting. There are also two cinemas in town.

Things to Do & See

Coral Coast Railway The greatest thing to come to the western side of Viti Levu in years is the Coral Coast Railway – a newly developed tourist line which has begun a service from the Fijian Hotel with the terminus at Natadola Beach. Future routes slated for Sigatoka and Nadi in mid-1986 will also take passengers to Natadola Beach. Not that a railway is new to Fiji at all. The sugar train has been around since the turn of the century, bringing the cane harvest from throughout the western side to the refinery in Lautoka. Up to the 1970s the old train

took passengers as well, but this practice was discontinued. It took a New Zealand entrepreneur by the name of Peter Jones to utilise the already existing railway infrastructure, add a few stations, rebuild a circa-1911 steam engine, construct carriages from scratch, and voila, the Coral Coast Railway was born.

The first line, which originates at the Fijian, hugs the coastline and rolls through rainforest, passes villages, and journeys through virgin land, canefields and even a fruit bat sanctuary. One hour and 15 minutes later you are deposited on unspoilt Natadola Beach for a barbecue or any number of activities such as hiking, swimming, snorkelling, windsurfing or conventional surfing. During the ride refreshments are served. At 4 pm the train departs the beach and returns to the hotel. Cost for the ride, which includes lunch, is about F$20. Tickets can be bought at any tour desk. The Coral Coast Railway has free pickup and return for passengers at any of the Coral Coast Hotels.

CORAL COAST RAILWAY CO.

The beauty of the train is that it travels through countryside that is off the main road and has not been developed. It is essentially the same landscape that a rail traveller would have seen at the turn of the century. Although the engine is on the surface a rebuilt steam locomotive, it actually contains a diesel engine more like the modern-day sugar train. Apparently Jones wanted to use the old-style steam locomotion but found that importing coal was too costly. The carriages, although modern in construction, are replicas of 19th-century cars with seating for 16 in comfort and style. The train consists of four carriages, one service car providing refrigeration for beverages and a caboose which acts as a brake car.

Places to Stay – bottom end

Hideaway (tel 50 177) is probably the best of the inexpensive hotel facilities in Fiji. Located on a beach 20 km from Sigatoka, they cater to a generally younger crowd. Accommodation ranges from dorm arrangements (F$8 per night) to *bures* priced at F$56 (up to three people) and F$70 (up to five people). The 15 *bure* units are not self contained but the resort does have an excellent restaurant.

Activities include horseback riding, snorkelling, glass-bottom-boat trips and excursions to a nearby cave. The local village puts on traditional dances or *mekes* for guests twice weekly and offers non-traditional dancing to the sounds of the house band.

The highlight of a stay at the Hideaway is a trip to the hot springs and waterfalls for F$10 by four-wheel-drive vehicle. This entails a hike through the rainforest and a dip in a steaming-hot pool or a swim beneath the falls. The trip departs from the hotel six days a week at 9 am. Other good news is that the Hideaway accepts credit cards.

Places to Stay – middle

Naviti Beach Resort (tel 50 444) is a highly recommended, moderately priced, family-oriented resort hotel situated roughly halfway between Nadi and Suva. Located an hour's drive from Nadi near Korolevu and situated on a bay, the 144-room Naviti (which occupies 15 hectares) has all the amenities. These include duty-free shop, boutique, service shop, restaurant, pizzeria/game room, pool and activities such as snorkelling, diving, horseback riding (donkeys for the kids), canoeing, bicycling, hiking, tennis (on a new all-weather court), nine-hole golf course, live music, local dance shows and firewalking exhibitions. This is a very good place to bring children; they are well cared for here. Prices are F$58 for a single and F$64 for a double. Car rentals are also available.

Crow's Nest (tel 50 230), located near Sigatoka, is a small but well-run resort. Operated by Paddy Doyle, a long-time builder of hotels in Fiji, it is not fancy but is comfortable. Eighteen individual *bure* units are fully self-contained and there is an inexpensive restaurant on the premises serving good food. Prices are F$50 for a two-person unit and F$57 for a *bure* that sleeps up to four. It is also a good place to bring children. In addition, the Crow's Nest has one of the best restaurants in the Sigatoka area. Their curries and fish are moderately priced at F$4-5 and are excellent.

Near Korolevu, *Man Friday* (tel 50 185) has 28 *bure*-style units (with utensils, refrigerator, toaster and coffee maker but no stove). It is 'acceptable,' meaning it's nothing out of the ordinary. It has a pool, bar, restaurant and badminton. Activities include snorkelling, deep-sea fishing, beach BBQ and live band. Rates start at F$45 for a single and F$50 for a double. A large *bure* which sleeps two to four people goes for F$60.

Also acceptable is the *Reef Hotel Resort* (tel 50 044) near Sigatoka. It has 72 rooms, a nine-hole golf course, live music, snorkelling and a restaurant. Prices begin at F$50 for a single and F$54 for a double.

Places to Stay – top end

The Fijian (tel 50 155) is a self-contained resort complex constructed on tiny Yanuca Island, connected to the mainland by a causeway. It is a gorgeous piece of real estate and the hotel is certainly one of the top five in Fiji. Located an hour's drive from Nadi Airport, this 316-room resort has all amenities including two pools, four restaurants, five bars, a general store, a boutique, a duty-free shop, convention facilities, a disco, and regularly scheduled traditional dance shows and firewalking exhibitions. Recreational activities are probably the most complete in Fiji. They consist of five tennis courts with professional coach, a nine-hole golf course, horseback riding, snorkelling, lawn bowling, sailing, volleyball, scuba diving, deep-sea fishing and water skiing. The hotel has excellent cuisine – the chef recently won a 'cookoff' competition naming him the best cook in the country. Price for a single is F$94, double F$103. Aside from standard rooms there are individual *bures* with living rooms that go for F$210 (one bedroom) and F$260 (two bedroom).

The Hyatt (tel 50 555) near Korolevu also ranks as one of the top five resorts in the country. This 250-room beachside hotel opened in 1979 and is one of the newest in Fiji. Amenities include four restaurants, four bars, boutique, duty-free general store, 24-hour room service, convention facilities and local entertainment such as dancing and firewalking shows. Sports include a nine-hole golf course, two tennis courts, pool, snorkelling, windsurfing, scuba diving facilities and canoeing. Rooms which have fully stocked bar and refrigerator start at F$67 for a single and F$83 for a twin. Cuisine is also very fine at this hotel, with the Wicked Walu restaurant serving some of the best seafood on the Coral Coast. Book ahead for reservations.

Casablanca Beach Resort (tel 50 527) in Korotogo, about eight km east of Sigatoka, is the newest property along the Coral Coast. Once a private home, the structure has eight self-contained units and has been given a 'hacienda' look. All units have individual balconies facing the sea, and each has an oyster-light peephole for security. There is also a swimming pool on the premises. Adjoining the hotel is a pizzeria called *The Hacienda*, which serves the best pizza in Fiji. Prices for the hotel are F$70 for a single or twin.

Places to Eat

Best place to eat in town is the restaurant at the *Sigatoka Hotel* (which isn't recommended for its accommodation). Meals are F$3-5 with an excellent variety of Chinese and Indian food on the menu. There is a less expensive *Chinese restaurant* on the corner across from the bus stand.

The Crow's Nest, a small resort a few km east of town, has one of the best restaurants in the region. Their specialities are seafood, traditional Fijian food and curries with a dozen condiments or 'chutneys' on the side. For visitors who have never sampled curry before, it is a good place to begin. Average price for main courses is F$4-6.

Inexpensive Indian food for F$2-3 can be had at the *Sigatoka Lodge* and the *Pacifica Lodge*, both near the market. Just outside of town (at Korotogo) is a good pizzeria (owned by the same man who runs the pizzeria in Nadi) at the *Casablanca Hotel*.

KINGS ROAD

The Kings Road, the route along the northerly coast of Viti Levu, is less often seen by visitors primarily because the road is much poorer, the area is less developed for tourism, and the distance to Suva is longer. However, there are attractions, the scenery is beautiful and the more adventurous visitor may want to rent a car and drive it. The two main

settlements along the way, Ba and Tavua, are primarily agricultural communities but do have small hotels. This route is described in detail in the 'Around the Island' section.

Places to Stay – bottom end

The only place to stay in Ba – indeed one of the few hotels on this side of the island – is the *Ba Hotel* (tel 74 000). It is a simple 13-room affair with restaurant and bar. Price for a single is F$20, double F$28. It is decent and clean with average food.

Nadarivatu Government Guest House is located about 30 km inland from Tavua and was formerly a mountain hideaway for bosses at the nearby gold mines of Vatukoula. Today it is primarily a facility for government workers but also accommodates visitors if they make reservations with the Forestry Department in Suva (tel 23 833) or Lautoka (tel 61 000). There is hiking and camping nearby. Cost for a room is F$4 per night. Close to these places is a store, but you should get your supplies in Tavua or Ba before reaching Nadarivatu. For more information on this area see the 'Around the Island' section on Kings Road.

A clean, spartan little place, the *Tavua Hotel* (tel Tavua 8) sits on top of a hill overlooking the town of Tavua and the nearby ocean. The old-style clapboard hotel is only a two-minute walk from the community of Tavua, a quintessential sugar town that certainly does not see too many visitors. Amenities include a good, inexpensive restaurant, pool, tennis and golf. Bowling is a 15-minute drive away in the gold-mining town of Vatukoula. Prices are F$14 for a single and F$18 for a double for non-air-conditioned rooms, and F$20 and F$28 for air-conditioned units. Excursions are available to Mt Victoria, the forest region of Nadarivatu, and Vatukoula.

Places to Stay – middle

Rakiraki Hotel (tel 94 101) bills itself as the northernmost hotel on Viti Levu basking in the driest and 'deliciously hottest' climate on the island. Located near the small community of Rakiraki at a point roughly halfway (about 120 km) along the Kings Road from Nadi, the hotel is a good overnight spot for those touring the northern coast. The 46-room hotel is nothing fancy but quite adequate, well run and comfortable. Amenities include air-conditioning, pool, refrigerator, nine-hole golf course (nearby), local entertainment, tennis court, lawn bowling, bar and restaurant. Prices are F$30 for a single and F$38 for a double.

Places to Stay – Offshore

Nananu-I-Ra Island has become very popular with visitors who wish to get away from the commercialism on the western side of Viti Levu and find a more 'local' scene. It is located five km offshore from Viti Levu. The accommodation on this island is highly recommended.

*Bethams Beach Cottages (tel 383 013) consists of four self-contained bungalows on Nananu-I-Ra. Each cottage has two rooms, refrigerator, cooking facilities, linen, shower, toilet, snorkelling gear and fishing. Bring the supplies you need from Rakiraki and catch the launch (F$20) from Ellington Wharf, 11 km west of Rakiraki. Price is F$25 per group using the cottage. Write Robin B Pitts, PO Box 1244, Suva, for information/reservations.

*Nananu Beach Cottages (tel 22 671) has the same setup as their neighbours the Bethams. This resort has five cottages, also with cooking facilities and refrigerators, so you must bring your own food. Activities include deep-sea fishing, shelling and snorkelling. Prices begin at F$30 for a single and F$35 for a double. Pick-up time at Ellington Wharf is 11 am and cost for the transfer is F$10 per person, F$25 if you are the only one on the boat. Write to Maxine Macdonald, PO Box 340, Suva or phone 22 671 or 27 274 for more information.

*Kon Tiki Island Lodge (tel 366; radiotelephone RB4) has three self-contained bures that sleep up to six. Accommodation includes bath and kitchen. At F$6.50 per person, this is the least expensive of the Nananu-I-Ra guest houses and is more or less equivalent in quality to the others. The beachfront for this property is excellent. The transfer from the mainland (F$4) is also the cheapest of all; contact any of the local taxis in Rakiraki.

MONASAVU DAM

The Monasavu hydroelectric project is one of the most ambitious public works ever undertaken by the Fiji government. Designed to reduce the country's dependency on imported fuels, the F$234 million project was begun in 1978 and completed in 1983. The most visible part of the scheme is the 82-metre-high earth-fill dam and its accompanying 17-km-long lake cradled in the Nadrau Plateau, about 1000 metres above sea level in the mountains of central Viti Levu. About 625 metres below the lake is the Wailoa power house – connected via a 5.4-km tunnel forcing water through a series of four 20-megawatt turbines. Overhead transmission lines then carry the electricity to Suva and to Lautoka in the west. The project will provide relatively cheap electricity – more than double the island's needs into the end of the 1980s.

AROUND THE ISLAND

Viti Levu has one main road around its perimeter. Most of it is well maintained, especially the stretches between Sigatoka and Nadi and Suva and Pacific Harbour, which make up a comparative super-highway. Portions of the road, due to flooding, hurricanes and other natural disasters, are not in such great shape and seem to be in a continual state of repair.

The highway that circles the island is actually divided into two portions: the Queens Road which covers the southern coast from Suva to Lautoka; and the Kings Road which includes the northern coast, also from Suva to Lautoka. Of the two, the Queens Road is the shorter route to Suva (221 km) and is paved (barring any repair work) all the way to Suva. Leisurely driving time is about three hours. The northern route is in poorer shape, longer (265 km) and certainly less travelled by tourists.

In theory the island could be circled in a day, but this would involve maniacal driving and certainly wouldn't be any fun. The best suggestion is to take your time and do it in two, three or even four days, stopping along the way to see all the points of interest and chatting with the local villagers. There are some interesting inland and coastal turn-offs mentioned in this guide but do not expect tar-sealed roads on these detours. Inclement weather (not unusual in Fiji) may make them even worse, so be forewarned. Drivers should also keep a lookout for locals walking along the edge of the highway and ubiquitous stray livestock at any time of the day or night.

For both legs of the tour (the Kings and Queens Road) the starting point will be Nadi Airport. The reason for this is that 99% of visitors arrive at Nadi International Airport first, and thus begin their journey there. Distances will therefore be from the airport to Suva.

The inland routes described here represent only a few of the options. Explorers may want to pick up a copy of Kim Gravelle's *The Fiji Explorer's Handbook*, which has an excellent selection of trips and can be purchased at any bookstore in Fiji.

SOUTHERN COAST: NADI AIRPORT TO SUVA

Newtown Beach (4 km)

As you head towards Nadi town, the turn-off for Newtown Beach will be on your right, about two km off the Queen's Road. This is popular with locals and is a venue for power boat racing.

Access Road to Regent Hotel (7 km)

This is the turn-off to the Regent, Fiji's 'showcase' hotel – the most expensive and luxurious in the country. The point of land on Denarau Beach where the resort is situated (about 5 km off the main road) is also the jumping-off point for cruise vessels to Castaway Island, Plantation Island, Musket Cove and Naitasi.

Nadi Town (9 km)

Nadi town is a hot, dusty agricultural community that has made it big as a 'duty-free' centre, chasing the tourists' buck. For a description of what to do and see here refer to the section on Nadi.

Inland from Nadi: Nausori Highlands Road

The turn-off to the Nausori Highlands is not well marked and the myriad of other unmarked roads makes it difficult to find. Best bet is to get directions from the hotel. Before leaving, the traveller might call the Public Works Department (tel 72 375), the police (tel 70 222) or the Forestry Department (tel 61 085) to get a report on the current road conditions in the mountains.

To get to the highlands road, take the Queens Road as far as Namaka (in between town and the airport) and turn inland; or from Nadi go east from Nadi's main street. If uncertain, ask a policeman – chances are other folks will shrug their heads. Parcel out a day for this trip and take a picnic lunch. The road will be rough but the scenery will be fantastic and well worth the drive. There are several options depending on how adventurous you are. You can go as far as the major junction at Bukuya and then go on to Ba in the north and connect with the Kings Road. This is a long and tortuous route (about a three hour drive) ideally suited for a four-wheel-drive vehicle which can be rented through UTC or Budget. The highlight is passing through Navala Village, deep in the mountains. The *bures* in this settlement are almost exclusively traditional thatched-roof homes, which are becoming a rarity in Fiji. Perhaps in 10 to 15 years they will be a thing of the past. To see this magnificent village perched on the side of a river valley is worth the trip.

The second option is to take the road to its eastern extremity at Bukuya Village and continue south 60 km along the Sigatoka Valley and eventually to Sigatoka town. Be sure and stop at Nakabuta Village along the Sigatoka River road, to purchase pottery. This is also a lovely route, but at least a three-hour drive.

A third option is to go as far as you feel comfortable, eat your picnic lunch and head back to Nadi. The scenery along the way begins with rolling hills studded with cane. About 15 to 20 km inland you get into mountains which tower over deep cleft valleys. Much of the land has been planted with Caribbean pine, which is already yielding valuable building material and may someday be an important export. Deeper into the interior the landscape becomes more rugged, precipitous and wet.

The inhabitants of the occasional villages are poor, eking out a living from their dalo and cassava patches. It is not unusual to see them walking along the road, bush knives at their sides, on their way to the family *teitei* (vegetable patch) or perhaps leading a pair of oxen. Some residents of the area, mounted on horses, hunt wild pigs using only bush knives and dogs to catch their prey. After school, children will be making the often long trek back to their homes. Perhaps you will see them toting their books, or village women with prawn nets heading for a stream.

Seashell Cove (37 km)
This is an inexpensive resort (see Places to Stay section under Nadi) highly recommended for backpackers or campers. It is located on Momi Bay adjacent to a fine public beach. Seashell Cove is also a jumping-off spot by boat for Tavarua Island, the only surfing resort in Fiji.

Uciwai Beach (39 km)
About two km before the Momi Gun turn-off is Uciwai Rd. The beach is about 5.5 km from the highway. Situated in the midst of cane fields, the area is perfect for a day's outing. There is also a racetrack with horse racing every other Sunday.

Momi Guns (41 km)
The Momi Guns are a WW II battery constructed in 1941 by the New Zealand army. They have been restored by the Fiji National Trust to their full camouflaged glory. The six-inch coastal defence guns had a range of 19 km and are attended to by several lonely caretakers who sometimes never see a tourist all day. The guns, as you might expect, were placed on a hill and the view is glorious; worthy of a picnic lunch. They are located about nine km off the main highway, a 10-minute drive down a winding dirt road (which was once the original Queens Road). The turn-off on the main road is not clearly marked other than 'Momi.' To get to the gun site, bear to your right through the Fijian and Indian settlements. There is intermittent public transportation to the villages from the main road but it stops nine km short of the battery. Note that in the hills cane land is beginning to be replaced by pine. The park is open seven days a week and admission is free. There are toilets, drinking water and plenty of parking space.

Natadola Beach (43 km)
This is probably the nicest beach on Viti Levu, isolated from any resorts and thus seldom visited by tourists. It has become known in surfing circles as having decent breaking waves and is also used surreptitiously by campers. Swimmers be advised that large waves break on the beach, which is great for body surfing but dangerous if you're not strong in this department. Hunting for shells here is great too. In theory you can camp here, but there have been problems with thefts by unruly locals and even a recorded instance of rape. I definitely do not recommend that you camp here – better to

picnic instead and even picnickers should not turn their back on their belongings while frolicking in the surf. Lock away all valuables in your car before taking leave.

The beach is accessible by public transportation from Nadi (buses leave at 4.30 pm) or Sigatoka (buses leave at 11.30 am); however, there is 20-minute three-km hike from the bus stop on the main road to the beach. To get there watch for the sign for Batiri. A few km further on, just over the crest of a hill, is Maro, where you turn right and continue toward the coast for about eight km. Turn left and cross a single-lane bridge and continue for another couple of km and there you are.

Natadola Beach is also the terminus for the new Coral Coast Railway. Here day trippers have a chance to enjoy their lunch, hike and return that afternoon by rail.

Vista Point (45 km)
Top the hill where a road sign warns you of a steep grade ahead. To the left are the green mountains and to the right below is the translucent blue reef. The resort island adjacent to the shore is Yanuca, where the Fijian Resort is located.

Cuvu Beach (58.5 km)
Those staying at the Fijian Resort may want to check out this beach. Walk or drive 1.5 km from the hotel to an unposted turn-off on the ocean side of the road. Continue another two km down the road and you'll be on Cuvu Beach – a great white sand beach with plenty of shade trees.

Fijian Resort (60 km)
This is another fine resort and is constructed on Yanuca Island, a tiny islet connected by a man-made bridge. This area is roughly the beginning of what is known as the 'Coral Coast' – that part of Fiji that stretches to Pacific Harbour.

Sand Dunes (68 km)
The sand dunes, located near Kulukulu village (about two km outside of Sigatoka town) rank as among the most beautiful sights in Fiji. Take the Kulukulu turn-off a few hundred metres and park the car to climb the dunes, which are 30 to 45 metres high. The undulating dunes look like something out of the Arabian nights. They hug the coastline for several km and their soft sand is as fine as flour. The tops of these sand hillocks afford a beautiful vista of green mountains to the east and the ocean to the west. Some of them have been planted with vegetation to resist erosion, while others near the roadside are being stripped of their sand for building materials. Occasionally you may see shards of ancient pottery poking through the sand. If you happen to find some, do not remove them from the beach – they are protected by law. Also, the surf may look inviting but it is treacherous. Drownings are tragically frequent.

Sigatoka Town (70 km)
Sigatoka is another sleepy market town and a duty-free centre. It is characterised by a huge mosque and the mighty Sigatoka River which flows through its centre. See the section on Sigatoka and the Coral Coast.

Sigatoka Valley (75 km)
This valley, known as the 'Salad Bowl' of Fiji, ranks with the Nausori Highlands as among some of the most magnificent scenery on the island. Follow the main road into Sigatoka town, then turn left and follow the river valley road about 20 km. The Sigatoka River ranks second in size and importance among the rivers of Viti Levu. It rises near Nadarivatu in the Nausori Highlands and flows some 136 km to the coast.

The Sigatoka River divides the rich valley into two distinct agricultural areas. The government stipulates that half the valley must be used for growing dalo (taro root), tavioka (cassava), corn, tomatoes, lettuce, green peppers, tobacco, cabbage, passion fruit and other vegetable or fruit crops. During harvest time the crops are transported down the river on handmade *bilibili* (bamboo rafts), on small boats or via truck to Sigatoka, where they are sent to other markets around the country. The eastern side of the valley is utilised for sugar cane. The government's reasoning is that if left to the farmers, all the rich valley land would be used to grow cane exclusively, or whatever crop fetches the highest price. Fiji would thus be without other important produce because of the whims of supply and demand. Farmers are restricted to growing no more than 15 acres of cane to make sure that no one crop monopolises the land.

Sigatoka marks the end of the cane-growing region. From here on precipitation begins to increase and the foliage becomes greener and denser.

Travelling up the valley road, you should first stop at the agricultural station (about seven km from town) and the nearby pottery village of Nakabuta. Continuing on up another five km or so, the road takes a turn to the east at Raiwaqa (towards the Yalavou Beef Scheme), which makes for an interesting detour. About four km along this route is an accessible bat cave. Ask around for directions. Back on the main road there are several other options. You can follow the valley road another 35 km up to a northern junction (a left-hand turn) a few km past the village of Tuvu. This will take you to the major junction at Bukuya Village. At this point, you can continue north to Ba or west to the Nausori Highlands and back to Nadi. Both rides are gorgeous. The northern route is a bit rougher and would be better negotiated with a four-wheel-drive vehicle.

The second option is to continue along the Sigatoka River Road (sticking to your right) to the bridge beyond the village of Keiyasi. Past the bridge are two interesting points. The first (and much closer to the bridge) is a cave about an hour's hike from

the village of Natuatuacoko. Ask around and the villagers will probably be happy to show you this cave, which was used as a fortress by local tribes during the Colo Wars of 1876. If they take the time to show you around, you should offer them a suitable gift of money or groceries. The second point of interest is reached by taking the road to the end of the line, beyond the village of Korolevu. From there you walk to Namoli – an old-style, thatched-roof community. When visiting the area you should not just barge into the village, but should wait until you're invited and come with suitable gifts.

At this point you can simply turn back to Sigatoka or double back to the junction described above and continue along the interior.

Korotogo Village (77 km)

Crow's Nest (77.5 km)

This hotel is owned by a pioneer in the Fiji Hotel industry, Paddy Doyle, one of the men who helped build the Mocambo and the Fijian. It is moderately priced and recommended as an overnight rest stop. Next door is the Casablanca, a pizzeria that is worth dining at.

Reef Hotel (78.5 km)

Korolevu Village (101 km)

There is an airstrip here and a nearby waterfall to visit. The falls, called Savu-na-matelaya, can be reached either on horseback through arrangement with the local hotels or on foot from Biasevu Village, about one km from the airstrip. Villagers charge F$1 per person to guide you to the falls and a hot spring in the vicinity.

Hideaway Resort (102 km)

Naviti (102.5 km)

Here the road crosses the mouth of the Sovi River, which has created a beautiful river valley. Nearby is a fine half-moon beach very close to the Naviti Beach Resort. Along the road you pass villages with tin-roof shacks which have replaced the traditional thatched *bures*. Keep an eye out for entrepeneurs who have set up coconut or fruit stands.

Vatulele Island

Thirty-two km offshore from Korolevu lies Vatulele, a small island (about 31 square km in area) which in places is honeycombed with caves. In one of these caves, Korolamalama, are large numbers of the creatures Vatulele is best known for – red prawns. Called *ua bua* or 'cooked prawns' for their already-been-cooked colour, they are sacred and no one is permitted to touch them. According to tradition they can be called to the surface by the villagers, much like sharks and turtles can be called up in other parts of Fiji.

There are no facilities for overnight guests on Vatuele but there may be day trips available from the Naviti Resort. Ask at the tour desk for information.

Hyatt Regency (103 km)

Another of the top resorts in Fiji.

Man Friday Resort (113 km)

This small resort is perched on a hilltop with a magnificent view of the beach and the crystal-clear water over the reef below. Even if you don't stay here, on a sunny day the drive is worthwhile to admire the vista.

Naboutini Village (113 km)

At the time of writing the road near the village is still under repair for about a km and may well be when you are travelling on it. At low tide you can see spear fishermen walking along the mud flats stalking their prey.

Serua Island (123 km)

This tiny island is on the far boundary of the Serua district, which is the end of the Coral Coast.

Qaloa Village (143 km)

Near the village is a famous mission school. The area was also a favourite vacation spot for Fijian statesman Ratu Sukuna. His summer cottage is about one km from the school grounds.

Coral Coast Christian Camp/Beach (148 km)

These motel units and dorm facilities are clean, comfortable and may be used by the average tourist. However, keep in mind that this is not a place for drinking or dancing. Across the way is a popular beach – the closest to Suva. You are also within walking distance of Pacific Harbour. Rates are F$15 double.

Pacific Harbour (148 km)

The 480-hectare Pacific Harbour complex consists of the Beachcomber Hotel, villas, an 18-hole golf course and the Cultural Centre and Marketplace. (See 'Around Suva' section for more information.)

Navua Delta (158 km)

The delta is a rich agricultural region. Readily visible are fields of corn, family plots and grazing cattle. Wooden shacks on the farmland are typical residences. From 1906 to 1922 the area was the site of a sugar mill and the land you see was mostly planted with cane. However, it was found that the sugar content was much higher in sunnier areas, and this is seldom a sunny place. Dairy farming and rice growing have since taken the place of sugar in the Navua region. Inland along the river are spectacular gorges shrouded in mist like a Chinese painting and serrated mountains that rise like spires.

Beqa Island

South of the Navua Delta (10 km) is the island of Beqa, best known as the home of Fiji's firewalkers. It is a compact island, seven km in both directions, and is visible for quite a distance along the coastal drive. There are eight villages, but only those from Rukua, on the west coast, are

Top: Boat (FVB)
Bottom: *Jubilee II* Ovalau ferry off-loading at Natovi, Viti Levu (RK)

Top: Mixing *yaqona* in Taveuni (RK)
Bottom: Warriors in traditional *yaqona* ceremony at Savusavu, Vanua Levu (RK)

custodians of secrets connected with the firewalking ceremony. Thanks to their unusual skills, Beqans are gainfully employed (at least on a part-time basis) throughout the resort industry as fire-walkers. Boats leave regularly from the Navua wharf for Beqa but there are no facilities for visitors on the island; so unless you're invited, it's better to try and arrange a day trip with the captain of the launch rather than an overnight excursion.

Orchid Island (188 km)

A miniature zoo/museum combined with a little showbiz, Orchid Island is fun and informative. Note the brick-red soil on the road cuts and the mangrove swamps along the coast. (For more information on Orchid Island see the 'Around Suva' section.)

Suva (197 km)

The capital of Fiji and a world unto itself. (See Suva section).

NORTHERN COAST: NADI AIRPORT TO SUVA

There are a few things to know about the road whether you decide to drive yourself or take a bus or hired taxi. The first is that it is much more hazardous than the southern route. The stretch of Queens Road from Nadi to Lautoka and the stretch of Kings Road from Nausori to Suva are the busiest in the country. These two stretches are paved and well monitored by police, but the accident toll along these roads is staggering, so extra caution is needed. Distances begin at Nadi Airport.

The Guns of Lomolomo (7 km)

Past Nadi Airport the rugged hills of the Sabeto Mountain end nearly at the foot of Queens Road. At this juncture watch for a school building. On the bluff above the school are two WW II coastal defence guns. Unlike the battery at Momi Bay, these have not been taken over by the National Trust and thus have been left in the state in which they were abandoned

after the war. The view from the top of the gun emplacement is outstanding. For those travelling by bus, the Lomolomo site is easier to reach than Momi Bay. Take a Lautoka or Viseisei bus from Nadi and ask the driver to let you off at the school. From there it is a short hike up the road at the right of the school grounds to the top of the hill.

Viseisei Village (9.5 km)

Around the bend from Lomolomo (on your left) is Viseisei. Legend has it that Viseisei Village is the oldest settlement in the country. Fijians say their ancestors first came to Fiji in great ocean-going canoes and landed at nearby Vuda Point. Coincidentally, the first Christian mission-aries also landed at Viseisei.

There is a crafts centre at the Nadi side of the village. You can stop there and ask if someone can take you to see the centennial monument (1835-1935) marking the arrival of the missionaries. Opposite the monument is the Chief or Tui Vuda's *bure*. The Tui Vada also happens to be the Minister of State for Forests. In the middle of the village is a large Methodist Church with a monument commemorating the arrival of the missionaries. Usually a small tip to the person who has shown you around the village is proper. Incidentally, after having visited this village you'll be in good company. Queen Elizabeth II, Princess Margaret and Prince Charles have also visited Viseisei.

Vuda Point/Anchorage Beach Resort (12.6 km)

The turn-off to Vuda Point and the Anchorage Beach Resort is on the left near the top of the first steep hill. About three km down, you pass several large oil storage tanks and then the road becomes very sandy. The beach is a short walk away (through a cane field between two fresh-water ponds). This is traditionally where the first Melanesians landed. There is not much to see, but the point is a popular picnic spot for families in the area.

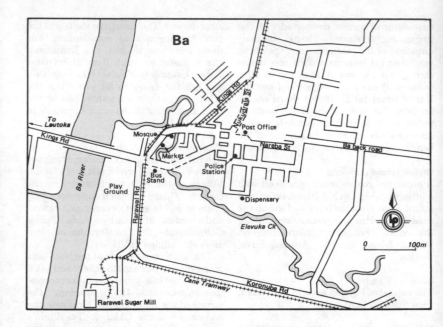

Situated on Vuda Point two km off the main highway, the Anchorage is one of two hotels between Nadi Airport and Lautoka. Considering the moderate price, the beautiful location on a bluff overlooking the sea, and the good restaurant, it is certainly worth considering.

Saweni Beach Hotel/Saweni Beach (15 km)

This is the only beachside hotel between Lautoka and Nadi. It has 12 self-contained units and a bar, but no restaurant. There are infrequent buses to Saweni Beach, but it might be easier to catch a Lautoka-bound bus; ask the driver to let you off at the junction and walk the two km past the cane fields and goat farms. The beach area has a parking lot, shade trees, toilets, picnic tables and a 'so-so' beach.

Lautoka (24 km)

The Port of Lautoka (see section on Lautoka) or 'Sugar City' is Fiji's second largest town and is the home of one of the largest sugar mills in the southern hemisphere. There are a number of popular day trips from Lautoka for visitors (see Getting Around section in this chapter).

Lololo Pine Forest (34 km)

Pronounced Lo-loló, this picnic area is nestled in a pine forest above Lautoka on the edge of a large creek that has been dammed to create a swimming pool. With plenty of picnic tables, it is a good place to get above the heat of the coast in summertime. The water is cool and refreshing, and with the pines you might easily think you were transported to the foothills of California.

To get there, take the Lololo bus from the Lautoka station. They run several times a day but make sure you check the time for the last returning bus, and then get to the stop a few minutes early.

By car or motorcycle: Head east on

Kings Road about 10 km from Lautoka, and look for the sign on the left side of the road pointing to the turn-off, which is on the right. Follow the road until you come to the large timber yard at Drasa. Just past the yard the road forks. Bear left down a steep hill and follow the road until you reach the edge of the Lololo pine station. You'll see the picnic area on the right. The distance from the main road to the pine station is about eight km.

From there you could also visit a forest fire watch station which offers an incredible view of the north-west side of Viti Levu and the Yasawa Islands off the coast. The trip is worthwhile only on a clear day because the road is very rough and not recommended for small cars or vehicles loaded down with passengers or luggage. To get there, go past the picnic area to an intersection at the centre of the station. Take a left turn and follow the road to the top of the mountain. The fire lookout tower will be on the left.

Ba (62 km)
Ba is a classic Indian sugar town that most tourists drive through. While the town's economy has always revolved around sugar, in recent years several small manufacturing firms have started up here. A walk through the main shopping area shows you what a 'blue collar' community this is. You can visit the Rarawai Sugar Mill on the edge of Ba. The most noticeable landmark in town is the large mosque near the Ba River in the centre of town.

There is only one hotel in town, the 13-room *Ba Hotel*, which has a bar and restaurant. Eateries include an inexpensive Chinese and Indian restaurant on the main street.

Tavua (91 km)
This is a relaxed market town where you can catch the buses for Vatukoula, Nadarivatu and Monasavu. If you are driving, visit the Tavua Hotel for refreshments or try the colonial-style local pub.

The Tavua Hotel has a classic 'South Seas' hotel feel about it and is far from the beaten tourist track. It is one of the best hotels along the Kings Road in which to 'overnight'. The Tavua town market is a good place to stock up on fresh fruit. If you plan to spend time in Nadarivatu, this is the last chance to buy supplies.

Inland from Ba & Tavua
Navala Village
The picturesque village of Navala, one of the last in Viti Levu with thatched roofs, is a two-hour (26 km) drive on rough road into the mountains above Ba. Your best bets for transport are a four-wheel-drive vehicle or a trail bike. The road is passable by ordinary car but the going can be brutal.

From Navala it is possible to continue on to Bukuya, where the road forks either to the Sigatoka Valley (it's about 66 km to Sigatoka at this point) or the Nausori Highlands and continues on to Nadi.

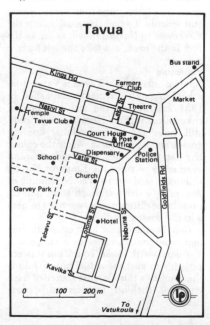

These are all-day drives, so pack food and be sure to have a full tank of fuel. For motorcyclists it is possible to purchase 'white benzene' from some of the village shops if needed. Do not make the trip on Sunday! The villagers in this neck of the wood are very religious and most people are in church or in repose most of the day. Even if it's not Sunday, don't simply stroll into the village and begin taking photos. The local chief will not be charmed. Your best bet is to stop short (on the Ba side of the road) and shoot from across the river – which gives you a great perspective.

To get there, from the Ba side of the bridge make a right turn on Rarawai Rd. Turn left at the next junction, just outside the sugar mill. Follow the road about two km where it forks and take the right fork.

Note An interesting alternative to the Kings Road to Tavua and Vatukoula is the 'Ba Back Road'. Along this road are sugar cane farms, rural Indian settlements and schools. To find this road, follow the directions to Navala above, as far as the fork in the road, and take the left fork.

Vatukoula

Nine km inland from Tavua is Vatukoula, a gold-mining settlement established in 1934 and one of the last bastions of colonialism in Fiji. Here the expatriate still rules the private clubs, bowling greens and a golf course. While the colour bar has faded since independence, and even more so since the Emperor Mining Company sold out to Western Mining of Australia, a drive through town quickly reveals the difference between the miners and the bosses.

Gold is mined here both open-pit style and underground. There are excursions to Vatukoula with Rosie Tours, but it is not possible to visit the actual mine. Gold is the country's third largest source of hard currency (behind tourism and sugar cane).

Nadarivatu

Approximately 30 km from Tavua is Nadarivatu, which is one of the nicest mountain getaway spots in Viti Levu. High in the mountains above the heat and surrounded by pine forests, the highlands of Nadarivatu are a far cry from the stereotypical 'South Seas' featured in most brochures. From Vatukoula follow the main road through the town. At the 'T' intersection, go left and at the next junction take a right. The road will take you on a dramatic 366-metre climb to the Nadarivatu Plateau. If you decide not to go to Nadarivatu via Vatukoula, the main highway to Nadarivatu is 2.5 km east of Tavua on the Kings Road. A large sign marks the road on the right if you are coming from Tavua. If you are coming west from Rakiraki the sign is not so apparent, so keep an eye out.

The nicest place to stay is the *Forestry Rest House*. Constructed originally for expat bosses at the gold mine (so their families could escape the summer heat), this large, rambling structure is now run by the Forestry Department. At F$4 per person per night the price is right, but make sure you have reservations in advance with the Forestry Department in Lautoka or Suva (tel 61 085). If you're told it's booked, ask if you can share a room until a vacant one is available. The house comfortably sleeps seven, cooking utensils are supplied, and there is a small shop nearby for basics. The best idea is to stock up on provisions in Tavua or Ba before you get there. Be prepared to cook on a wood-burning stove or benzene primus.

Nadarivatu is one of the few areas in Fiji where camping is permitted and the pine forest makes quite a nice setting. Make absolutely sure you have a permit from the forestry people first – the 'DC' (district officer) has been known to be very tough on squatters.

Hike to Fire Watch One of the nicest short hikes you can take in Nadarivatu is a three-km trek to the fire watch post on the mountaintop behind the Forestry Department training centre, across the road from the rest house. The post is easily seen from the rest house; follow the trail past the training centre to the governor general's swimming hole. From there the trail winds through dense vegetation to the peak. The view from the top is fantastic but try to make it in the morning before the clouds move in. Stop for a dip at the swimming hole on the way back. Allow 2½ hours for the climb and back.

Hike to Mt Victoria About 10 km beyond the Forestry Rest House is Mt Victoria (Tomanivi), Fiji's highest peak at 1323 metres. Three large rivers originate in the shadow of this mountain — the Sigatoka; and the Wainimala and Wainibuka, which eventually join to form the Rewa River. The bridge at Navai Village (about eight km past Nadarivatu) is where the trail begins. Follow a wide track about 100 metres and take the trail on the right to the top. Stay on the main trail; markers pointing elsewhere may be misleading. The top is almost continuously cloud-covered, so don't expect a great view. However, you will be able to tell your friends that you hiked to the summit of the highest mountain in Fiji. Allow five to six hours for the climb. Guides are available at the village.

Navai Area
Nadarivatu translates as 'stone bowl.' It is easy to understand why when you see the large valley near Navai. In recent years that valley has become known as a major agricultural area, producing lettuce, cauliflower, cabbage and carrots which thrive here because of the cool climate. In 1938, during the colonial era, a potato-growing scheme was established in the Navai area but the programme failed.

Koro-ni-O
Another 25 km down the road from Navai is Koro-ni-O or 'village in the clouds', an apt name. Today this area is headquarters

for the F$234-million Monasavu hydro-electric scheme, the largest development project ever undertaken by the government (see section on Monasavu Dam). An 82-metre dam was built on the Nanuka River to provide water which is piped down to four 20-megawatt turbines on the Wailoa River, 625 metres below the level of the dam. The lake behind the dam is the larger of Fiji's two lakes (the other is on Taveuni). Fishing is possible in this lake, if Malayan carp is to your liking.

There are buses from Koro-ni-O to Suva across the interior of the island. It is an interesting but rough ride. If you're thinking of driving this stretch with an ordinary car this is positively the worst road on the island and the rental agency will not let you near their cars if they catch wind of your plans.

Yaqara (107 km)
Halfway between Tavua and Rakiraki is Yaqara, Fiji's biggest cattle ranch — a 7000-hectare estate with 7000 head of cattle. Visitors should not be surprised to see Fijian cowboys astride horses and wearing Western hats, rounding up cattle.

Rakiraki (132 km)
From Tavua to Rakiraki is a long and dusty 41 km. A few km east of Tavua the paved road ends. The government has been slowly paving a few km each year, but the project is still far from completion.

About 10 km before Rakiraki, watch for Navatu Rock. It is a small island about 1½ km from the coast, jutting about 180 metres from sea level. Fijian legend holds that this is the jumping-off point for disembodied spirits journeying into the afterlife.

If locals tell you Rakiraki is where you can refuel, get a tyre repaired or buy supplies for your stay at Nananu-i-Ra Island, they are really referring to the town of Vaileka, which is one km off Kings Road. There is a well-marked triangle with a sign pointing toward Suva, and another to Vaileka.

Just prior to the triangle, on the south side of the road, is the tomb of Ratu Udre Udre, a chief famous for his appetite for human flesh. This gentleman is said to have consumed 999 human beings before his death in the late 19th century. The stones surrounding the base of his tomb are how he kept tally of his grisly meals.

Continue on Kings Road three km past the Vaileka turn-off to the *Rakiraki Hotel*, the only accommodation (other than Nananu-i-Ra Island) between Tavua and Korovou (Tailevu province) 107 km away. The hotel is a good place to overnight for those making the round-the-island circuit. The large lunches and dinners are well worth the moderate cost of F$3-6. For eating on the cheap there is also a few mediocre curry houses in Vaileka. Prices are between F$2 and F$4 for a meal.

Turn-off to Volivoli or Ellington Wharf (142 km)

This junction is about five km past the Rakiraki Hotel. From here you catch the boat to Nananu-i-Ra (see Places to Stay section under Kings Road) and ferries to the outer islands (see schedule in Getting Around section). Snorkelling is so-so on Nananu-i-Ra but fishing and shelling are first class.

Naiserelagi (177 km)

This village, about 45 km east of Rakiraki, is the home of the church with a mural of the 'Black Christ' by French artist Jean Charlot. This is an exquisite work, blending Fijian motifs with the teachings of Christ. Charlot painted the mural in 1962 at the invitation of Monsignor Franz Wasner, the then caretaker of the mission. (Prior to coming to Fiji Monsignor Wasner was at one time the singing teacher of the Von Trapp family of *Sound of Music* fame.) The mural was painstakingly completed by the dim lamplight of the church – apparently Charlot had a great deal of trouble applying the fresh mortar to the wall.

The central image of the mural is the figure of a black Christ on the cross wearing tapa cloth around his waist. He is being paid homage to by a number of Fijian figures. In the immediate background are breadfruit leaves and fruit which express his close relationship with nature and according to Charlot's wife are a vital symbol in the fresco. The Fijian word for breadfruit, *uto*, is also used for 'heart.' At Christ's feet is a *tanoa* or kava bowl, symbolising the Eucharist. To his right are a child in a mission school uniform; St Peter Chanel (a martyred Saint in the Pacific); Father Mataca, the first Fijian (Catholic) priest; a Fijian woman bringing Christ an offering of woven mats; and a Fijian man offering Christ a *tabua* (whale's tooth), the highest form of respect a Fijian can confer. To Christ's left an Indian woman is portrayed offering a garland of flowers and an Indian farmer is pictured with a pair of oxen. Also shown are St Francis Xavier (whom the Church is named after) and an acolyte.

According to accounts, when the mural was complete the entire parish of Naserelagi had a feast in Charlot's honour. Cows were slaughtered and the traditional yaqona ceremony was observed. As in the mural, women presented the artist with mats.

After visiting what has to be the finest non-Fijian work of art in Fiji, you should not forget to drop some money into the donation box at the door. Proceeds are used to maintain the church.

There is no express bus to this settlement but a local bus will let you off near the church if you ask the driver. Visit in the early part of the day because buses are less frequent in the afternoon. Those driving may find the church easy to miss. Watch for Nanukuloa village; Naiserelagi is the next village to the east. Once there, keep an eye out for the Ra Maternity Clinic. Take an uphill right towards the Navunibitu Catholic Mission School.

A few km past Nanukuloa the road turns inland, leaving the sugar cane and coconut trees behind. Now the vegetation becomes lush and dense. For approximately the next 80 km the Kings Road follows first the Wainibuka River and then the smaller Waimaro River all the way to Korovou. Stop at one of the many fruit stands along the way and sample mandarins, oranges, bananas, pineapple and watermelon. Buses usually stop at a choice fruit stand or two so riders will have the opportunity to stock up.

Wailotua Village No 1 – Home of Snake God (216 km)

Fijian legend is rife with snakes. About 23 km west of Korovou is a cave (formerly a meeting place for chiefs) known as the 'Home of the Snake God.' As you approach Korovou from the west, watch for Wailotua Village No 1, on the left-hand side of the road. Enquire about the cave and someone will show you around, admission is F$2. Ask to be shown the six-headed snake (stalactite).

Waterfall (225 km)

Nine km past the cave, a small bridge crosses a large stream. Keep your eyes open and you'll see a wonderful waterfall here.

Korovou (239 km)

There are nine villages named Korovou (including one previously mentioned on the Queens Road) on Viti Levu alone, but for our purposes Korovou (which translates as 'new village') is in the Tailevu province. This is the centre of Fiji's dairy industry, which was established by several English veterans at the end of WW I. In a magnanimous gesture, the local Fijian chiefs gave the 'European' farmers 4000 hectares of the finest land in the province to 'keep forever.' Some of the descendants of those veterans still run a few of the dairy farms around Korovou. During the period immediately prior to independence many of the farmers began selling their land to the highest bidders, in most cases Indians. This incensed the Fijian chiefs, who said that if the Europeans did not want the land anymore, it should be given back to the villages. The government has since worked out a system whereby as the original farms come up for sale, the former native landowners have the first chance at purchasing them.

Near Korovou is Natovi Landing, the terminus for the Ovalau and Vanua Levu ferries.

In Korovou, a nondescript one-horse town and government centre, the *Tailevu Hotel* offers inexpensive accommodation. It is a good place to stop along the way for a break and wash down some of the dust with a cold Fiji Bitter. It's wise to drink in the main part of the hotel; the public bar around back for the locals can get a bit wild for the visitor.

From Korovou it's 31 km to Nausori and paved roads once again.

Nausori (270 km)

Only 19 km from Suva, Nausori grew as a city around Fiji's second sugar mill (1881-1959), located where the Rewa Rice Mill now stands. The golf course and some of the old colonial homes constructed for expatriates are about all that remain of Nausori's days as a sugar mill town. The end of the sugar mill marked the final attempt at growing sugar on the eastern side of Viti Levu. Today Nausori is much like Ba, a working-class town and agricultural centre. The airport (which serves Suva) is located in Nausori, a 20-minute drive from the capital.

Near Nausori are three landings from which you can hire punts or 'water taxis' to explore the Rewa Delta or to visit snorkelling areas or Toberua Resort. The landings are Nakelo, Wainibokasi and Bau. Buses leave frequently for these points from the Nausori bus station. Nakelo Landing is where boats depart for Toberua Island, a very fine resort.

Bau

Bau Landing is a few metres from tiny Bau Island, to this day the seat of traditional power among native Fijians (see History section). Fiji's recently retired governor general, Ratu Sir George Cakobau, is still considered 'the Paramount Chief' of Fijians and lives on Bau. The island is not a place where visitors may casually drop in – it is in fact against the law to visit Bau without permission from someone who lives on the island or from the Ministry of Fijian Affairs. This applies to locals and visitors alike.

Bau has the oldest church in the country, a fascinating cemetery for chiefly families and an impressive stone near the church that was once used to crush skulls in the days of cannibalism.

If you really want to visit the island, the best way to go about this is to try and befriend someone on the bus ride to Bau Landing in hopes that the person may offer to show you around. Make sure and take a large bundle of waka (yaqona root) with you and dress conservatively (this applies especially to women).

At certain times all non-Bauans are forbidden on the island, so don't attempt to reach it without permission; and if by luck you get there, never walk around unescorted. Some tourists reportedly have tried this but it is a grave insult. Getting on the wrong side of a high Fijian chief is akin to getting on the wrong side of the law. In many remote parts of Fiji the chief is still the one who lays down the law. Even the courts have ruled that in some cases a chief's word takes precedence over the law books.

Naililili Mission (272 km)

Naililili is the largest church in Fiji. It was built at the turn of the century by Father Rougier, who left the priesthood later to become a well-known trader in Tahiti. Apparently Rougier accidentally inherited a tidy sum from a down-and-out convict from New Caledonia who was in reality heir to a fortune. At that point he left organised religion to seek a more worldly life. To get to his church take the first left at the junction past the Nausori Bridge. Water taxis cost F$2 to cross the river.

GETTING THERE

The vast majority of travellers arriving in Fiji by air will come first to Nadi International Airport. See the introductory Getting There section about flying to Fiji. Nadi and Nausori (the airport near the capital of Suva) are the two major hubs of air travel throughout Fiji. The visitor heading to the more remote islands via plane or boat will find it necessary to travel to Suva in order to catch the right flight or vessel. Otherwise, the majority of tourist destinations can be reached from Nadi. See the introductory Getting Around section for details on domestic flights and sailings, or see individual sections for details of transport there from Viti Levu.

GETTING AROUND

Tours Rosie Tours' series of 'Road Tours' that leave from the Lautoka/Nadi area are recommended for the individual who doesn't want to drive but would like to see outlying areas not served by public transportation. The best of these trips are the Nausori Highlands Tour and the Sigatoka Drive. Both visit inland areas that offer spectacular vistas not usually seen by the visitor.

The Nausori Highlands tour begins in the sugar cane lands past farmhouses and mosques, progresses to rolling hills, and culminates in the craggy green mountains overlooking the sea. The road is bumpy but you will see bucolic countryside that hopefully developers won't get to. Cost of the half-day tour is F$15.

The Sigatoka tour also takes the visitor through caneland and the verdant Sigatoka Valley, the salad bowl of Fiji. The drive continues into the mountains through the planted pine forests above Sigatoka, passing several villages. For the benefit of shoppers, the tour stops in Sigatoka town to check out the duty-free stores. I realise that the visitor may feel assaulted with superlatives as far as Fiji goes, but the varied landscape on this drive is breathtaking and unlike anything else in the

South Pacific. Cost for the all-day Sigatoka Drive is F$26 and includes lunch. Phone 72 607 for more information.

If you are down Sigatoka way (either staying at the Fijian or a nearby resort), the Baravi River Cruise up the Sigatoka River is an alternative way to see the salad bowl of Fiji and catch a bit of local colour. There is a pickup at the Fijian Hotel or you can simply get to Sigatoka Jetty at 9.30 am or 2.30 pm for the twice-daily cruises. There are great views of Fijian villages and agriculture on the banks. You'll see people fishing or collecting freshwater shellfish and watch *bilibilis* (bamboo rafts) loaded with produce ply the waters en route to town. Twenty minutes after the vessel's departure, you call on Naroro Village for a traditional yaqona ceremony and *meke* (dancing). Price is F$12 per person. Call 50155 or ask at your tour desk for more information. There is another, newer river trip called the Pioneer Cruise up the river which also has had good reports.

In the more offbeat arena, Wilderness Adventures (which also departs from the Lautoka/Nadi area) has one of the more creative tours in Fiji – a rafting trip down the Ba River. Visitors are taken to the headwaters of the river – an area completely removed from the tourist mainstream – and float down the white water on Avon rafts. The river winds through narrow gorges and past villages. Along the way the rafts are tied up and lunch is heartily consumed. While this doesn't match the whitewater rapids of North America, the ride is exciting enough and the landscape is certainly exotic. There is an abundance of birdlife along the river and the trip is definitely recommended for folks with an ornithological bent. Cost is F$55 (including lunch).

This same firm, which is a branch of Burnsmoore Travel in Suva, also has less adventurous but equally interesting day-trips for those on the Suva side of Viti Levu. Their Navua excursion is particularly interesting. The boat travels up the rich Navua delta past the grazing lands of the floodplain and into the deep river gorges to an altitude of 1000 metres. At this point the air is thick with mist while sheer cliffs and spires rise almost vertically from the valley floor like a Chinese landscape. If you are in Suva and want to get out of your hotel room and see something unusual, this is the trip to take. Cost is F$29 for adults and F$14 for children, phone 313 500 for information. At this time Adventure Tours is in the process of negotiating rights to raft the river in the interior of Viti Levu, starting from the village of Naitavoli in the Naitasiri region. I've been on this tour and highly recommend it.

The only true 'adventure travel' programme operated in Fiji is a two-week trip put on by Pacific Outdoor Adventures, a Honolulu-based tour operator. The basic programme, called 'Fiji Shakedown,' includes camping, exploring, snorkelling, ocean kayaking, and natural history tours of four islands (Viti Levu, Vanua Levu, Qamea and Taveuni), all accompanied by guides. Natural history tours include mountain and stream hikes, village visits, reefwalks, shelling and bird watching. The itinerary, which covers a lot of geographical territory, seems to cover as much natural history and cultural aspects as you can cram into a two-week period. The price of US$1499 includes round-trip airfare from Honolulu (add US$100 from Los Angeles or San Francisco), eight nights of hotel accommodation, seven nights of camping on remote beaches, all meals (except two), all ground transfers, and inter-island airfare. Phone 808 988 2188 or write PO Box 61609, Honolulu, Hawaii 96822, USA for more information.

Inland Safari Tours (tel 312 129) has the only guided hiking tour in all of Fiji. The tour is combined with a visit to Levuka (the old capital) and two nights on Motoriki (a beautiful island near Ovalau). It is a good programme at a very low price. Inland Safari will meet you at Nadi Airport, put you up in a hotel for the night, and pick you up the next day for a chartered bus ride along the Kings Road up into the hill country between Tavua and Rakiraki. From there it's hiking in the mountains and a series of overnight stays in four different villages for a total of eight nights. From all reports the hiking is not terribly strenuous and Eli of Inland Tours tells me the participants are of all different ages. After the village visits the journey turns to Levuka (via Fiji Air) and Motoriki, where visitors stay in more conventional accommodation. The trip is led by an energetic senior citizen by the name of Eli Nabose, a native of the mountains of Viti Levu. He will not take groups of less than 15, but you are accompanied by four Fijian guides. Cost is F$28.50 per day, meals and transportation included. Write to PO Box 3014, Lami, for more information.

For those wishing to stay in a village without the hiking or outside trips, the best person to contact is Mere Nawaqatabu. Mere has excellent connections with villages throughout Viti Levu, Vanua Levu and Lau. She has spent years taking visitors around the country, including the likes of Sir Edmund Hillary and hosts of journalists from Australia and the United States. She will arrange village stays as well as transportation and food. Her knowledge of both western and Fijian cultures also provides great guidance and insight. As far as I am concerned, there is no better person to take you to a Fijian village than Ms Nawaqatabu. Her tours are F$50 per day, not including transportation and other expenses. She can be contacted by writing Mere Nawaqatabu, Fiji Village Tours, PO Box 3119, Lami. She has no phone but can be contacted through Endeavour Investments (tel 23 103 or 25 913) in Suva.

Day Cruises The vast majority of these cruises are on the western side of Viti Levu and visit the many resort islands of the Mamanucas. While they are not 'adventure travel,' they are fun if you've never been to a small island, and if you're travelling alone they are a fine way to meet people. They range from half– to full-day trips and the price (anywhere from F$32-35) includes lunch. For the visitor with an unplanned day at his/her disposal the day trips are a good thing to do. The following come highly recommended:

South Sea Island Cruises has a half-day sightseeing cruise with pickups at 8 am and noon from all Nadi hotels. They depart at 9 am and 1.30 respectively from Regent Jetty. The boat stops at Plantation Island Resort, Musket Cove, Castaway, Club Naitasi and Mana Island. You can't get off unless you plan to stay; the trip is just a shuttle to drop off and pick up guests. However, the trip does give you a chance to at least see the various resorts and perhaps decide which island appeals aesthetically for a long-term visit. Pack your own lunch on this trip. Drinks are served on board. The boat is the speedy *Island Express*, a catamaran with sundeck and air-conditioned level below.

The Mana Island Cruise, also offered by South Sea Island Cruises, is the above trip aboard the *Island Express*, but you get off at Mana, which might be considered a first choice because it has the best beach in the Mamanuca Islands. Pickup is at 8 am at all Nadi hotels; you'll depart Regent Jetty at 9 am and stay a full day at Mana. Cost is F$34 per person including lunch and transfer. Passengers are dropped off via launch rather than the *Island Express*. The vessel (as above half-day trip) also visits Castaway, Plantation and Musket Cove (which share the same island) and Club Naitasi for other optional day trips. Phone 70 144 or enquire at the tour desk for more information.

Daydream Cruises is a bit offbeat in that it visits Malamala, a 2½-hectare, uninhabited island that is excellent for snorkellers and shell collectors because of the nearby reef. The isolation and the proximity of the reef are the chief advantages of this cruise through the same islands visited by South Sea Island Cruises. Pickup for Daydream Cruises is around 9 am at most Nadi-area hotels; from there the bus goes to Nadi to pause for a half-hour shopping break. At 11.30 the vessel departs for Malamala from Newtown Jetty and an hour later the boat reaches the islet. By 4.30 that afternoon you are back at Newtown Beach, hopefully with a better tan. Despite the shopping trip in Nadi, you still have more beach time on this cruise than on the South Seas Cruises (another advantage) because the boat goes directly to the island instead of shuttling people to other points. Price is F$31 including buffet lunch, which is served on a small *bure* on the island – the only man-made structure there. Phone 72 061 or ask at your tour desk for information.

The Beachcomber Cruise is one of the most popular excursions because it was originated by Dan Costello, one of the pioneer/showmen of modern tourism in Fiji. Pickup from Nadi hotels is around 8 am and departure is from Lautoka Wharf for Beachcomber Island, a tiny resort about 90 minutes' sail away. It is the only budget resort island on the western side and is extremely popular with young travellers. The beach here is nice, there are free glass-bottom boat rides and lunch is a sumptuous buffet. Price with lunch is F$32. If you are considering staying at Beachcomber, the day trip is an opportunity to give it the once over. Phone 61 500 or enquire at the tour desk for information.

Yachting aboard the *Red Velvet* is another option. For F$45 per person (not including a F$5 hotel pickup fee), you can cruise in style on the 44-foot *Red Velvet*, eat a great lunch and even troll off the boat if you like. The boat stops at an uninhabited island where you can sunbathe, swim, shell or snorkel with gear provided by the boat. The *Red Velvet* has the advantage of privacy (if you don't like big crowds) and lets you visit tiny islands that most visitors will never see. These cruises depart only on Sundays and Mondays from the Lautoka wharf. Phone 61 120 for information or ask your hotel's tour desk.

The Plantation Island/Musket Cove Day Trip is an alternative for those who prefer air travel to that of a boat. Flights depart on Sunflower Airlines from Nadi Airport at 8.30 am and 10.30 am to Malololailai Island. Malololailai (which means 'small Malolo Island') is half of a beautiful horseshoe-shaped island separated from the other half by a shallow inlet. Aside from having a beautiful bay, the island has the second best beach (after Mana) in the Mamanuca group. Both Plantation Island and Musket Cove, two very different but excellent resorts, share Malololailai, and a day trip would certainly be a good way to check them out. Cost is F$28, lunch included. There are also a variety of watersports (including windsurfing, snorkelling and water skiing) available, but you must pay extra to rent the gear. Phone 73 016 for information.

The Yasawas

Of all the Fiji islands the Yasawas are perhaps the most archetypally 'South Pacific.' From a distance they suggest a string of blue beads lying on the horizon. Up close they are characteristically steep and precipitous with long stretches of sandy beaches fringed by azure waters. In a word, they are gorgeous, and except for one resort are completely undeveloped. The islands are a major attraction for cruise vessels originating in Lautoka (see 'Getting Around' in this chapter), and several Yasawa villages derive much of their income from the tourist industry. The islands' beauty as a tourist attraction is doubly fortuitous for villagers because arable land is limited. With some crops difficult or even impossible to grow, tourist income is all the more valuable for economic survival. Population of the Yasawas is approximately 2000.

Geography

The Yasawa group is volcanic in origin and comprises six large islands and many smaller ones, having a total area of 135 square km. From a point 40 km north-west of Lautoka, they stretch for over 80 km in a north-north-east direction, forming a broken ribbon of land rarely more than five km wide and generally much less. The principal members of the group are high, their summits ranging from 250 to 600 metres. Except for the south end, the land formation is so straight that a line could be drawn through a map of the islands with a ruler.

Westward of the Yasawas there is an extensive area of unsurveyed water littered with reefs, many of which are still uncharted. The only safe passage for ships is between Yasawa and Round Island to the north. This was the route used by Captain Bligh, though how he managed to find it – especially when one considers he was being chased at the time

by a speedy war canoe filled with cannibals – is a mystery. The maze of barrier reefs lying between the islands and the open sea effectively intercepts ocean currents and prevents the free flow of tidal water into the lagoon, thus creating unfavourable ecological conditions for the growth of coral. Thus there are a few massive formations in the open water but except for the northernmost island there is little coral development. Snorkellers need not fear that lack of coral growth inhibits fish-viewing – snorkelling is excellent.

History

The islands were sighted by Captain Bligh in May 1789, a few days after he began his legendary voyage in the *Bounty's* launch. It was in Yasawa waters that Bligh's tiny boat was pursued by a *drua* (war canoe) which he miraculously managed to elude. Five years later the islands were visited by Captain Barber in the ship *Arthur*, but little seems to have been known of them until 1840, when they were roughly surveyed and charted by officers of the United States Exploring Expedition under Commandant Charles Wilkes.

In the past the residents had the reputation of making fine sail mats, the dry climate being excellent for the production of the best fibre for this purpose. During the mid-19th century the Yasawans were harassed by Tongan raiders who levied tribute of these mats on the islanders or bartered for what they couldn't steal.

For the most part the islands were of little interest to European traders or settlers and for many years they remained one of the most isolated parts of Fiji. During the war the islands were used by the American military as communications outposts. Paradoxically, today they are probably seen by more visitors than any other of Fiji's outer islands.

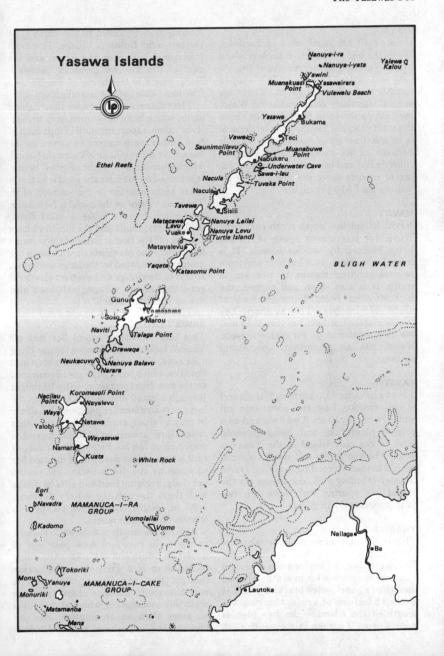

Yasawa Islands

Nanuya-i-ra
Nanuya-i-yata
Yalewa Q Kalou
Yawini
Muanakuasi Point
Yasawairara
Vulawalu Beach
Yasawa
Bukama
Vawea
Teci
Saunimolilevu Point
Muanabuwe Point
Nabukeru
Ethel Reefs
Underwater Cave
Sawa-i-lau
Necula
Tuvaka Point
Nacula
Tavewa
Sisili
Matacawa Levu
Nanuya Lailai
Vuake
Nanuya Levu (Turtle Island)
Matayalevu
Yaqeta
Katasomu Point
BLIGH WATER

Gunu
Leumaoma
Soso
Marou
Naviti
Talaga Point
Drawaqa
Naukacuvu
Nanuya Balavu
Narara

Nacilau Point
Koromasoli Point
Wayalevu
Waya
Natawa
Yalobi
Wayasewa
Namara
Kuata
White Rock
Eori
Navadra
MAMANUCA-I-RA GROUP
Kadomo
Vomolailai
Vomo
Nailaga
Ba
Tokoriki
Monu
Yanuya
MAMANUCA-I-CAKE GROUP
Monuriki
Matamanoa
Lautoka
Mana

WAYA

Located 40 km north-west of Lautoka, Waya, the highest and most broken island in the Yasawas, measures about 6½ km long and almost five km wide – shaped roughly in the form of an 'H.' There are several singularly sharp peaks on Waya, including a towering bluff directly above the main village of Yalobi. This settlement is on the itinerary of many cruise vessels because of its excellent anchorage on Alacrity Bay and beautiful beach. According to reports there are guest *bures* for visitors for F$10 per night.

NAVITI

Naviti Island lies north-north-east from Waya, the intervening space of 13 km being bridged by smaller islands. It is irregular in shape, 14.5 km long and from several hundred metres to five km in width. It is also steep and rugged, the highest point being Vaturuayalewa at about 388 metres. The southern bay (Soso) and the northern bay (Somo Somo) are also regular stops for cruise vessels. Naviti has an important agricultural station.

TAVEWA

Tavewa lies about 1.5 km from Nacula and is only two km long and about one km wide. For many years it was worked as a private plantation, and being freehold land, is the only island in the Yasawas where the visitor doesn't need a special permit to visit. According to author David Stanley (*Finding Fiji*), conditions on the island are spartan but there are two families who take in guests.

YASAWA

This is the northernmost large island of the group to which it gives its name. Yasawa is about 22 km long and is several hundred metres to a km in width – shaped much like a punctuation bracket,]. It has a steep backbone of a ridge that runs the length of the island – the two highest points being Taucake in the south (233

metres) and Cololevu in the north (194 metres) near Bukuma Village. The most traditional village on the island and the seat of the Yasawa group is Yasawa-i-Rara, which is the home of Tui Yasawa (the head chief of the island group).

The villagers are noted for their fishing skills, which have developed from necessity because important staple crops such as taro and cassava cannot be grown on the island. Near the village is Vulawalu Beach, which translates as 'eight months' beach. It is named so because the sand is so fine it takes eight months to rid yourself of it. The main village on the island is Nabukeru, whose inhabitants make a good living selling mats, shells and the like to visitors coming off the boats. Sales of these items have made the residents the richest in the group, as indicated by the large amount of concrete dwellings and even an electrical generator in the village. Nabukeru also has an excellent beach.

SAWA-I-LAU

This tiny limestone island lies just off Yasawa Island and is famous for one thing – its cave. Visitors off the boats step into the cave, which has a large pool illuminated by the sun. Next you swim with a flashlight through a small orifice that connects the large cave to a smaller pool, which is dimly lit only by dissipated light from the other cave. Here, according to Fijian legend, a young chief hid his betrothed – a lady of rank whose elders would have married her to someone she did not want. He visited her daily, bringing food and gifts by diving with them through the watery doorway, until at length the couple escaped to friends on another island.

Although normally not shown to visitors, in the main cave are rock paintings of uncertain origin and antiquity. According to historian R A Derrick, one observer thought that the 'inscriptions bear a resemblance to Chinese characters; and upon this assumption, which at present is no more than an assumption, has put forward the hypothesis that a Chinese junk was at one time blown south and wrecked on Yasawa Island. The possibility that the inscriptions are the work of an itinerant Chinaman suffering from nostalgia is not to be excluded.' According to Museum Director Fergus Clunie, other similar rock engravings exist in Vanua Levu, Viti Levu and Taveuni but there is no explanation of their origins. The inscriptions are likewise a mystery to the local Fijian population and presumably are of ancient origin.

NANUYA LEVU (Turtle Island)
Turtle Island, about two km wide and several hundred metres long, is well known as one of Fiji's most exclusive resorts. It was also the backdrop of the most recent version of the movie *Blue Lagoon*. The original *Blue Lagoon* was also filmed in the Yasawas just after WW II.

GETTING THERE
Vessels headed for the Yasawa group depart from Queen's Wharf in Lautoka at least once a week (usually Saturday mornings). Sunrise Barge Services (tel 63 737) also has vessels and may have additional schedule information. Your best bet is to go directly to the docks on a Thursday or Friday and enquire. Visitors on commercial vessels must have a permit from the 'DO' (District Officer) located in Lautoka at the Agriculture and Fisheries Department before you set foot on the Yasawas. This can be obtained only if you have a personal invitation from a member of the community or a letter from the chief.

GETTING AROUND
Cruises Over the past few years organised cruises to the Yasawa Islands, located 40 km off Viti Levu's western coast, have increased tremendously in popularity and either of the two cruise companies described here can be highly recommended. Both cruises are so much in vogue that it would be wise to book passage before you get to Fiji.

Although hard-core vagabonds might scream that 'commercialism' has come to the outer islands, the area that these vessels visit in the three– or seven-day cruises would be otherwise difficult for you to see – unless of course you have access to a yacht. The itinerary entails visits to beaches and villages, snorkelling, and partially submerged caverns. Food with both cruises is served buffet style and is excellent. Much of the fare is what you might expect – seafood, caught right on the spot. There is also plenty of alcohol on hand. Locals at some of the villages have set up makeshift markets on the beach where they sell shells, carvings, necklaces, mats and other handicrafts. Prices are generally much less expensive than you'd pay in town.

The differences between the itineraries offered by the two cruise companies are negligible but there are distinctions between the firms. Blue Lagoon is a much bigger operation, with six modern ships. In contrast, at the time of writing, Seafarer is in the process of acquiring a new ship to replace the 1930s era *Matthew Flinders*.

Seafarer Cruises, part of Islands in the Sun (Fiji) Ltd, has three day/three night voyages and the price is in the F$300 range for a shared twin. The price covers all meals, entertainment, shore excursions, transfers, and a special feast or *lovo*. The *Flinders* departs from Lautoka and the itinerary includes overnight stops in Waya, Yasawa-i-Rara and the Vomo Islands. The ship departs twice weekly from the Lautoka wharf and picks up passengers from Treasure, Beachcomber, Mana and all Nadi-area resorts. For information in Australia call 008 221 318, 808 949 3778 in the USA, 604 682 3858 in Canada; in New Zealand call Air Pacific at 792 404.

Blue Lagoon Cruises has five 39-metre vessels with 22 cabins on two decks and a brand-new flagship, the 54-metre *Yasawa Princess* with 33 staterooms on three decks. There are two classes of service, and prices for the three-day voyages (only done on the smaller ships) run (per person) from F$242 triple to F$315 twin. Prices include all meals, excursions, feasts, visits to villages and beaches, snorkelling and fishing. The seven-day cruise on the *Yasawa Princess* is priced from F$504 triple to F$656 twin. Cruises depart daily from Lautoka Wharf for the three-day voyages and each Monday for the seven-day trip. Blue Lagoon does not have transfers from hotels. For information call 61 622 in Fiji, 231 6755 in Sydney, 51 1478 in Melbourne, or 77 3790 in Auckland.

Top: Fijian woman (FVB)
Left: Traditional *meke* dance (RK)
Right: Fijian warriors (FVB)

Top: *Bure* near Suva, Viti Levu (RK)
Bottom: *Drua* catamaran at Pacific Harbour, near Suva, Viti Levu (FVB)

The Lomaiviti Group

Lomaiviti, which translates as 'central Fiji,' accurately describes the location of this group of seven large islands and a few small ones in the geographic centre of the archipelago. With an aggregate area of 409 square km, the group includes the islands of Ovalau, Gau, Nairai, Koro, Makogai, Wakaya and Batiki. Of these, Gau and Koro are some of the most important of the purely volcanic islands in Fiji, exceeded in size only by Taveuni and Kadavu.

The Lomaiviti group was first recorded by Captain Bligh of the *Bounty* in May of 1789, less than a week after the mutiny. In 1792, he revisited the area in the *HMS Providence* to complete the survey that he had begun under less than ideal circumstances three years earlier.

As a historical footnote, Koro, Batiki and Gau were for a short time claimed by the United States government but were never occupied. In July 1867, when the *USS Tuscarora* visited Levuka, the old capital of Fiji, in an attempt to settle the long-standing debt against Cakobau (who owed the US Consul a large sum of money), these three islands were demanded as security for the promised payment of the debt. Two years later the money was paid, although neither on the due date nor by Cakobau himself, and American interest in the islands waned.

According to historian R A Derrick, the climate of these islands is not as wet and humid as it is in the windward areas of the large islands, nor as dry and hot as it is in the leeward regions.

From the standpoint of creature comforts, the group represents Fiji at its best. The islands' temperatures are mild, rainfall is moderate yet ample, and sunshine is plentiful. The villages of Lomaiviti, most of which are on the coasts, stand open to the wind.

OVALAU

Ovalau is the principal island of the Lomaiviti group and may justly be called the birthplace of modern Fiji. Levuka, the largest settlement on the island, was Fiji's first capital and in the mid-18th century was one of the main ports of call for trading ships and whalers in the entire South Pacific. Today the old capital is a quaint backwater town – an archetypal South Seas port looking much the way it did at the turn of the century when Rudyard Kipling visited and wrote, 'The palm-grove's droned lament, Before Levuka's trade.' Levuka is a fascinating destination well off the beaten tourist track. With weather-worn clapboard buildings, narrow streets and ever-friendly residents, it seems to hark back to an earlier time when one knew one's neighbours and life was much simpler. The feeling of the past is a palpable presence in Levuka, so thick you can cut it with a knife, so dense it can be smothering.

Levukans are a stubborn breed, intensely proud of their history and their town. Several years ago the Levuka Cultural & Historical Society was formed with the sole intent of preserving the town's architectural heritage. When one developer from Suva wanted to raze an old building and put up a flashy disco, his plan was bitterly attacked by the members of the society and eventually quashed by the town council. 'If he wants to build a disco,' said one resident, 'let him go back to Suva. We like things here just the way they are.'

Among the historical firsts in Fiji that occurred here: the first public school was established in 1879, the first Masonic Lodge in the Pacific Islands was founded in 1875, the first newspaper (*The Fiji Times*) was founded in 1869, and the first bank (Bank of New Zealand) opened in 1876. Of these, the school and the lodge

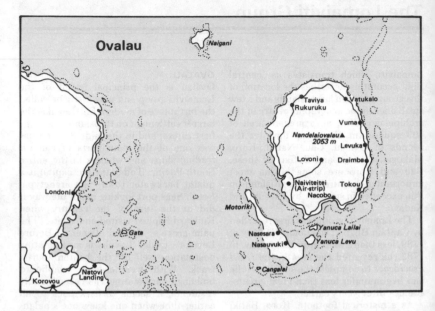

still stand, as does the oldest operating hotel in the South Pacific, the Royal Hotel, opened in the late 1850s.

Visitors will find there is no shortage of inexpensive accommodation. On the other side of the island in Rukuruku there is a budget resort with one of the few 'legitimate' camping areas in Fiji and the main beach area on the island. History buffs will find plenty of interesting sites, and snorkellers and spear fishermen will find no lack of quarry in the harbour or offshore. For the person with an inclination towards a quiet, bucolic setting I highly recommend Ovalau.

Geography

Ovalau is roughly oval in shape, about 13 km in length and nearly 10 km wide; its area is about 100 square km. Except for the Lovoni Valley in the middle of the island, and at the mouths of the various streams, there is little flat land. The Lovoni Valley, about 18 square km, was once a crater walled by naked rock. Today vegetation covers the earth and the valley is home to Lovoni villagers, a fiercely

independent tribe who were one of the last peoples in Fiji to be subjugated.

The east coast in particular is rugged, with bluffs rising abruptly from the sea and sharp pinnacles thrusting their way into the skyline. Almost all the surface area is covered with dense vegetation. The highest peak on the island is Nadelaiovalau ('the top of Ovalau' at 625 metres), which overlooks the east coast near Levuka. The north end of the island is dominated by Tomuna (526 metres), whose isolated position and sharply conical form are set against the more massive summits of Korotolutolu ('the triple mountain') a short distance beyond.

LEVUKA

Levuka is nestled at the base of steep bluffs on Ovalau's south-east coast. Its natural harbour and anchorage set the stage for the first traders who arrived in the early 1830s. These early settlers were a mixed bag. Some were honest and industrious men who built small sailing vessels for trading in the outer islands, while others were shiftless rounders or opportunists looking for an easy buck. Among the earliest settlers was David Whippy, a Connecticut sailor who jumped ship and eventually became one of the leading citizens of the town. Whippy acted as an advisor to the local chief and served as a translator to Commodore Wilkes during his expeditionary visit to the islands. The offspring of these original settlers, many of whom took Fijian wives, were the beginning of Levuka's racially mixed 'part-European' or Creole society.

In 1844 some of the settlers offended the paramount chief, who banished them from his territory; but five years later they were allowed to return and re-establish the settlement. Despite raids and burnings by the Lovoni tribespeople, Levuka grew and flourished. Joining the early traders were cotton growers who came during the brief cotton boom of the 1860s, coconut planters, missionaries and professionals. Soon Levuka's beachfront street (known as Beach St) was crowded with shops, shanties, offices, boarding houses and saloons. The growing number of permanent residents built homes on the hillsides and reached them by steps which were and still are Levuka's 'streets.' By 1870 the population exceeded 800.

Ships from every nation crowded the harbour and the bars were bubbling with sailors of every nationality, awash with gin. An early issue of the *Fiji Times* described the atmosphere thus:

We have had rows enough during the last week to satisfy everyone for two fortnights, and if broken heads, black eyes and narrow escapes from a Japanese disembowelling with the broadsword, or a few gentle prickings with a fourteen-inch ham slicer are not sufficient to make us all go about with revolvers in our belts, as many of the more cautious do, yet they make us all wish either for a magistrate that would be a terror to evildoers, or for a beacon to sweep the beach of the drink maddened ruffian.

Unfortunately there was no magistrate in those days because there was no govern-ment. In 1871 there was an attempt to form a local government with Chief Cakobau as head, but this only led to discontent culminating in riots. Cakobau was under tremendous pressure to compensate for looting claims stemming from a 4th of July fire at the American consul's home. The grave of Consul Williams, who did not live to see his debt paid, can still be visited in the old Methodist Cemetery.

While Cakobau stalled on payment of the debt, anarchy filled the air and a potential race war loomed over the islands. The aging chief felt the need for a strong outside power to control the situation. His wish for peace was realised on 10 October 1874, when Cakobau and his fellow chiefs ceded the country to Great Britain and the Colony of Fiji was born. A monument to this occasion can be seen in Nasova, the small village outside of town where the signing of the Deed of Cession took place.

Levuka became the first capital of Fiji but this did not last long. The founding fathers were concerned about the need to expand the capital. Because the town was confined by cliffs, there really was no room for Levuka to grow. In 1881 the capital was shifted to Suva. Levukans were a chauvinistic lot who thought that even though the capital had been moved, the town would always be the centre for trade. They were wrong. Over the years businesses left and the town's economic life became ever more difficult. The *coup de grace* came in the late 1950s when Levuka, which had always been a trans-shipment point for the copra trade, lost that last dribble of commerce.

Fortunately, through negotiations with a Japanese firm the town fathers brought a fish cannery into Levuka which provided jobs for fishermen and workers and kept the community going. Recently the town has lost even more government jobs due to a budget austerity program.

The several small hotels and guest houses do provide some income but the scale of tourism in Levuka is so small it has little effect on the general population. Levuka's isolation has kept it off the beaten tourist track and the economic mainstream but it has helped preserve the town's architectural integrity.

Levuka, population 1400, can be seen in a relatively few hours by the ambitious traveller, but a stay of several days is recommended to really savour its 'lost-in-time' ambience.

Information

A new tourist information office has been established in Levuka and is located opposite the post office close to the Fiji Air bureau. Brochures, ferry schedules and general transportation information are available. Bookings at any of the local resorts can be made. Phone 44 329 for information/confirmations.

By arrangement with the Visitors' Centre, historical tours of Levuka and its environs can be organised for F$5 for a three-hour tour.

Things to Do & See

Community Centre/Museum This completely revamped storehouse originally belonging to Morris Hedstrom, a trading company established in the early days of Levuka and still in business in Fiji. The first-rate rebuilding was carried out by local craftspeople under the auspices of the Levuka Historical & Cultural Society, financed by donations of time, money, labour and materials from businesses and individuals throughout Fiji. The structure, originally built in 1878, was given by Morris Hedstrom to the National Trust of Fiji in 1980. It was refurbished with salvaged Oregon timber from a nearby storage shed and now houses a branch of the Fiji Museum, a public library, crafts centre, kindergarten, squash court and meeting hall. It represents the evident desire of Levuka's residents to have their town remain a living museum. Historical tours of the town can be organised through the museum for F$1 for an hour.

Queen's Wharf With a maximum depth of eight metres alongside, the wharf is used by local and sometimes foreign vessels. Levuka is one of three official ports of entry (Lautoka and Suva are the other two) and the wharf has recently been upgraded. The harbour entrance is indicated by a pile light, marking the passage through the barrier reef. In the distance is Wakaya Island, scene of the capture of Count Von Luckner during WW I (see history section in Facts about the Country) and now subdivided for expensive homes. To the left is the island of Makogai, which until recent years was a leper hospital. The entrance to the wharf area, which is adjacent to the Community Centre, also houses the post office, Customs Office and the Port Authority of Fiji office. A drinking fountain on Beach St, directly opposite the post office, was once the site of a carrier pigeon loft which in the late 1800s was the Levuka terminal of a pigeon post service to Suva. The birds covered the 65 km distance in about 30 minutes.

Pacific Fishing Company Founded in 1964 by a Japanese firm, Pacific Fishing is used as a centre for freezing and exporting tuna. Under a joint venture with the Fiji government, the cannery was opened in 1976 and is the primary private employer on the island. The deal to bring the facility to Levuka was put together by local citizens when the copra shipments were diverted from the port for economic reasons. This act saved the town from economic extinction.

Nasova A km south of the wharf (towards the airport) is the village where Fiji's Deed of Cession was signed on 10 October 1874. The signing took place in the Government House, which was located below the residence of the district commissioner. On the seaward side of the road, beyond a small creek, is a fence surrounding what are known as the three 'cession stones' (and a flag pole), which

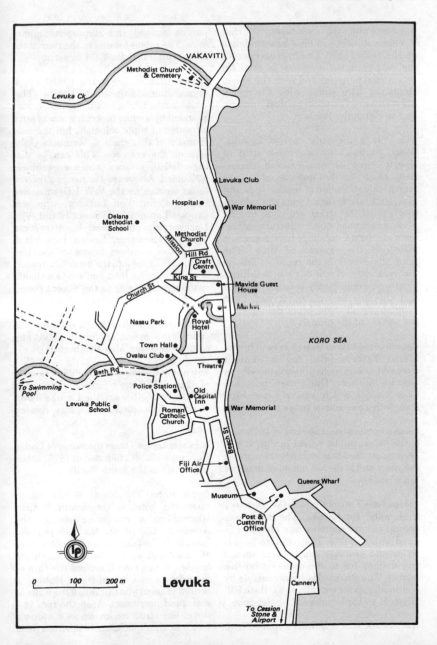

Levuka

commemorate the centenary of that ceremony in 1974 and Fiji's independence on 10 October 1970. The large *bure* across the road from the memorial is used for ceremonial purposes and is on the site of an earlier *bure* where King George V (then Duke of Clarence) resided during a visit to Fiji in the 1860s.

Beach St In the early days of Levuka, Beach St was only 'a narrow strip of shingly beach' between a row of houses, built close to the water's edge – a ramshackle collection of shacks, bars and makeshift businesses. Today the saloons which lined the street are gone but its peeling, columned storefronts and weather-worn clapboard buildings have somehow withstood the ravages of time. The present sidewalk is the result of linking the verandahs of the original buildings. The town council only recently learned that title to the walkway it had been maintaining all these years belonged to the owners of the property!

Church of the Sacred Heart was built by the Marist Fathers, who, led by Father Breheret, established themselves in Levuka in 1858. The church boasts a French clock which strikes twice each hour, with a one-minute pause in between.

Levuka Public School opened in 1879 and is the oldest public school in Fiji. It has been maintained immaculately throughout the years and is the old school of many of Fiji's leaders.

Totoga Falls Totoga Creek is the source of fresh water for Levuka. The creek has several swimming holes, one of which is lined with concrete. The concrete pool is on private property and bathers should pay a small fee to the owners who live nearby. The other holes are accessible by continuing up the trail known as 'Bath Rd' adjacent to the Levuka Public School.

Nasau Park This is Levuka's sports field,

parade ground and all-purpose grassy area. The rooms located to the rear of the Royal Hotel face the field directly.

Ovalau Club is one of the oldest social organisations in the South Pacific. This white-washed, clapboard structure surrounded by a white picket fence was once a bastion of white colonials, but the only remnant of that era is a 'Members Only' sign on the entrance. This can be disregarded by visitors, who are genuinely welcomed. Above the bar hangs a framed letter written by the WW I German sea raider, Count Von Luckner, who was captured on nearby Wakaya Island. Von Luckner, who abandoned ship after it ran aground elsewhere, landed in a small launch on Katafaga Island in the Lau group. He broke into the home of a trader, 'liberated' some food and wrote a thank-you note explaining to the absent owner that he was sorry about the inconvenience but he was on a South Seas sporting cruise and in need of provisions. The conscientious count left some money for the goods and signed the letter 'Max Pemberton.'

Town Hall Constructed in 1898 in honour of Queen Victoria's jubilee, the hall is home of the offices of the Levuka Town Council, Fiji's oldest municipality, created in 1877.

Masonic Lodge This is the home of Lodge Polynesia 562 SC, founded in 1875, and is the oldest in the South Pacific.

Royal Hotel The Royal is the oldest operating hotel in the South Pacific. Resembling a roadhouse out of the American Old West, the 125-year-old hotel is the last one remaining of the over 50 bars and saloons built in Levuka's heyday. It was rebuilt around the turn of the century by Captain David Robbie, a retired seaman who thickened the walls to withstand hurricanes. Atop the roof is a turret-like structure known as a widow's watch or ship's lookout. Just across from the front entrance is Levuka's small municipal market.

Mission Hill Atop Mission Hill are some of Levuka's finest old buildings, including Methodist Mission homes and the Delana Methodist School. To climb the 199 steps to the top, begin at the historic Methodist Church. The vista from the hill is worth the climb. At the foot of Mission Hill is the Levuka Government Hospital.

Niukaubi Hill is the site of one of Levuka's two war memorials. (The other is on Beach St, opposite the Roman Catholic Church.) The Supreme Court and Parliament House were on Niukaubi Hill. On the other side of a small boat harbour is an area once occupied by the Mechanics Institute, Levuka's principal recreational centre before and at the time of cession.

Church of the Holy Redeemer The Reverend William Floyd, who came to Fiji in 1870, built the first Anglican church on this location. The present church was consecrated in 1904. Stained-glass windows commemorate early Levuka residents.

Levuka Fijian Town This village was home to Tui Levuka, the chief who first befriended early European settlers. On the opposite side of a small creek is a Methodist church, constructed in 1869, where Ratu Cakobau once worshipped.

Old Methodist Cemetery Here lie the remains of at least 135 of Levuka's early settlers, many of them German immigrants. The most famous resident of this graveyard is John Brown Williams, the somewhat unscrupulous American consul whose exaggerated financial claims helped cause the downfall of the Cakobau government and were a major factor in the cession of Fiji to Great Britain.

Gun Rock Situated above Levuka village, this point was used in 1849 as a target by the *HMS Havannah* to impress upon Cakobau the power of the warship's cannons. The rock was again battered by naval guns in 1874 by Commodore Goodenough, to entertain Fijian chiefs in Levuka. Visitors who inspect the rock can still see the scars left by cannonballs. In a more peaceful vein, Roman Catholic missionary Father Breheret said his first mass beneath the shelter of Gun Rock after his arrival in Levuka in 1858.

Vagadaci Village Lying beyond Gun Rock, this village became headquarters of the Royal Engineers who built the town of Levuka (and later Suva) as well as the roads after cession. The area was also a boatbuilding centre. The concrete ruins of a large house were once the former home of the Palmer family who were boatbuilders and merchants. The Duke of York (later King George V) and his brother the Duke of Clarence played cricket at Vagadaci but much of the old sports field is now occupied by the homes of government employees.

Places to Stay
All the places listed here are downright inexpensive compared to most places in Fiji or anywhere else in the world for that matter. Ovalau has simply not been discovered by the moneyed set and lacks the beaches on the populated side of the island to make it a desirable locale for large-scale resort development.

The *Royal Hotel* (tel 444 024) is a landmark in its own right and the most 'upscale' of Levuka's accommodation. Constructed in the 1850s, it has been managed by the Ashleys, a local 'part-European' family, for two generations. Never mind that the hot water isn't so hot or an American Express card is an unknown entity here. The Royal is loaded with atmosphere, found in such particulars as an old-style balcony facing the cliffs, polished brass shell casings for ashtrays, a winding staircase, a haunted room and a century-old billiard table. The Ashleys, who are very kind people, do run a restaurant but you must tell them ahead of time whether or not you're eating at the hotel. The Royal has 14 rooms and a bar full of local rowdies; prices begin at around F$8 for a single and F$12 for a double. It's the place to stay in Levuka.

The *Old Capital Inn* (tel 44 057) is run by an enterprising man of Fijian and Chinese extraction by the name of Emosi Yee Show. The Old Capital Inn is a clean and well run backpacker's haven. Emosi is a most engaging character who will grab the visitor by the hand (much to the chagrin of his wife Mary) and take you out snorkelling or spearfishing, lead you to the city lights (of which there are few) or drive you around the island in his van. After a few days at the establishment, you can't help but feel like a member of the family. The Old Capital Inn also runs a moderately priced and fairly good restaurant, the only one of two in town. Aside from the main building, which is more dorm-style in nature, the Inn has an annex on Beach St with individual rooms more conducive to couples. Prices begin at F$3.50 for dorm accommodation, F$6 single and F$11 twin (including breakfast).

Emosi offers snorkelling trips for F$4.50 (including gear), land tours to Rukuruku for F$8.50 (including lunch), and an overnight visit to Cagelai, one of the smaller outlying islands for F$20.50 (including four meals). Those wishing to extend their stay on Cagelai must bring their own food and pay F$2.50 per night. Cagelai is a jewel of an islet with a great beach, swaying palms and clear water for excellent snorkelling/fishing. There are six *bures* there, each of which can accommodate up to four persons. The boat ride over takes about one hour.

The *Mavida Guest House* (tel 44 051), run by George Thomas, a native son of Levuka, is also quiet, clean and inexpensive. His accommodation is located on Beach St, next door to his own home. George is proud of his family's role in local history and he'll probably dig out a photo of himself escorting Prince Charles, who

visited Levuka during the centenary celebration of Fiji's cession to England in 1974. Prices begin at F$8 per person (including breakfast). The Mavida serves good, homecooked food – F$5 for lunch or dinner. George also has one self-contained unit behind his house.

Places to Stay – Outside Levuka

The *Ovalau Holiday Resort* (tel 44 329) is the newest resort on the island of Ovalau. Located about four km outside of Levuka (heading in the opposite direction of the airport), it has three tidy chalet-style units that are fully self-contained. The resort is nestled in a shady grove of palms at the base of a hill facing a small, rocky beach and a 100-year-old lighthouse, the oldest in Fiji. Amenities include shower, toilet, washing machine, refrigerator and gas burner. The resort, very much a family-run operation, will either feed you from their cabin (which they dub restaurant/bar) or allow guests to fend for themselves. The owners, Stephen and Rosemary Diston, are currently rebuilding a 100-year-old whaler's cottage which will be the new bar/restaurant. They have a boat for fishing. The resort is a very quiet locale and will appeal to those who want to be out of town. Transportation from the resort to anywhere on the island can be arranged through Tuni Tours. The fare from town to the Ovalau Holiday Resort is only F$0.50. Rates are F$10 single, F$18 double or F$26 triple. You may also pitch a tent for F$7 double.

Rukuruku Resort (tel 444 329) is located on the opposite side of the island 16 km (about 35 minutes) from the town of Levuka. Buses or Tuni Tours carriers run regularly from the old capital, or taxis are available. This modest resort is good for families and has one of the few 'official' campgrounds on the island, complete with shower and toilet facilities. There is a small restaurant (prices range from F$2-5) and bar on the grounds, the beach is nearby and snorkelling and spearfishing are excellent. There are six *bures* (which can accommodate four people) at F$35 per unit. The campground costs F$10 per night if you rent the tent and F$3 if you have your own camping gear. There is also dorm accommodation for F$8 per person (including breakfast). Tuni Tours supplies transportation twice daily to town for only F$1 one way. Excursions are also available from Tuni.

Places to Stay – Offshore

Islanders Village Resort (tel 44 364) is an attractive, out-of-the-way spot on Naigani Island, which lies eight km north-west of Ovalau and about 10 km from Tailevu Point on Viti Levu. The resort has 12 villas (all with cooking and refrigeration facilities) and one building large enough to house 34 persons. Accommodation is comfortable, snorkelling is excellent and there is big-game fishing, windsurfing, waterskiing and canoes to paddle about. Prices begin at F$60 single or double, F$10 dorm. Transfers to the island are F$12 by launch from Natovi, F$80 by helicopter and F$45 via seaplane. Phone 22 062 or 23 160 in Suva for more information.

Places to Eat

The pickings are mighty slim in this small town. The most popular place is the small restaurant at the *Old Capital Inn*. They serve home-style cooking – mostly fish, beef and a local variation of Chinese food. Prices range from F$2-4 per meal for dinner and lunch. Breakfasts, usually eggs and toast, are even cheaper.

There are also three small curry shops on Beach St, all about the same quality, with food ranging in price from F$2-4. The *Royal Hotel* serves food but they usually cater only to guests. Ask Eddie Ashley, the manager, what his current policy is. For a cup of tea or a scone during the day the place to stop is *Matt's Corner*, near the library/museum.

Entertainment

Levuka residents have the dubious dist-

inction of consuming more alcohol per person than anywhere else in the Fiji islands. During a beer strike several years ago their stockpile of Fiji Bitter held out for the entire duration of the labour dispute, keeping them happy while the rest of the nation ran dry. Adjacent to the town hall is the venerable *Ovalau Club*, a whitewashed clapboard structure and one of the finest watering holes in the entire South Pacific. Above the dance floor is a portrait of the Queen (circa 1957) and various other members of the Royal Family – which Fijians seem to be crazy about. Framed above the bar is a letter from none other than Count von Luckner, the notorious German Sea raider captured on nearby Wakaya Island. The Ovalau Club, once an exclusively white colonial hangout, is no longer an austere bastion of the Empire's faithful servants. Chances are that after one hour in this convivial hangout you will learn enough about Levuka's inhabitants to last a lifetime. Don't be surprised if bottles of beer suddenly appear at your table. People buy one another quite a bit of beer at the Ovalau Club.

The second drinking establishment is the *Levuka Club*, located on the oceanfront on Beach St. The Levuka Club is also a fine place to drink but is a newer structure and doesn't seem to have the character of the Ovalau Club.

There is a movie theatre in town but the acoustics are so tinny that they make serious movie-going a real chore.

LOVONI

Lovoni village is located in the crater of an extinct volcano. Early residents of Levuka feared the Lovoni tribespeople, who burned the town down on several occasions and were well known for their ferocity. The tribe was subdued only by treachery. In a peace offering by Cakobau the warriors were invited into Levuka and seized while they were unarmed. They were then forcibly scattered around the Fiji group where they wouldn't present a security risk. Only much later were they allowed to return home. To this day they are a fierce lot. Several years ago a land dispute caused them to don their war paint and gather their clubs. The dispute was settled peaceably, but not before the tribespeople made their wishes known by blocking the road and forcing the landlord in question (accompanied by a policeman in a jeep) to turn back. You can visit the village by catching a bus in Levuka (for about F$0.50) and getting off at the bridge. If possible, bring some yaqona (there are several grog shops in town) and try to get a youngster or another resident to take you across the bridge and lead you into the village. Many of the villagers come into town during the day and chances are you will meet someone if you ask around.

GETTING THERE

Air Ovalau has twice-daily air service from Suva via Fiji Air – the fare is F$17 one way and about half that amount on a standby basis. The flight is only 10 minutes long. The bus ride from the airstrip into town is about twice as long as the flight and costs F$2.50.

Boat The island is also served by four ferry boats. *Princess Ashika* departs on Sunday at 4 pm from the Princess dock in Suva and returns on Monday at 5.30 pm (via several other stops) and on Saturday. *Princess Ashika* schedule information can be had by phoning 385 388 in Suva, or 44 059 in Levuka, where you purchase tickets at R S Goundar Store. The Patterson Brothers' *Ovalau* and *Jubilee* depart Natovi Landing (an hour's ride outside of Suva) for Levuka on Tuesday, Wednesday, Friday and Saturday at 3.15 pm for the 1½-hour trip. The *Romanda*, a WW II-vintage sub-chaser, offers daily

service to Levuka for passengers only (no vehicles). The Patterson Brothers' ferry departs Levuka for Natovi at 5.30 am on Monday and Thursday. Fare is F$9. Call the Patterson brothers (who are native sons of Levuka) in Suva at 315 644 or in Levuka at 44 125 for schedule information.

GETTING AROUND

Getting around Levuka is no problem. The town is so small you can walk from one end to the other in 10 minutes at a brisk pace. Since no one walks briskly in Levuka, figure 15 minutes. There are always taxis available and buses leave four times a day for the outer villages.

Tours *Tuni Tours* (tel 44 329) is based at Rukuruku Resort but operates out of the Tourist Centre in Levuka. They offer transport between Levuka and the Ovalau Holiday Resort, as well as to Rukuruku, the airport, Buresala and the Patterson Brothers ferryboat landing five km beyond the airport. Janet Tuni, the owner/driver, offers regular tours around Ovalau to Rukuruku which leave at 9 am from the tourist office and return to town between 3-4 pm. The tour includes swimming, snorkelling, lunch and village visits to Lovoni and other communities to purchase handicrafts or just watch them being made. The cost is F$10 per person (minimum of four).

Trekking There are a multitude of hikes around Ovalau, most of which are never taken by tourists and require a guide. The more popular treks are from Levuka to Lovoni, Rukuruku to Lovoni and Ovalau Holiday Resort to Rukuruku. Cost for a guide is only F$3 for a half day. Contact the Tourist Centre for more information.

Vanua Levu

Vanua Levu, with a population of approximately 125,000, is the second largest island of the Fiji archipelago and is situated only 64 km north-east of Viti Levu. Although very near Viti Levu in distance, it is miles apart in development – particularly tourism infrastructure – and is little-known to the average visitor. This is changing with the recent introduction of ferry services, which enables an easy and inexpensive commute to and from the capital. The added advantage of the ferry is that the visitor can rent a car in Suva, take it on the boat and drive the very beautiful (although generally unpaved) road from Savusavu to Labasa and the Hibiscus Highway starting from Savusavu and running along the southern coast.

Because the island is such virgin territory for the visitor and the local economy does not rely on tourism, the residents are particularly friendly and interested in strangers. In the same vein, Vanua Levu offers the guest an ideal opportunity to observe relatively untarnished island life. Compared to the facilities on Viti Levu, there are few places to stay. The several resorts on Vanua Levu are equally distributed in the old copra port of Savusavu in the south and the sugar mill town of Labasa in the north. The offshore islands of Taveuni, Qamea and Laucala also have small hotels.

Geography

Vanua Levu is about half the size of Viti Levu, with an area of 5538 square km. It has a squiggly, irregular shape, about 180 km in greatest length and from 30 to 50 km in width. Geologically it is a complicated structure – evidently formed by the amalgamation of several volcanic islands whose coasts melded together during successive stages of uplift. A rugged mountain axis runs through the main part of the island from end to end, but it is discontinuous and asymmetrically placed. On each side of the island are equally precipitous parallel ranges with lowlands in between. Highest point on the island is Batini (1111 metres), located about 13 km from the southern coast, followed by Dikeva or Mt Thurston (1030 metres) about 16 km to the north-east of Batini.

The principal ranges stand near the windward (southern) coasts, causing most of the rainfall to drop on this side of the island. Like Viti Levu's western side, the north of Vanua Levu is dry eight months out of the year, making it ideal for growing sugar cane. Not surprisingly, cane is the major agricultural product of the north.

Between Bua (the south-west portion of the island where the sandalwood trade took place in the 1880s) and Lekutu to the north is an area the Fijians call *talasiga*, which means 'sunburnt land.' This 'rain-shadow' is barren with desert-like vegetation and arid soil. Just east of this region is the Seatovo Range, which was once said to be the home of albinos.

To the south-west, in the hilly area known as Dradramea, are the Nasavunimuku Falls, which Fijian folklore says was a favourite suicide spot. The Dradramea region was used as a mountain stronghold during the ancient Fijian tribal wars, and the remains of a fort can still be seen 91 metres from the summit of Dradramea, the highest peak in the chain.

The rivers of Vanua Levu are short and second rate when compared to those of Viti Levu. None are navigable by large vessels.

The most important bay in the south is Savusavu, an early European settlement ringed by high mountains. The area is known for its hot springs (some of which send their steam directly over the main street). Savusavu's hot springs are among the more than 20 distributed over almost the entire island.

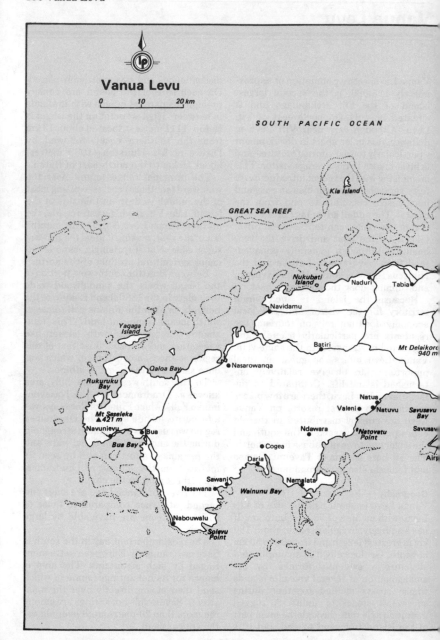

Vanua Levu

0   10   20 km

SOUTH   PACIFIC   OCEAN

Kia Island

GREAT SEA REEF

Nukubati Island ● ○ Naduri   Tabia ●

Navidamu ●

Yaqaga Island

Batiri ●

Mt Delaikoro 940 m

Qaloa Bay   ○ Nasarowanqa

Rukuruku Bay

Natua ●

Valeni ●   ○ Natuvu   *Savusavu Bay*

Mt Seseleka ▲ 421 m

Navunievu ●   ● Bua

Ndawara ●   *Natovatu Point*   Savusav

Bua Bay

● Cogea

Daria ●

Sawani ●   Namalata ●

Nasawana ●   *Wainunu Bay*

Nabouwalu ●

Solevu Point

Airp

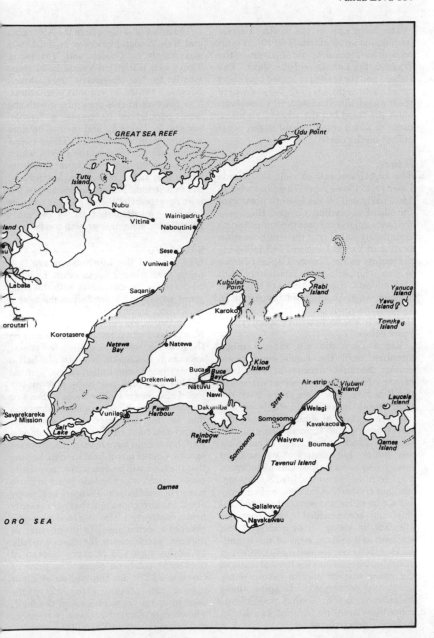

The main city in the north, Labasa (population approximately 5000), is built on a delta formed by three rivers – the Wailevu, the Labasa and the Qawa. The Labasa and the Qawa are joined by a short canal about eight km from the sea where the town is built. Shallow draft vessels can enter the canal but the larger freighters, many of which come to load sugar, must anchor on the coast.

History

The first European to visit the Vanua Levu region was Abel Tasman, who in 1643 navigated off the eastern portion of the island's coastline. Captain Bligh was the next explorer to come through when he dauntlessly sailed past the south-western portion of Vanua Levu in 1789 following the mutiny on the *Bounty*. Captain James Wilson, skippering the missionary ship *Duff*, added to the discoveries of Bligh and Tasman when he explored the region in 1797 and narrowly escaped the same reefs that nearly ended Tasman's journey 154 years before.

Vanua Levu did not receive much attention until the sandalwood trade during the first decade of the 19th century. This began in 1805 or earlier, in the Bua Bay area. Ten years later the sandalwood thickets were depleted and only the occasional whaler or beche-de-mer trader came through, looking for supplies. The first European to make his way into the hill country of Vanua Levu was a young sailor by the name of Jackson, who late in 1840 jumped ship at Somosomo, leaving a crew of 'freebooters' he evidently did not trust. He was adopted by the local chief and accompanied a war party to Maucata; in doing so he explored the northern and eastern arms of the island. Jackson, however, seemed more interested in making inroads into the lives of some of the young women than in taking notes about the countryside. Despite these distractions, much of what was known about these areas up to 1850 was due to Jackson's descriptions.

The influx of settlers from the Australian and New Zealand colonies in the 1860s was mainly to Ovalau and Viti Levu. Those who settled on Vanua Levu came mostly to the Savusavu area, which became a centre for coconut plantations. The planters in this area mixed with the local population to create a 'creole' society in Levuka, and many became wealthy from copra sales. Their riches ended with the crash of the 1930s, which depressed the price of copra and from which they never recovered. Meanwhile, the industrious Indian community to the north created the thriving sugar town of Labasa – an area that shows the most promise for economic growth today.

SAVUSAVU

Like Suva to the south, Savusavu is a pretty town when it doesn't rain. Located on gorgeous Savusavu Bay with towering green mountains shrouded in mist for a backdrop, it consists of one main drag about half a km long, facing the water. Nawi Island sits directly offshore and on the harbour there are usually a few yachts anchored. Lining the streets are half a dozen Chinese and Indian shops, painted in blue and pink pastels – now mostly faded and dingy. Unlike those in Suva or Levuka, many of the small businesses, due to the depressed local economy, simply can't afford a new paint job or a roof that should have been replaced years ago. Residents are upbeat though, hoping that the town will be designated an official port of entry, which should bring in more business and tourism. Planters are happy about the new copra mill that has recently been constructed. The new facility means cheaper coconut meal (a by-product of milling), which means they can diversify by raising pigs and chickens instead of depending solely on copra. The price of copra is F\$330 per ton and an efficient planter can make up to 75% profit depending on the workers and the land. The average planter has about 16 hectares and can make about F\$10,000 a year.

Things to Do & See

Hot Springs Visitors should not miss the hot springs for which the town is famous. Most are located near the elementary school grounds across from the Hot Springs Hotel. The bubbling holes are lined with rocks on which locals often place pots filled with dalo or tavioka to cook while they attend to shopping or visiting. As you walk from the hotel to the main part of town you'll see a steaming spring just a few metres from the sidewalk, sometimes covering the ground with vapour.

Savarekareka Mission The most noteworthy attraction is the mission at Savarekareka. A 10-km ride north outside of Savusavu, the venerable chapel (circa 1870) was the first Catholic mission on Vanua Levu and is still in use. The compound is beautiful and the view spectacular.

Hibiscus Highway The highway runs from Savusavu to land's end at Darigala and is delightful. Local buses will get you there but it's more comfortable to hire a driver and pay him for his services (a three-hour cab drive to the end of the road is about F$35). Along the roadside, nestled among the numerous coconut groves, are some of the oldest homes in Fiji. Some, like the Lepper place (circa 1880), are perfectly preserved, while others such as the Simpson home (circa 1850 and perhaps the oldest European house in Fiji) have fallen into disrepair. The key to why some of the homes are in good shape while others have deteriorated rests in the ups and downs of the market and family fortunes. The highway, which runs along the coast, is unpaved but is generally in good shape. The ride offers some quintessential South Pacific vistas – cobalt-blue waters lapping at a shoreline studded with palm trees.

Yachting Emerald Yacht Charters has four vessels in its fleet, which is moored in Savusavu. They measure 11 to 14 metres in length and each is well equipped with food, beverages and linen. Prices range from F$1360 to F$1955 for seven nights. Phone 10 or write Private Box, Post Office, Savusavu for more information.

Places to Stay

The *Hotsprings Hotel* (tel Savusavu 86 or 96) is the best place to stay in town. Situated on a bluff facing Savusavu Bay, it affords a spectacular view. The hotel was formerly a Travelodge but recently has been taken over by new management, which eventually hopes to build a spa. They are continuously revamping this forgotten property but the process is slow. Although not upscale in service or demeanour, the hotel is quite adequate if you're not too fussy. It has 48 rooms, a pool, a bar which is one of two hot spots in town, and a restaurant which is OK. Prices begin at F$25 for a single and F$30 for a double.

Lovinuvu Point Beach Apartments (tel 85 250) are the newest development in the Savusavu area. They are located five km from town and 15 minutes from the airport. Each unit is fully furnished and self-contained with kitchen, bedroom and lounge, accommodating up to six people. The tariff is F$40 per night for the entire apartment, or F$210 per week.

Budget Holiday House, located near the hotel (behind Burns Philp) is a cheap bed-and-breakfast rooming house with five single bedrooms, two doubles and a shared bath. It is clean but very spartan. Prices are F$10.50 single and F$17.50 twin.

Places to Stay – Outside Savusavu

Last Resort (tel Diloi exchange K-4) is located at Kubulau, the easternmost point and the end of the Hibiscus Highway, which is three hours by car (a F$35 taxi ride) from Savusavu. Aside from riding from Savusavu you may fly directly to the island of Rabi and take a launch to the resort. Like Namale, it is a family-style working plantation. The old plantation house can accommodate up to 12 people and the property has three km of ocean frontage. They offer rainforest walks, a beach, windsurfing and plenty of isolation. Price is F$20 single and F$35 double (including meals).

Kon Tiki Lodge (tel Savusavu 262), about 15 minutes by car from Savusavu, is run by Robin Mercer, one of the most established hoteliers in Fiji. Robin, a native-born Fijian (and former manager of Namale) is also a renowned ornithologist. He provides seven self-contained units with electricity and hot and cold water for F$25 complete. For the self-sufficient visitor to this beautiful area, this is the place to stay.

Wina Estate, located about 14 km outside of town, is the best bet for the backpacker or frugal traveller. Situated on a plantation and run by Ann Lepper, the one *bure* is comfortable and is only F$10 a single. Cook your own food and get to know the colourful Lepper family. Enquire at the butcher shop in town for further information on this good-value place.

Namale Plantation (tel Savusavu 117), at the top end of the scale, has the best accommodation and perhaps the best kitchen in the Savusavu area. Surrounded by an actual working plantation (complete with cattle and goats), it consists of three 'family' *bures* and four double *bures*, some of which are built adjacent to huge volcanic outcroppings and conform to the terrain. Managed by an American couple, Liz and Curly Carswell, the plantation claims one of the largest collections of plants in the South Pacific. They offer flora and fauna walks, garden tours, copra plantation tours, snorkelling and four-wheel-drive land tours, fishing, windsurfing and yacht cruises. Prices (including meals) are F$74 single and F$103 double. *Bure* accommodation (sans meals) begins at F$50 single and F$55 double. Cost for meals is F$5 breakfast, F$7 lunch and F$12 dinner.

Places to Stay – Offshore

Moody's Namena Island (radiophone 388M-RP6) is a 44-hectare resort/nature reserve located 24 km south of Vanua Levu (off Wainunu Bay) and 32 km northwest of Koro. Because there is no water supply, it has never supported a permanent population; consequently the flora and fauna have been undisturbed. According to the owners there are land and sea birds which have become extinct on the other islands because of the introduction of the mongoose. The island has superb diving and snorkelling, windsurfing, shelling, bird watching and fishing. There are 10 *bures* which limit the number of people to 20-25 maximum on the island. Transportation is either by seaplane from Nadi to Namena or by scheduled Fiji Air service to Savusavu and then by speedboat to the island. Price per day is F$110 for single or double plus F$40 for three meals. A deposit of F$600 is required. Scuba equipment is provided for F$25 extra per dive.

Places to Eat

Wing Yuen, located on the main street next to the bank, is by far the best place to eat in town. It has good, basic Chinese food, the staple of travellers around the world. Prices are F$2.50-6 per person. Down the street is *Ping Ho's*, an awful-looking place from the outside but the food is OK. Price range is F$2-5. Open during the day is *Khan's Cool Corner*, which serves fine vegetarian food from F$1.50-4 as well as ice cream.

Entertainment

Savusavu is a quiet town in the evenings but on the weekend there just may be a dance at the *Planters Club*, located down the street from the Hot Springs Hotel. The Planters Club, not unlike a grange hall in the USA, is a turn-of-the-century clapboard building with a long bar. It was constructed by and for the once prosperous community of plantation owners and is still the social heart of Savusavu. Here is

Top: Navala village, Nausori Highlands, Viti Levu (RK)
Bottom: Village scene in Tailevu, Viti Levu (RK)

Top: Ovalau Club, Levuka, Ovalau – oldest social organisation in the South Pacific (RK)
Bottom: Levuka, Ovalau – the old capital of Fiji (RK)

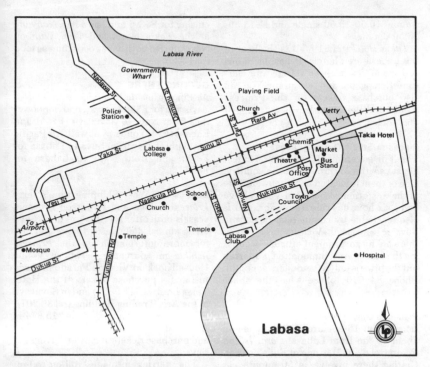

Labasa

the place to drink, gossip and discuss the depressingly low price of copra. Although it is a private organisation, visitors are made to feel very welcome by the locals, who are more than likely to buy a stranger a tall cool one. Dances, which are chock full of friendly natives, are likely to be punctuated by a semi-innocuous drunken brawl at the end of the evening. The only other place of significance to drink is the *Hotsprings Hotel*, which has a modern lounge facing the bay.

LABASA

Labasa is a hot, dusty sugar mill town, pure and simple. Although growing in importance economically as an agricultural community, the town is still very quiet and provincial. The surrounding countryside is beautiful (much like on Viti Levu's western side), with golden, sunburnt hills

and miles of green canefields. In general, the area is not geared towards visitors, but there is a new tourist development – the Coral Island Resort on Nukubati Island near Labasa. It is receiving good reviews in the local press and attention from the diving community.

As far as attractions go, there aren't that many except the municipal market and the Labasa sugar mill.

Places to Stay
The Grand Eastern (tel 81 022) is a venerable, 18-room classic roadhouse affair with a restaurant/bar and pool. Recently acquired by a locally owned Best Western (Budget) Hotel chain, it *supposedly* is undergoing improvements. There is air-conditioning and private bath in some of the rooms, fans and shared bathroom facilities in others. Price ranges

from F$10.50-19.50 single and F$15.50-25.50 double.

Takia Hotel (tel 81 655) is the best of the Labasa-area hotels. It has 34 rooms and amenities such as refrigerator, air-conditioning, bar and restaurant. You can also purchase tickets for the Princess Ashika and Patterson Brothers ferries at the hotel.

Places to Stay – Outside Labasa
The Fiji government has several guest houses scattered throughout the country. One of them is located in Nabouwalu, one of the westernmost points of Vanua Levu and a six-hour bus ride from Labasa. It is also reachable by commercial boat from Suva or Savusavu. Visitors may stay if there are no government officials occupying the bunks. Accommodation is spartan but the price is only a few dollars per night. Phone 84 010 to see what the space situation is.

Places to Stay – Offshore
Located on 16-hectare Nukubati Island about 40 km from Labasa, *Coral Island Resort* (tel 82 955) is one of Fiji's newest. Getting there involves a 50-minute car ride followed by a five-minute boat shuttle. There are 14 units (eight air-conditioned) each capable of sleeping four. Amenities include restaurant, bar, live music, hot and cold water, refrigerator and ceiling fan. Activities include snorkelling, scuba diving, water skiing, glass-bottom boat, deep-sea fishing, outrigger canoes and a great beach. Prices are F$45 single and F$70 double, including meals. Specialty of the area is diving, which is provided by the hotel for an extra charge. According to owner Paul Jaduram, the hotel has become a favourite for honeymooners who really want to get away from it all.

Places to Eat
Labasa is not a gourmet's delight, but there are several decent places to dine. *Isa Lei* on Sangam Avenue has good Indian

cuisine for F$3-6 and has a bar. *Nanyang* at the Takia Hotel and *Wun Wuh* on Nasekula Rd both have good Chinese food for F$2-5.

GETTING THERE
Air Fiji Air has daily service from Suva to Savusavu for F$36 one way, and Sunflower flies from Nadi to Savusavu (F$55) and Labasa (F$57) one way as well. Air Pacific has daily flights from Suva to Labasa for F$38, and from Nadi to Labasa for F$57.

Boat North West Shipping Line's ferry *Princess Ashika* and Patterson Brothers vessels both offer services to Vanua Levu on an almost daily basis. Phone 385 388 for more information on the *Princess Ashika* and purchase tickets at Vanua House Kiosk on Victoria Parade in Suva. In Labasa purchase tickets at the Hotel Takia Lobby (tel 81 655) and in Savusavu at the Arm Trading Building (tel 86 201). For Patterson Brothers phone 315 644 in Suva and 82 646 in Labasa for schedules, and purchase tickets at Epworth House in Suva.

The ferries provide roll-on/roll-off service for cars. The more adventurous may want to rent a car in Suva, disembark in Savusavu and then drive over the mountain from Savusavu to Labasa or along the Hibiscus Highway. To book ferry-*cum*-auto passage call Thomas Cook Travel at 23 861 in Suva. The price for three-day rental including ferry is about F$150. Fares for the ferry are F$18 with Patterson Brothers from Suva to Savusavu or Nabouwalu, and F$28 on the *Princess Ashika* from Suva to Savusavu. Labasa fares are slightly higher because they include bus fare from Savusavu.

GETTING AROUND
The road system is not as extensive on Vanua Levu as on Viti Levu, but the three-hour drive over the hump from Savusavu to Labasa is filled with wonderful mountain scenery. Although the road is unpaved,

it's not bad. Likewise, the Hibiscus Highway from Savusavu along the southern coast is unpaved but is scenic and quite drivable.

Car Rental Both Budget (tel 81 199) and Paul's Rent A Car (tel 81 595) have cars available in Labasa. Rates at Paul's are F$20-25 per day plus F$0.20-.25 per km depending on the model.

Bus Buses run four times daily from Savusavu to Labasa and vice versa; the fare is about F$3. Buses also make the six-hour run to Nabouwalu on the western side of the island. It is an arduous journey and there is no accommodation on that side of the island except the government rest house.

Taveuni

Taveuni, known as the 'Garden Island' of Fiji, is extremely rugged, wet and verdant. Located only seven km off the coast from Vanua Levu, it has excellent air and sea transportation from Viti Levu and Vanua Levu but remains relatively non-touristed. Its primary attraction is the landscape – stands of virgin rain forest, a rare array of flora and fauna, two waterfalls and a legendary lake. There is one major moderately priced hotel on the island (Taveuni International Resort), a smaller upscale establishment (The Maravu), an inexpensive guest house (Kaba's) and a condo development known as Taveuni Estates. Everyone on the island (even the Indians) speaks Fijian. The local dialect is characterised by the absence of the consonant 'k', which becomes a glottal stop.

A little-known fact about Taveuni is that it is one of the few places in the archipelago with traditional surfing. Because ancient surfers were here long before the sport ever reached Tahiti or Hawaii, Taveuni may actually be surfing's home.

Taveuni is also remarkable for its diversity of birdlife. It is the home of the orange dove – the male of the species, whose green-speckled plumage changes in season to flaming orange. Years before the European arrived, Taveuni was famous for its *kula* – a species of parrot indigenous to the area. In ancient times trading parties of Tongans would journey to Fiji in order to barter for the brilliant maroon feathers of this bird, which they then took to Samoa to exchange for fine mats. Taveuni is also one of only two islands in the Lau group (the other is Cicia) where the Australian magpie was introduced to control coconut pests. Though a conspicuous part of the fauna, this successful introduction is admired for its melodic song.

Geography

Taveuni is more or less tied with Kadavu as the third largest island in the archipelago. It is still a fraction of the size of Viti Levu or Vanua Levu, but is triple the size of Gau, the next island in order of size. Taveuni is about 42 km long and between 10 and 11 km in average width, its area being 435 square km. The island is wholly of volcanic origin (having had volcanic activity as recently as 2000 years ago) and has a uniform backbone of volcanic cones forming a 900-metre ridge over 16 km long. Among the four summits contained in this ridge, two (Uluigalau, 1241 metres high at the south end; and Des Voeux Peak, 1195 metres in the centre) are among the highest mountains in Fiji. Mt Uluigalau, the highest point in Taveuni, also has the distinction of being directly under the 180th meridian (also known as the international dateline) 12 hours east and west of Greenwich. Though the dateline no longer officially runs through Taveuni (it was changed for the sake of convenience), the marker can still be seen on the beach near Waiyevo and visitors can purchase T-shirts commemorating the landmark.

The high ridge of Taveuni lies directly in the path of the prevailing winds, in a perfect position to intercept moisture, and much of the time lies hidden in a cloud. The higher slopes on the windward side may receive over 1000 cm (30 feet!) of rain per year and, as you might expect, are smothered with dense forest.

The 'Garden Island of Fiji' possesses some of the nation's best coconut plantations and its rich, reddish loam soil is ideal for agricultural development. It was on this land that high-grade cotton was raised and exported to Europe during the civil war in the United States. Later sugar cane was grown. Although coffee and tropical fruit grow in profusion and sheep, cattle and poultry have been raised, the staple of the island's economy has always been copra.

History

The first European to sight Taveuni was Abel Tasman in 1643. Tasman was northeast of Taveuni in the stretch of water that now bears his name, and though visibility was poor he most likely glimpsed points of land which he took to be separate islands but were probably the peaks of Taveuni and islands to the north.

Taveuni's inhabitants were feared throughout the Fiji group as fierce warriors who relished the taste of human flesh. In prehistoric times the village of Vuna was the most important settlement on the island, but it eventually lost this status to the more northerly village of Somosomo in a series of tribal wars. Perhaps the most memorable battle in Somosomo occurred when the Tongan warlord Ma'afu was defeated by the Fijian chief Tui Cakau in a skirmish that took place several years before Fiji's cession to Great Britain. Somosomo currently holds the title of 'chiefly village' and is also the burial site of one of Fiji's most important missionaries, William Cross. The William Cross Memorial Church, established in 1839, suffered a great deal of damage during a 1979 earthquake and has been rebuilt in Somosomo.

Except for tribal struggles and later settlement by planters, Taveuni remained out of the historical spotlight. Perhaps the most interesting visitor to come along was Commandant Charles Wilkes of the American expedition, who visited Somosomo in 1840.

One of the more fascinating historical incidents concerns the villages of Lovonivonu and Kanacea. Both are populated

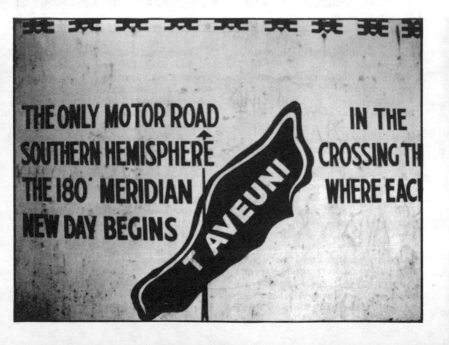

THE ONLY MOTOR ROAD IN THE
SOUTHERN HEMISPHERE CROSSING TH
THE 180° MERIDIAN WHERE EAC
NEW DAY BEGINS

TAVEUNI

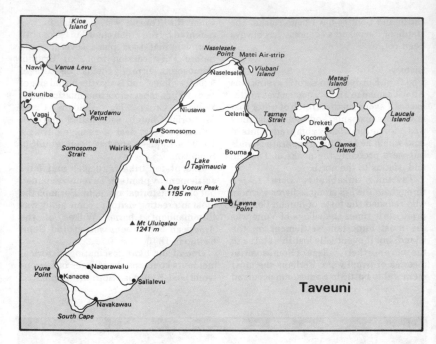

Taveuni

by descendants of inhabitants of several other islands sold by the chief, 'Tui Cakau,' to Europeans. The inhabitants were deprived of their land as punishment for taking sides with the Tongans against Tui Cakau during a war.

Things to Do & See

Perhaps the most famous geographical landmark on the island is **Lake Tagimaucia**, which is located in an old crater 823 metres high in the mountains. Difficult to hike to, the lake is filled with floating masses of vegetation and is home to Fiji's most famous and beautiful flower, the tagimaucia, which produces red blooms with white centres. Contrary to popular mythology which suggests that the tagimaucia flower grows nowhere else but on the shores of the lake, the epiphytic plant does flourish elsewhere. Still, any attempt to transplant the flower at a lower altitude has failed.

There are at least two legends attached to this lake. The first relates to the greenish hue imparted to its perimeter by the submerged vegetation. The legend asserts that the fat of all turtles killed on Taveuni are taken by spirits to the lake. The more famous tale (or at least one version of it) is attached to the flower and concerns a small girl who lived above the shores of the lake. It seems one day she was playing when she should have been attending to her chores. Annoyed by her behaviour, her mother spanked the daughter and chased her out of the home. She ran sobbing and blundered into a tree full of thick vines in which she became entangled. As the tears rolled down her cheeks they turned to blood, which fell on the vine and turned to flowers. The girl did manage to free herself and lived happily ever after. According to historian R A Derrick, the derivation of the name is as follows: The child of a local chief, having seen the flower, cried 'Tagi' for it; but as it could not be transplanted crying was useless, (maumau), for there was nothing that resembled it (ucia) to put in its place.

Getting to the lake, as I can personally attest to, is no easy matter and necessitates hiring a guide for anywhere from F$10-20. Leave yourself a full day for the arduous trek, which begins near the Mormon church in the village of Somosomo. A guide can be recruited from the village, or enquire at the nearby hotel. This is not for the faint-hearted; trekkers should be in above-average condition for this journey.

The **administrative centre** isn't a renowned attraction but visitors might like to know that it is situated in Waiyevo, above the site of the International Hotel. Nearby are a hospital, dock, schools and police station.

Aside from Lake Tagimaucia, **Bouma Falls**, 36 km from the International Hotel (on the opposite side of the island from Somosomo), is definitely worth seeing. To get there, take the local bus (which departs at 9 am from the hotel) heading towards the north end of the island. You can also take a taxi but the round-trip fare is F$25. Walk 100 metres past the village and take the track inland 200-300 metres to the falls. They cascade over 24 metres into a pool which is swimmable. Admission to the falls, which are on native land, is F$1.

Near Lavena Village (past Bouma Falls) is another **waterfall** that plummets off a cliff directly into the sea. During WW II, ships requiring fresh water could actually go beneath the falls and fill their tanks with ease! To get a guided tour there, contact Rafaele Manaseva c/o PWD Depot at Waiyevo.

A few km past the falls is **Lavena Beach**, a gorgeous white-sand beach with fine snorkelling and swimming. You can take the local bus here as well or a taxi for F$35. Combining the falls and the beach for a day's outing is an excellent idea.

Prince Charles Beach, towards the airport coming from the hotel, is also of the white-sand variety and has plenty of shade and picnic tables. Swimming is great with plenty of shallow areas for kids.

Another option is the **Salialevu Plantation**, the island's largest copra/beef plantation. It is located about 35 km from the International Hotel. On the plantation grounds are the ruins of the 100-year-old Billyard Sugar Mill. There are also freshwater pools and a beach, but avoid swimming in the ocean – it's treacherous here. Ask permission of the plantation manager before entering because it is private property.

Nearby is **Dolphin Bay**, where you can water ski and picnic. Arrange transportation with the hotel (approximately F$35) or take a rental car.

There is a great **water slide** on the Waitovala Estate, owned by Burns Philp. The estate is about two km south of Somosomo, near the government station. Ask permission first of Ben Johnson, the local manager of Burns Philp.

Also of interest is the **coconut cream and cheese factory** at Nagasau, about 17 km from the International Hotel, towards the airport.

For sporting types **Taveuni Estates** offers golf, tennis and lawn bowling for 'moderate' fees. Enquire at the hotel for information.

Diving in Taveuni is world class. Rick Cammick is the dean of Taveuni divers – he dives solely in the Somosomo Straits which has the now famous 'Rainbow Reef,' an unusual drop-off with a soft white coral wall. The Somosomo Straits are known for very strong currents, a characteristic that promotes the growth of soft coral. Cammick has two boats, one measuring 10 metres, and the other a 13-metre aluminum catamaran designed specifically as a dive vessel. At no charge, Cammick will transfer a diver staying anywhere on the island for a day's dive which costs F$50 per day. The rate includes lunch, two tanks and backpack.

Shell collecting Taveuni's reefs offer some of the best shelling spots in the world. The island is currently under government study as a source of shells for commercial sales.

Places to Stay

Accommodation on Taveuni is limited. The largest place on the island is the *International Hotel* (tel 87 286), formerly Castaway Taveuni. The 35-room hotel fronts the sea three km south of Somosomo. The hotel is adequate for most people and the staff is friendly. However, it needs refurbishing. The resort has a pool, sauna, restaurant, bar and nightly entertainment. Activities include deep-sea fishing, water skiing, diving, snorkelling, and nearby golf, tennis and lawn bowling at Taveuni Estates. Prices begin at F$45 single, F$50 twin and F$60 triple. Rates include airport transfers as well as complimentary use of golf, tennis and lawn-bowling facilities. The menu is good (F$5-12) and the best dish is the local fresh fish. The hotel organises trips to the lake either with guides (F$20 for the four-hour hike) or via four-wheel-drive truck (a half-hour drive and another half hour on foot for F$10). There is a nearby cave where those with a plague (*lamulamu*) were sealed inside and buried alive. The hotel will take you inside to see the ancient bones. Also available is windsurfing (F$5/hour), catamarans (F$10/hour) and mopeds (F$5/hour).

The inexpensive alternative to the hotel is *Kaba's Guest House* (tel 58, ask for Taveuni operator), located in Somosomo. They have three double rooms with communal cooking facilities for F$8 per night single and F$15 double. It is very clean and there is an excellent supermarket (also owned by Kaba) nearby.

Maravu Plantation Resort (tel 401 A) is the upscale resort in Taveuni. Located one km from the airport, it is a working plantation with 10 large *bures*. The resort is perched on a gentle slope in a grove of coconut trees and has the advantage of having a small beach within walking distance. It is owned and operated by Ormand and Robert Eyre, both of whom were born on Taveuni but spent years in Europe – and it shows. They serve the best food on the island; the cuisine is European, Indian, French, Italian and local. Despite the rustic environment, the resort lends a definite air of refinement to the Taveuni hotel scene. The Eyres provide tours of their 54-acre plantation, which has cattle, pigs, goats and chickens. Visitors can see the stages of copra production, from collecting the nuts all the way to bagging and weighing. Other activities include nature treks (with guides available), four-wheel-drive excursions, windsurfing, snorkelling, fishing and bicycling. Rental cars are available. The family owns four horses and there is a multitude of trails nearby. There are also visits to some of the uninhabited islets nearby where you can be left alone for the day with a fresh fish to barbecue in an open pit. Rates are F$80 per day for a double in finely crafted *bures* and F$25 per day for three great meals.

Dive Taveuni (tel 406 M) located near the airstrip (just across the road from Maravu) is not only one of the best dive operations in Fiji, but also has four *bures* for rent for F$45 per person per day including three meals. Amenities include solar-generated electricity and solar-heated water. The food is good and the accommodation is more than adequate. No booze is served on the premises so you must bring your own.

GETTING THERE

Air Both Fiji Air and Sunflower Airlines serve Taveuni. Fiji Air flies daily for F$41 (one way) from Nausori Airport. Sunflower has one daily flight from Nadi to Taveuni for F$64, a flight from Savusavu to Taveuni for F$24 (one way), and a Labasa-Taveuni flight for F$25 (one way).

Boat Ferryboat service from Suva via the *Princess Ashika* leaves on Thursday at 6 am from Princess Wharf. Return service from Taveuni to Savusavu, Labasa, Levuka and Suva leaves at noon on Friday. Fare is F$34.

GETTING AROUND

A good (although not wholly paved) highway runs the entire length of the western side of Taveuni. It runs from

Vuna in the south around the northern end of the island to Lavena Point midway around the opposite side. There is also a cross-island route from Vuna to Salialevu on the southern side. There is a local bus service throughout the island three times daily (9 am, 12.30 and 5 pm), leaving from Waiyevo. Taxis are always available but are expensive for long jaunts.

Qamea & Laucala

Qamea, Laucala and tiny Matagi are volcanic islands grouped immediately to the east of Thurston Point, Taveuni. Qamea and Laucala are surrounded by one barrier reef. Until only a few years ago these islands were never visited by tourists because there was no accommodation. Today Qamea has one small resort, and Laucala, which is owned by American financial publisher Malcolm Forbes, has the most exclusive resort in Fiji.

QAMEA

Situated 2.5 km from Thurston Point, Qamea is 10 km long and varies in width from several hundred metres to five km. Its area is 34 square km. Like its large island neighbours, Qamea is rugged and covered by dense forest. Steep-sided valleys lie between high hills, some of which approach 300 metres in height. Qamea's Naivivi Bay is known geographically as a 'hurricane hole' – in other words, it is sheltered naturally from hurricanes. During these periods many vessels anchor offshore of the hotel.

For its size, Qamea is a populous island, having six villages (Kocoma being the largest) and a population of 500. Both Qamea's and Laucala's original populations were displaced during the 19th century by Tui Cakau, a chief who was angry with the original inhabitants for having taken the side of his enemy, Ma'afu, during a tribal conflict.

Like Taveuni, Qamea is of interest to naturalists because the mongoose was never introduced here; thus the indigenous fauna, especially birdlife, was never interfered with. For some reason (unknown to me), natives of Qamea are referred to as *kai-Farani* (Frenchmen) – not a compliment. They prepare a local food called *paileve* – a concoction fermented in a pit.

Places To Stay

There's only one place to stay, *Qamea Beach Club* (tel 87 220), an eight-*bure* resort located on 17 hectares of land. Activities include water skiing, fishing, windsurfing, snorkelling, sailing, shelling, canoeing, a waterfall tour and crab hunts. Qamea is a comparatively big island compared to the Mamanucas (offshore from Viti Levu) so you don't get the claustrophobic feeling of being on a small island. There is plenty of room for nature walks and there are organised visits to the local village of Vatusogosogo, which has traditional thatched *bures* and is quite beautiful. The hotel also has two dive masters, two dive boats and all the equipment. Reefs in the area are reportedly magnificent. Accommodation is in private *bures*, all facing the beach, with verandah, overhead fan and hammock. The food is excellent and is included in the price of F$90 single and F$110 double.

Getting There

Clients of Qamea Beach Club are picked up by boat from the airport at Taveuni, which is only a 15-minute, four-km ride away.

LAUCALA

Laucala lies east of Qamea, separated by a strait which is only several hundred metres wide. It is five km long and and from 1½ to three km wide, with an area of 12 square km. It was sold by Tui Cakau – who was once kept a prisoner on the island – to Europeans who turned it into a copra plantation and later sold it to the Carpenter Group, an Australian corporation. In 1972 the owners sold the island to Malcolm 'Capitalist Tool' Forbes for a cool US$1 million. When Forbes purchased Laucala, the workers' housing – ramshackle tenements – were in a sorry state of disrepair. Since then the American millionaire has spent an undisclosed fortune constructing over 40 modern homes for his workers, all of which have water seal toilets, piped-in spring water for washing, individual cisterns for drinking water, modern kitchens and electricity. He has also built a home for himself, four guest houses, a school complex, a copra plant, a store, workshop, dormitory, boathouse, refrigeration plant, airstrip and other facilities. Primary education is free on Laucala (unlike the rest of Fiji) and 'Fiji Forbes' will pay for up to one half of a youngster's secondary education, including the university level.

Workers' paradise? Perhaps. However, Laucala is different in other ways. Because the island is a private estate – one of many owned by Forbes around the world – manager Noel Douglas, a fourth-generation European of Fijian birth, has the authority to expel anyone from the island. This he does without hesitation to drunkards or other troublemakers he feels are detrimental to the well-being of the community.

For precisely this reason, he is disliked by some of the younger people who do not care to be the objects of his discipline. Douglas, who speaks the local dialect fluently, does not seemed worried about winning popularity contests. He says, 'You have to carry the big stick every once in a while. The older people on Laucala understand this reasoning and support it.'

Although the island has all the trappings of a Fijian community, there are fundamental differences between it and a typical village. Since it is a private estate, the traditional authority of village government is non-existent. In some instances, as in cases where people are removed from the island, Douglas wields even more power than a chief might.

The lack of traditional authority accounts for other differences between the Laucala and more typical communities. A University of the South Pacific student whose father lives on Laucala told me, 'Dress is different on the island. For example, some women wear pants which they would never do in a village. Also, church attendance is much poorer than you would expect in an average community. There is no chief or village elder to watch over you, which is a sort of unnatural situation for villagers.'

In Douglas' opinion, improved hygiene and housing serve to strengthen the islanders' culture. He feels that because locals don't have to compete for jobs and thus fall into the western 'rat race' syndrome, there have been few changes in their lifestyle. When asked if they were satisfied with their lives on Laucala, the residents replied that they liked their homes, were pleased with their jobs, were happy that their children's education was paid for, and agreed unanimously that the quality of life had improved since Forbes took over.

Roughly half the workers on the island are native Laucalans, while the other half come from neighbouring villages on nearby Qamea or elsewhere. The plantation supplies jobs to people in an area where outside employment is nil and people live largely in a subsistence economy. Cash inevitably filters down to the non-resident relatives of those who work on Laucala, thus spreading the wealth.

Because copra farming is not the most profitable enterprise, Fiji Forbes has invested money into the island's future by diversifying industry through the introduction of animal husbandry (cattle and goat ranching) and the establishment of a small-scale resort for high-rolling tourists. To date, the island is not yet self-supporting, but with one of the world's pre-eminent capitalists running the show, chances are good that one day it will be in the black.

Places to Stay

One very well-travelled airline pilot has called Laucala 'the ultimate tropical paradise' – he and his wife had no bad words for the island's exclusive resort.

Certainly on Laucala, which specialises in game fishing, Robinson Crusoe never had it so good.

When you disembark from your scheduled flight in Nadi, you are met by your own personal pilot who skippers a twin-engine, green-and-gold Navajo Chieftain (with 'Capitalist Tool' inscribed on the side). You are whisked to Laucala, 90 minutes away by air. Guests have their own private *bure* complete with fully stocked bar, including wines (which are part of the price). A chef makes your dinner in your own home and reports are he knows how to cook pretty damn well. Since fishing is the main attraction, a fishing boat (with skipper) and tournament-quality tackle are provided. You apparently need the tournament quality because fishing is superb. You can expect to hook black Pacific sailfish up to 90 kg, yellowfin tuna up to 45 kg, barracuda up to 45 kg, mahimahi up to 45 kg, and even black marlin up to 225 kg.

The coves and inlets around Laucala also offer great fishing, especially for those using light spinning tackle and lures. Twenty-two km away from Laucala is a great reef for snorkelling and scuba diving. Near the reef is also a small sandy island for picnicking or diving excursions. Naturally Forbes 'throws in' amenities such as scuba tanks and water-skiing gear so you can dive or ski to your heart's content. For those who want to explore Laucala itself there is even a jeep with which to explore the island.

Other amenities include jet ski, wind-surfing, VCR with supply of movies, tennis, volleyball and swimming pool.

The resort has four air-conditioned guest *bures* which sleep up to eight people. Two are equipped with two bedrooms and baths, and two have one bedroom with bath. All have a living room, bar and kitchen. The price is US$1650 per person for seven days and eight nights (minimum stay). A 10% deposit secures your reservation and the balance must be paid at least four weeks prior to arrival. The price, as mentioned, includes everything.

Contact Fiji Forbes Inc, c/o Forbes Magazine, 60 Fifth Avenue, New York, New York 10011, USA, tel 212 620 2461. Or write to Fiji Forbes Inc, Laucala Island, Waiyevo PO Box 41, Taveuni, Fiji. Direct phone is 87 Taveuni; request Laucala 120.

Getting There

There is air service for Forbes' clients, and local boats ferry from Qamea.

Kadavu

The Kadavu group lies between 88 and 96 km south of Suva. Aside from the main island of Kadavu, which ranks fourth in size in the archipelago, the group includes the island of Ono and a number of smaller islands lying within the Astrolabe Reefs and comprising its northern extension.

Kadavu, with a population of approximately 8700, is not one of the tourist hot spots and retains a conservative, traditional culture. It is an island known for its headstrong, independent thinkers – its chiefly system is different from that in other parts of Fiji, allowing for stronger local chiefs rather than a few 'big chiefs' running affairs.

There is one resort on Galoa (formerly a whaling station) in the south, and several village-style accommodation possibilities are being planned on the main island. The area is best known for its fantastic diving in the Astrolabe Reef, considered one of the finest 'dive destinations' in the world. Some villagers of Kadavu are also known for their ability to call turtles up from the depths of the sea. Other more arcane facts about the island are that it's the home of a rare parrot; it's famed for raising goats; the local yaqona is very strong; and fishing between Kadavu and Beqa is excellent.

Geography

The Kadavu group is volcanic in nature, the main island being Kadavu, which is 93 km long and varies in width from several hundred metres to 13 km. It has an area of 408 square km. All its coasts are deeply indented, some bays biting so far into the land that they almost divide the island. One geographer has suggested that the shape of Kadavu resembles a wasp whose head, thorax and abdomen are linked by narrow waists. Thus Vunisea (where the adminstrative center is located), Namalata Bay and Galoa Harbour are separated by only a sandy isthmus standing a few metres above sea level; and at Vunisea the heads of Daku and Soso bays approach within 1100 metres of each other with only a low ridge between. This same characteristic occurs elsewhere on the island on varying scale – the shape and arrangement of these bays suggests they may have been drowned valleys.

Kadavu is rugged and its mountains are high for so narrow an island. Several peaks rise over 600 metres high, many are half that size. Coasts are generally fringed with coral reefs, the most famous being the 48-km loop of the Great Astrolabe Reef on Kadavu's northern extension.

The island can be divided into several main areas. The west end is 24 km long and dominated by Nabukelevu (Mt Washington), 822 metres high. Flanking the mountain on the south side are lovely crescent-shaped beaches. From this peak a spur runs west to Cape Washington – a rocky bluff crowned by a lighthouse – and continues in a range terminating in a steep cross range overlooking Galoa Harbour. One of the most beautiful villages in Fiji, Daviqele, is located in this area. The northern part of this region is called Yawe, known for its large earthenware cooking pottery still made by the women of Nalotu village. Most of the northern coast extending to the Sanima and Yale districts further east is dry and sheltered with reed-like vegetation and reefs offshore. Much of the goat raising is done here.

The link between the island's west end and its centre is Namalata Isthmus, known to Fijians as *Na Yarabale* (the place where the canoes are dragged across). On the isthmus are located Vunisea, the government station, high school, hospital, administration and airstrip. There are a few small stores and a public market in this vicinity. In the same area is the village of Namuana, home of the people who can call turtles from the sea.

Opposite the isthmus on the southern side is Galoa Harbour, and in the harbour is 2.5-km-long Galoa Island (for which the harbour was named). On the southernmost point of this part of the island is a tiny islet, Tawadromu, which at one time was home to an American Indian – the sole representative of his race among the mixed population of the period. Why he stayed and what he was doing there is anyone's guess. Further along the southern coast is the Naceva area, perhaps the most untouched and primeval in nature, with forests, mangrove swamps along the water's edge, many waterfalls and an ever-present mist hanging over the mountains.

The Ono Island group, enclosed by the Great Astrolabe Reef, has wonderful fishing and diving. Cruise ships sometimes stop at Dravuni Island, perhaps because there are great white-sand beaches. There is also a fisheries station. Yachts find the area appealing but must first get a permit to stop there. Locals still practise an ancient ritual of fermenting stored foodstuffs (breadfruit, plantains and dalo) underground. A hole is dug in the ground, the food is placed in it and is stored up to several years as an insurance in times of need. This used to be done throughout Fiji but is now rare.

History

Kadavu was first sighted by Captain Bligh on his return voyage to Fiji aboard *HMS Providence* in 1792. Seven years later, the American vessel *Ann & Hope*, skippered by Captain C Bently, touched on Kadavu while on a voyage from Australia. In 1827 the French commander Dumont d'Urville brought the *Astrolabe* to the island, nearly running it on the great reef that envelops the northern extension of the Kadavu group. He named the reef after his ship. Today this reef area is considered one of the finest diving areas in the world.

In later years, Tavuki Bay on the island

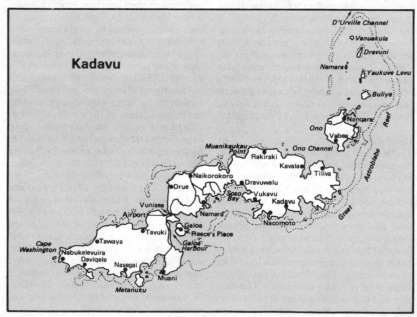

was frequented by beche de mer traders and by whalers from Sydney in Australia and from the New England ports of the United States. By this time whale teeth (chiefly those of the Cachalot species) had replaced the ancient form of *tabua* in religious ceremonies and became an important item of barter with the whalers. The teeth were in such demand that on one occasion a Fijian chief kidnapped a mate and ship's crew of the *Nimrod* from Sydney in exchange for whale teeth he had seen on the ship. As years passed and overseas shipping increased, Galoa Harbour in Kadavu became a regular stop for mail ships from San Francisco, Sydney and Auckland. At Galoa (which was once considered as a possible capital for the Fiji Colony), passenger cargo and mails were trans-shipped to the steamers of the branch line running to New Zealand, and to the small vessels plying between the port and Levuka. Galoa was not a busy port; even though the anchorage was spacious and well protected, it was only used for about three years. The shore accommodation, according to Derrick, was 'wretched,' consisting of a few huts, several small shops and a whisky store. After this brief flurry of activity the island reverted to its former sleepy nature.

Vunisea

This is the largest settlement on the island. Located near the airstrip, it is a government station and has stores, a hospital, school, post office and a jetty. There are several beaches in the vicinity. Nearby also is Mbiana, an 'off-licence' store where the only beer on the island is sold. West of Vunisea is the traditional turtle-calling stone where the Namuana villagers have called turtles from the depths of the sea for generations.

Beaches

There is a good beach north of Vunisea's jetty (on Crown land) and another (with a waterfall after it rains and great swimming) at Udulevu just around the western corner of Vunisea Bay. The Udulevu beach is actually on village land but it's OK to visit if you wade along the shore and stay away from nearby Namuana village.

Waikana Falls

About two km south of the airport and a short hike off the road is Waikana Falls, which has two nice pools for swimming.

Better yet is another, wonderful, more secluded **waterfall/pool** five to six km east of Vunisea – probably on village land but not close enough to any one settlement, so it's generally considered public.

Places to Stay

Reece's Place on Galoa Island is a F$5, 20-minute boat ride from the administrative centre at Vunisea. Situated off the southern coast, the resort is on a small peninsula surrounded by reefs and great beaches. Fishing and snorkelling are excellent. Joe and Mona Reece operate a working farm, thus providing plenty of fresh vegetables and fruit. There is no electricity nor, as Joe Reece points out, is there any noise. Food is homestyle family cooking and there is accommodation for eight in several Fijian-style *bures*. Price including accommodation and three meals is F$12 per night per person. Campers pay F$2 per night. Write to Joe and Mona Reece at PO Box 6, Vunisea, Kadavu for more information.

Visitors interested in staying in a Fijian village may contact a man named Vavu in *Murani village*, south of Vunisea along on the coast. Visitors may either stay with the family for about F$10 per night or pitch their tents on a deserted beach about three km from the village for F$3 per night. The F$10 price is approximate because it is best to do things Fijian style – presenting small gifts such as cloth, T-shirts, tools, tobacco, and then leaving a parting gift of cash (about F$50 if you stay a week). You should bring the obligatory yaqona for the arriving ceremony.

Places to Eat

There is a miniscule coffee shop at the airport, but short of that and *Reece's Place*, there really is no formal eatery.

GETTING THERE

Fiji Air has daily (except Sunday) flights to Kadavu for F$36 (one way). Sunflower has two flights (Friday and Sunday) for F$39. Inter-island vessels leave twice a week from Princess Wharf (behind Suva Market) and the best way to get a berth is to go down personally and talk to the captain. Boats go to Vunisea and it is an easy matter to catch one to Galoa.

GETTING AROUND

There are a few buses on the island that will get you to the outer villages, but Kadavu lacks a good road system. The best way to get around is by foot or boat. Vavu in Murani village has a boat and is willing to take people fishing or on excursions for a fee. Organise that with him. Boats are also undoubtedly on hire in Vunisea. Check with the local police or government station for information.

Top: Taveuni sunset (RK)
Left: Government vessel off coast of Taveuni (RK)
Right: Children sampling *yaqona*, Levuka, Ovalau (RK)

Top: Village scene, Rotuma (JP)
Bottom: Village scene, Qamea (RK)

The Lau Group

The islands and atolls of the Lau or Eastern Group are scattered over an area of 114,000 square km to the south-east of Viti Levu. The main islands of the Tongan group extend in a parallel chain less than 320 km to the east; and in fact southern Lau is closer to Tonga than it is to Suva. Here Tongan influence has been important for as long as 1000 years, and during the mid-19th century it was dominant. Students of the South Pacific will note that Tongan place names are common throughout the area; and on many of the islands Tongan was spoken as freely as Fijian. Likewise, material culture, customs and traditions were all modified by Tongan contacts.

The aggregate area of the Lau group is about 461 square km, which exceeds that of Taveuni or Kadavu; but since one third of this is compound of the three Islands of Moala, Lakeba and Vanua Balavu, and there are five others above 26 square km in area, the majority of the 60-odd islands that make up the group are very small.

History
European discovery of the Lau group was piecemeal, being spread over nearly 50 years, from Cook's visit to Vatoa in 1774 to Bellingshausen's discovery of the Ono group in 1820.

As early as 1814 there existed charts of the archipelago which contained more reliable information about the area than about any other part of Fiji; but the names of the islands were unrecognisable because the written Fijian language had not been developed and the European discoverers had scarcely any contact with the islanders.

Although the islands are classified for administrative purposes as one group, until the middle of the last century they comprised three different territories: northern Lau, Lau proper, and the Moala group. Northern Lau extended as far south as Tuvuca, and paid tribute to the chiefs of Cakaudrove (Vanua Levu) until about 1855, when the Tongan warlord Ma'afu acquired the right of sovereignty over the area and established his headquarters at Lomaloma in Vanuabalavu. Lau proper, which extended from Cicia to Ono-i-Lau in the extreme south, was under the authority of Tui Nayau, the paramount chief of Lakeba. (This title incidentally is now held by Ratu Sir Kamisese Mara, the prime minister). With the advent of Ma'afu, however, the Tui Nayau's influence waned; and although he kept title as 'king' of the region, he was dominated by the Tongans. The Moala group historically had affiliations with Lomaiviti and Bau, rather than with Lau, but shortly after Ma'afu established himself at Lomaloma he extended his influence over the Moala area as well.

Under Ma'afu's control during the mid-19th century, the Lau group was united and attained a degree of prosperity and peace unknown before. Ma'afu created a title for himself, 'Tui Lau' (King of Lau), encouraged the settlement of Europeans, and developed a constitution and set of laws. His Lau Confederation proved to be the most successful of the early attempts at constitutional government in Fiji.

LAKEBA
Lakeba, with a population of about 2000 inhabitants in eight villages, is the largest island in the Lau group, and politically the most important. It is one of the few places in Lau that has visitor accommodation. Lakeba is also the home island of Ratu Sir Kamisese Mara, the prime minister of Fiji. The main source of income on the island is copra production, which is expedited by the presence of a coconut mill four km outside the government station at Tubou.

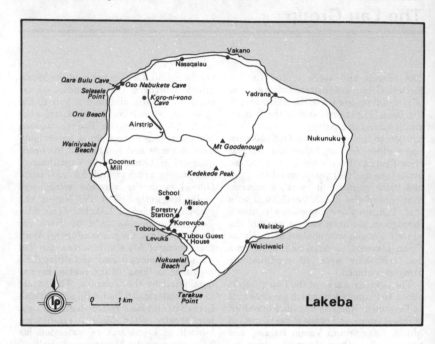

Lakeba

Geography

Lakeba is irregularly oval in outline, shaped somewhat like a shark's tooth, with a tongue of land jutting out from the south coast. The island is about nine km long and nearly as wide, has an area of 57 square km, and ranks as the 10th largest island in the archipelago. The central mass of Lakeba is volcanic in origin, the highest point rising to 219 metres. On the west and north-west slopes are masses of coralliferous limestone forming steep bluffs, cliffs and several major caves near the village of Nasaqalau. The soil of Lakeba is fertile and the once bare hills have been planted with pine trees. Of late Lakeba has been the subject of a thorough archaeological excavation which has revealed the presence of a massive fortification, built perhaps a thousand years ago as a defence against Tongan invaders. The fortification was believed to have been large enough to house 2500

people, the entire population of the island.

Culture & Customs

As has frequently been mentioned, Tongan influence in language and culture is strong in Lakeba. The cultural manifestations of Tongan culture even appear in the shapes of the houses, which are rounded (as in Samoa and Tonga) rather than square-ended as in the rest of Fiji. Even when homes are constructed with wooden materials, the ends are sometimes rounded. Church services also exhibit Tongan origins, notably a special evening service called *polotu* which features many Tongan hymns. On formal occasions Tongan clothing is worn, especially a mat which is tied around the waist. Tongan *mekes* (dances) may also be performed.

Shark Calling There is one clan in the village of Nasaqalau where live the only people in Fiji who can call sharks. They do this annually in October or November – though generally not for the benefit of visitors. The power to do this comes from the village of Wainikeli in Taveuni, where some of the settlers from Nasaqalau originate. Not only are these folks imbued with the power to call sharks, but according to tradition, the same force serves as a protection from sharks if a boat capsizes.

The ritual goes something like this: About a month before the ceremony a post is stuck in the reef with a piece of *masi* (tapa cloth) attached to the end of it (something like a pennant) in the area where the sharks are to be called. No one is allowed in the vicinity of the post. A *bete* or traditional Fijian priest performs a daily yaqona ceremony nearby and checks the area daily to make sure no one fishes or trespasses.

When the big day comes, the caller (a man or woman) wades in the water, neck high, and begins chanting. Within 30 minutes to an hour a school of up to 50 sharks, led by a white shark, will circle the caller. The sharks are then led to the shallows where all of them (except the white shark) may be killed and later eaten.

In former times many sharks were killed as part of the annual event, but it has been about 40 years since sharks have been killed during this ceremony. Currently, the prime minister is encouraging the revival of the complete ritual. Visitors lucky enough to attend should be prepared to offer donations to a charitable Fijian institution. No money should be offered as payment for this ceremony. According to my source, villagers believe the 'leader shark' was formerly incarnated as a young man and would dislike commercialisation, which would be sacrilege. Should the villagers not respect tradition, it is believed the sharks may decide not to show up one day. There is no scientific explanation for the seemingly obedient sharks. One theory is that the arrival of the sharks may be connected to an annual migration.

Stopping the Sun As if calling sharks wasn't challenging enough for the villagers of Nasaqalau, I am told they also have the power to stop the sun, if just for a few minutes. Galu Veitokiaki, an old friend and native of Nasaqalau, told me that if someone is on their way to the village around dusk, he/she may want a little extra daylight in order to get home in time for dinner. If this is the case, the villager goes to Saubukbuki (near the village) and picks a certain type of reed. After that, he calls to the sun to let it know what he's up to, and ties the reed into a knot while simultaneously hiding it in his fist, out of the light. He then runs home quickly (with light to spare) and upon returning, opens his hand. At this very moment darkness encloses him like a tidal wave.

Bat Balolo Up to the early 1960s fruit bats were also herded like cattle to one end of the island and then clubbed and eaten. This was a very involved process requiring that some of the village women from Nasaqalau don special costumes and live in the bush for three months. The practice was stopped because someone in the village died mysteriously. It is believed the reason for the death was an incorrect following of the ceremonial procedure, so the ritual ceased altogether.

Tubou

The main village on the island is Tubou, which is located on the south coast and is the home of the prime minister. The village has a government station which includes a telephone exchange, hospital and post office. The lovely Methodist church beside the village green is cross-shaped, an unusual feature of Methodist churches in Fiji. In Tubou are also the graves of perhaps two of the more influential personalities in Fiji over the last century – the Tongan leader and warlord Enele Ma'afu, who conquered much of Fiji; and Ratu Sir Lala Sukuna, who helped transform the colony into nationhood. Behind the village is a church compound where many of the early missionaries are buried. A climb to the Catholic church on the hill west of Tubou gives you a nice view of the immediate environs. To the north and the south of the village are good beaches. When visiting them or the village, show respect by wearing suitable clothing. Bathing in the nude anywhere in Fiji is strictly taboo.

Levuka

Adjacent to Tubou is the village of Levuka (not to be confused with the old capital of Fiji). It is home to a tribe of fishermen who according to legend came from Bau.

Caves

Near Nasaqalau are several caves, the most famous being Oso Nabukete, known as the 'Pregnant Womens' Cave'. It is called this because legend has it that a woman hiding her pregnancy will not be able to slip through the cave's opening. To visit this marvellous cave, see the Turaga-ni-matagali (chief of the clan), Nautogumu, in Nasaqalau. He will provide a guide for a fee of approximately F$5. The guide should furnish a benzene lamp, but you should still bring a torch (flashlight) to really appreciate the size of the caverns and the many stalagmites and stalactites therein. There are many narrow passages to squeeze through and plenty of bat guano around, so wear your grubbiest clothing and oldest tennis shoes. In the cave is a stream with icy cold water, so you may want to bring a bathing suit for a refreshing swim. The entire tour takes from one to 1½ hours. Outside the entrance is the grave of Sapuga, the Tongan who legend has it brought fruit bats from his homeland to Lakeba. Once outside the cave, you are several metres from the beach. This might be the opportunity to wash the bat guano from your clothing and ask one of your guides

(most likely a young boy) to climb a coconut tree for a few drinking nuts.

Adjoining Oso Nabukete is Qara Bulu, a smaller cave once used as a jail in times of tribal war but generally not shown to visitors. You may see this by contacting Tiko Veitokiaki in Nasaqalau.

There is a third cave, Koro-ni-Vono, located inland from Oso Nabukete. It is even more spectacular, but remains hidden to even many of Nasaqalau's residents. In the good old days those who acquired the dreaded *lilabalavu* disease were shunted inside and left to perish while the cave was sealed. To this day villagers say that the moaning of the victims can be heard when you go near the entrance. If you want to find out for yourself (and see the old bones), talk to Tiko Veitokiaki and he will have you guided there for F$5.

Places to Stay

There is a government guest house in Tubou which has four rooms at F$8 per person per day including breakfast. Lunch and dinner may also be eaten for F$4 per meal. This is a government facility and before going to Lakeba you should telephone 42 090 to make sure there is room. If you can't get a room there, do not go to Lakeba unless you are invited ahead of time to stay in a village.

GETTING THERE

Fiji Air has two flights a week F$59 (one way) to Lakeba, or you can travel the old-fashioned way on a copra boat or government vessel. Check the shipping companies listed in this book or the government Marine Department for schedules.

GETTING AROUND

There is a 29-km road circling the island but little traffic, except for a few carriers which are generally unscheduled.

Rotuma

Located 386 km north-north-west of the
Fiji archipelago, the island of Rotuma has
an indigenous population of Polynesians
(as opposed to the Fijians who are
Melanesian), related most closely to the
Samoans. Rotuma is governed as a
dependency of Fiji, and its people follow a
lifestyle as traditional as that of the
Fijians. Measuring 13 km long and about
four km wide, the island has rich volcanic
soil which will grow just about any type of
tropical fruit. The best oranges sold in Fiji
are grown in Rotuma.

The first visit by Europeans was in
1791, when the crew of *HMS Pandora*
landed in search of *Bounty* mutineers.
Later contact with the European world
came in the form of runaway sailors and
escaped convicts, who eventually killed
each other off or were killed by Rotumans.
In 1842 Tongan Wesleyan ministers
found their way to the island, followed by
Marist Catholics five years later. The
result was actual warfare between followers of the two groups.

Weary from the chaos caused by the
fighting, Rotuman chiefs ceded the island
to Britain in 1881. Rotuma became a
province when Fiji gained independence,
and today some 3000 Rotumans live on
the 'island' while another 8000 live in the
Fiji archipelago.

The main attractions on Rotuma are the
beaches and reefs, which are a fisherman's
paradise. The drawback for potential
visitors is that there is no accommodation
on the island. As recently as 1985, the
leaders on the island voted 7 to 1 against
opening Rotuma up to tourism. For the

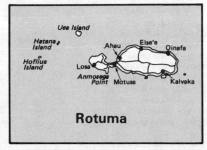

Rotuma

determined traveller with plenty of time,
it is possible to see Rotuma; but you had
better have a Rotuman friend on the
island because without an invitation you
will be told to leave.

GETTING THERE
Air Fiji Air flies twice weekly to the island
for F$110 one way, but the flights are
frequently booked in advance.

Boat The most frequent visitors come
aboard yachts. Permission for anchorage
can be obtained at the government station
on Ahau on Maka Bay. Government ships
and a couple of commercial vessels make
monthly visits to Rotuma, but getting
passage can be difficult. Even if the
Marine Department or a private shipping
firm says there is a berth, the captain has
the final say. Your best bets are to talk to
the skipper ahead of time or to have a
Rotuman friend make the arrangements.
Keep in mind that if you depend on a ship
for transportation, your stay on the island
may be a month or more, depending on
space availability.

Index

LONELY PLANET NEWSLETTER

We collect an enormous amount of information here at Lonely Planet. Apart from our research we also get a steady stream of letters from people out on the road – some are just one line on a postcard, others go on for pages. Plus we always have an ear to the ground for the latest on cheap airfares, new visa regulations, borders opening and closing. A lot of this information goes into our new editions or 'update supplements' in reprints. But to make the most of the info that comes our way we also produce a quarterly newsletter packed full of the latest news from out on the road. It comes out in January, April, July and October every year. Cost of the yearly subscription (including postage) is $7.50; or single copies of the newsletter cost $2. That's US$ in the US or A$ in Australia, write to:

Lonely Planet Publications
PO Box 88, South Yarra, Victoria, 3141, Australia
or
Lonely Planet Publications
PO Box 2001A, Berkeley, CA 94702 USA

If you're travelling further in the Pacific region look at what else we have:

Tahiti & French Polynesia – a travel survival kit
The idyllic tropical islands of French Polynesia are many peoples' image of the South Pacific. Our guidebook takes you from Papeete to the other islands of the Society Group and to the more remote islands of this scattered French colony.

Australia – a travel survival kit
The continent island of Australia is currently enjoying a travel boom as more and more travellers discover its amazing travel possibilities.

Papua New Guinea – a travel survival kit
North of Australia the wild and rugged country of PNG is truly 'the last unknown'. It forms a bridge from the islands of the Pacific to the countries of South-East Asia.

Bushwalking in Papua New Guinea
If you intend to explore PNG on foot then this is the book.

New Zealand – a travel survival kit
Calm lakes to smoking volcanoes, snow-capped peaks to sunny beaches, the islands of New Zealand have it all and our guidebook tells you were to find it.

Tramping in New Zealand
New Zealand is also famous for its wonderful walks and this guide takes you along all the major walks including the Milford Track.

Traveller's Tales

an illustrated journey through Australia, Asia and Africa

Anthony Jenkins

lonely planet

Cartoonist Anthony Jenkins has spent several years on the road, travelling in 55 countries around the world. Along the way he has filled numerous sketchbooks with his drawings of the people he met.

This is a book of people, not places. A tattooed Iban tribesman in Sarawak, a mango seller in Cameroon, fellow travellers in Nepal . . . all are drawn with perception and (in most cases) affection.

Equally perceptive are Jenkins' written comments and descriptions of incidents during his travels. The combined result is like a series of personal illustrated letters.

This is a traveller's travel book. If you have ever endured an Indian train, watched the world go by in Kathmandu's Durbar Square or tried to post a letter in southern Africa, then opening these pages will be like meeting old friends and will probably give you itchy feet to be on the road once more.

Lonely Planet travel guides
Africa on a Shoestring
Alaska – a travel survival kit
Australia   a travel survival kit
Bali & Lombok – a travel survival kit
Bangladesh – a travel survival kit
Burma – a travel survival kit
Bushwalking in Papua New Guinea
Canada – a travel survival kit
China – a travel survival kit
Ecuador & the Galapagos Islands
Fiji – a travel survival kit
Hong Kong, Macau & Canton – a travel survival kit
India – a travel survival kit
Indonesia – a travel survival kit
Japan – a travel survival kit
Kashmir, Ladakh & Zanskar – a travel survival kit
Kathmandu & the Kingdom of Nepal
Korea & Taiwan – a travel survival kit
Malaysia, Singapore & Brunei – a travel survival kit
Mexico – a travel survival kit
New Zealand – a travel survival kit
North-East Asia on a Shoestring
Pakistan – a travel survival kit kit
Papua New Guinea – a travel survival kit
South America on a Shoestring
South-East Asia on a Shoestring
Sri Lanka – a travel survival kit
Tahiti – a travel survival kit
Thailand – a travel survival kit
The Philippines – a travel survival kit
Tibet – a travel survival kit
Tramping in New Zealand
Travel with Children
Travellers Tales
Trekking in the Indian Himalaya
Trekking in the Nepal Himalaya
Turkey – a travel survival kit
USA West
West Asia on a Shoestring

Lonely Planet phrasebooks
Indonesia Phrasebook
China Phrasebook
Nepal Phrasebook
Thailand Phrasebook

Lonely Planet travel guides are available around the world. If you can't find them, ask your bookshop to order them from one of the distributors listed below. For countries not listed or if you would like a free copy of our latest booklist write to Lonely Planet in Australia.

Australia
Lonely Planet Publications, PO Box 88, South Yarra, Victoria 3141.
Canada
Milestone Publications, PO Box 2248, Sidney, BC V8L 3S8, Canada.
Denmark
Scanvik Books aps, Store Kongensgade 59 A, DK-1264 Copenhagen K.
Hong Kong
The Book Society, GPO Box 7804.
India & Nepal
UBS Distributors, 5 Ansari Rd, New Delhi.
Israel
Geographical Tours Ltd, 8 Tverya St, Tel Aviv 63144.
Japan
Intercontinental Marketing Corp, IPO Box 5056, Tokyo 100-31.
Malaysia
MPH Distributors, 13 Jalan 13/6, Petaling Jaya, Selangor.
Netherlands
Nilsson & Lamm bv, Postbus 195, Pampuslaan 212, 1380 AD Weesp.
New Zealand
Roulston Greene Publishing Associates Ltd, Box 33850, Takapuna, Auckland 9.
Pakistan
London Book House, 281/C Tariq Rd, PECHS Karachi 29, Pakistan
Papua New Guinea see Australia
Singapore
MPH Distributors, 3rd Storey, 601 Sims Drive #03-21, Singapore 1438
Spain
Altair, Riera Alta 8, Barcelona, 08001.
Sweden
Esselte Kartcentrum AB, Vasagatan 16, S-111 20 Stockholm.
Thailand
Chalermnit, 108 Sukhumvit 53, Bangkok, 10110.
UK
Roger Lascelles, 47 York Rd, Brentford, Middlesex, TW8 0QP.
USA
Lonely Planet Publications, PO Box 2001A, Berkeley, CA 94702.
West Germany
Buchvertrieb Gerda Schettler, Postfach 64, D3415 Hattorf a H.

Lonely Planet guidebooks are available around the world. For a copy of our current booklist or a list of our distributors write to:
Lonely Planet, PO Box 88, South Yarra, Vic 3141, Australia
Lonely Planet, PO Box 2001A, Berkeley, CA 94702, USA